FAMOUS
LAST
WORDS

Also by Jonathon Green
in Pan Books

A Dictionary of Contemporary Quotations

FAMOUS LAST WORDS

compiled by
JONATHON GREEN

PAN BOOKS
London and Sydney

First published 1979 by Omnibus Press
This edition published 1980 by Pan Books Ltd,
Cavaye Place, London SW10 9PG
3rd printing 1983
© Omnibus Press 1979
introduction © Jonathon Green 1979
ISBN 0 330 26205 x
Made and printed in Great Britain by
Richard Clay (The Chaucer Press) Ltd, Bungay, Suffolk

CONTENTS

INTRODUCTION

This is a collection of the last words of some two thousand two hundred dead people. Kings, courtiers, doctors, lawyers, poets, painters, philosophers, generals, priests, saints, villains, murderers, martyrs and sportsmen – a panoramic view, in their own words, of the way some of the better known members of humanity have faced their own extinction.

Two factors have made these final sentences famous: usually the person has been sufficiently well known in life for whatever reason, good or bad, for there to have been general interest in his or her parting words to the attendant world. On the other hand there are some final phrases that have brought their originator a fame in death that they never found possible in life.

There are infinite ways of dying and the last words included here reflect them all. Nevertheless, certain moods, certain styles do persist, and this book has been divided into eighteen loosely generalized sections that show these ranges of feeling.

People face their death in many ways. Some, the professional phrase-makers, seem to have been trying out a number of quotable last words almost as soon as they realize that their time is growing short. It is with this in mind that some notables appear more than once in the index. Others, in the main clergymen, are content to fall back on the established formulae of their creed. Yet more, inevitably, call for their Mother, a person one might expect them to be meeting almost as soon as they are wishing. Military men seem brave or patriotic, villains prefer bravado, the aristocracy try to maintain their hauteur, even on the scaffold. Saints reveal the qualities that duly bring them canonization.

The difficulties for the compiler of such a book, obviously, are the omissions. While every effort has been made to gather in as many last words as possible, and to set them in context and chronology, gaps inevitably appear. Quite simply, all too many famous names, with no thought for posterity, have died silent or unremarked. To note just a few personal losses, why were Evelyn Waugh, P. G. Wodehouse, Raymond Chandler and Lenny Bruce reluctant to leave something for an attendant public? Or all those unfortunates from show business whose lives have fascinated the millions but whose lifestyle has laid them prematurely low. More important, what of the unsung heroes and heroines of countless battlefields, prison camps and similar hells. It is to fill some of these gaps that I have unashamedly bent the rules on occasion. Perhaps not all the last recorded words originate on the actual deathbed, but for the record, they must stand.

Fortunately there remain the many who did remember to sign off in style. It is they who have found some small and posthumous fame in this collection. In an era when death is perhaps the supreme taboo, we can draw some comfort in the way these men and women have coped with their impending demise. They fill these pages: fearful, resigned, exultant, arrogant, surprised, with a shout or a murmur, shrinking from the inevitable or embracing it with fond relief. One might not look forward to death, one might well wish profoundly to avoid it, but when the inevitable arrives all that one can hope, like so many of the people included here, is at least to do it well.

JONATHON GREEN

THE END
IS NIGH

ABD-ER-RAHMAN
Caliph, died 961.
Oh man, place not thy confidence in this present world.

LOUISA M. ALCOTT
Authoress of children's books, died 1888.
Is it not meningitis?

EDWARD ALDERSON
Judge, died 1857. Asked how he felt . . .
The worse, the better for me.

HENRY ALFORD
*Clergyman, died 1871. Making the arrangements for his
funeral . . .*
Will you tell the Archdeacon? Will you move a vote of thanks
for his kindness in performing the ceremony?

STEWART ALSOP
*American journalist and political commentator, died of
Leukaemia 1973. The final words of his autobiography
Stay of Execution . . .*
There is a time to live, but there is also a time to die. That time
has not yet come for me. But it will. It will come for all of us.

FELIX ARVERS
French poet, died 1850. To his confessor . . .
Ah, Coquereau, I forgot to mention one of the greatest faults of
my life. I have spoken badly of Charles X.

☠

'LA RIVIERE' DE BAILLI
French doctor, died 1605. After disposing of all his
possessions he looked around his room . . .
I must hasten away since my baggage has been sent off before me.

GEORGE BANCROFT
Historian, died 1891. Turning to a friend he admitted . . .
I cannot remember your first name.
He was told 'It is George, like yours . . .'
Then what is your last name?

JOHANN BARNEVELDT
Dutch patriot, executed 1619.
Oh God! What then is man?

SIR JAMES M. BARRIE
Author, died 1937.
I can't sleep.

CLARA BARTON
Founder of the American Red Cross, died 1912.
Let me go! Let me go!

THOMAS L. BEDDOES
Author of Death's Jest Book, *died 1849.*
I am food for what I am good for – worms. I ought to have been among other things a good poet. Life was too great a bore on one peg, and that a hard one. But for Dr Elkins above mentioned, Reade's best stomach pump.

MAX BEERBOHM
Writer and wit, died 1956. Asked whether he had slept well . . .
No. Thanks for everything.

BISHOP BEHAINE
Clergyman.
I willingly leave this world where I have been thought happy in that I have had public admiration, been respected by the great, esteemed by Kings. I can't say that I regret these honours – it's just that they add up to vanity and trouble.

LUDWIG BORNE
Political satirist, died 1837.
Pull back the drapes, I'd gladly see the sun. Flowers. Music.

ANNE DU BOURG
French priest and martyr, executed 1559.
Six feet of earth for my body and the infinite heavens for my soul is what I shall soon have.

NATHANIEL BOWDITCH
American mathematician and astronomer, died 1838.
Tasting a final glass of water . . .
How delicious. I have swallowed a drop from 'Silva's brook that flowed fast by the oracle of God.'

CHARLES BRACE
Social services campaigner, died 1890. Reading of a
new sanatorium . . .
I wish you would send this to Mr Potter.

JAMES BRINDLEY
Engineer, died 1772. Instructing a group of canal
builders whose plans continued to go wrong . . .
Then puddle it, puddle it and puddle it again.

EMILY BRONTË
Authoress, died 1848.
If you will send for a doctor I will see him now.

SIR REDVERS BULLER
Colonial administrator, died 1894.
Well, I think it is about time to go to bed now.

BISHOP BURGESS
Died 1837.
I will lie down now.

FRANCES HODGSON BURNETT
Author, died 1924.
With the best that was in me I have tried to write more happiness into the world.

SAMUEL BUTLER
Author, died 1902.

Have you brought the chequebook, Alfred?

LORD GEORGE BYRON
Poet, died 1824.

Now I shall go to sleep.

☠

HENRIETTE CAMPAN
*French educator, died 1822. After making a brusque
demand from a servant . . .*

How imperious one is when one no longer has the time to be
polite.

CANIUS
Died 1st Century.

I have determined with myself to mark well whether in this short
pang of death my soul shall perceive and feel that he goes out
of my body. This point I intend fully to take heed of, and if I
can, I will surely bring you and the rest of my fellows word,
what I felt and what is the state of our souls.

JANE CARLYLE
*Died 1866. Last letter to her husband, Thomas, who
had requested her to buy him a certain picture . . .*

I will go back for it, if you like, and can find a place for it on my
wall.

THOMAS CARLYLE
Historian and essayist, died 1881.

So this is death, well . . .

ANDREW CARNEGIE
*American railroad baron, died 1919. Replying to his
wife who had wished him a good night's rest . . .*

I hope so.

LEWIS CARROLL
Author and academic, died 1898.

Take away those pillows – I shall need them no more.

VISCOUNT CASTLEREAGH
British Foreign Secretary, suicide 1822.
Oh Bankhead, it is all over!

NEVILLE CHAMBERLAIN
British Prime Minister, died 1940.
Approaching dissolution brings relief.

WILLIAM ELLERY CHANNING
'The Father of American Unitarianism', died 1842.
You need not be anxious concerning tonight. It will be very quiet and peaceful with me.

JOSEPH CHOATE
American lawyer and diplomat, died 1917.
I am feeling very ill. I think this is the end.

JOSEPH CLARE
Poet.
I have lived too long. I want to go home.

THOMAS COLE
Artist, died 1848.
I want to be quiet.

SAMUEL COLT
Arms manufacturer, died 1862.
It's all over now.

GEORGE COMBE
Phrenologist, died 1850.
From my present sensations I should say that I were dying and I am glad of it.

CONFUCIUS
Died 479 BC.
No intelligent monarch arises. There is no-one in the kingdom that will make me his master. My time has come to die.

JAY COOKE
American banker, died 1905. Overhearing the reading of a prayer for the dead . . .
That was the right prayer.

OLIVER CROMWELL
Lord Protector of England, died 1658.
My desire is to make what haste I may to be gone.

MADAME MARIE CURIE
Scientist, died 1934. Offered an injection to ease the pain . . .
I don't want it.

JOHN PHILPOT CURRAN
Irish author and wit, died 1817. Replying to his doctor
who commented 'You are coughing with more difficulty' . . .
That is surprising, since I have been practising all night.

☠

SIR WILLIAM DAVENANT
British playwright and Poet Laureate, died 1668. Putting off
the conclusion of a poem on which he was working . . .
I shall have to ask leave to desist, when I am interrupted by so
great an experiment as dying.

STEPHEN DECATUR
Killed in a duel, 1820.
I am mortally wounded, I think.

MADAME DE STAEL
Political and literary hostess, died 1817. When asked if she
would sleep . . .
Heavily, like a big peasant woman.

EMILY DICKINSON
American poet, died 1886.
I must go in, the fog is rising.
Offered a glass of water . . .
Oh, is that all it is ?

DIOGENES THE CYNIC
Greek Philosopher, died 4th Century BC. Waking for the
last time . . .
One brother anticipates the other: Sleep before Death. Everything will shortly be turned upside down.

PHILIP DODDRIDGE
British non-conformist divine, died 1756.
There is a hope set before me.

SIR HOWARD DOUGLAS
British general, died 1861.
All I have said about armoured ships will prove correct. How little do they know of the undeveloped power of artillery.

PAUL DOUMER
President of France, assassinated 1932. The statesman never knew a bullet and not a car had hit him. His aides refused to reveal the truth . . .
Ah, a road accident . . . a road accident.

TIMOTHY DWIGHT
American author, died 1817. As he finished his last manuscript . . .
There, I have done. Oh, what triumphant truth!

MORGAN EARP
American lawman, killed 1882. As he died at the OK Corral, Morgan finally accepted his brother Wyatt's refusal to believe in an afterlife . . .
I guess you were right, Wyatt. I can't see a damn thing.

EUGENE FIELD
Children's poet, died 1895.
Good night.

GEORGE FORDYCE
Died 1802. Dismissing his daughter who had been reading to him . . .
Stop. Go out of the room. I am about to die.

EDWARD A. FREEMAN
Historian, died 1892. Final entry in his diary . . .
Very weak. Rail to La Encina and Alicante.

HENRY CLAY FRICK
American industrialist, died 1919.
That will be all; now I think I'll go to sleep.

REV. CHRISTOPHER P. GADSEN
American clergyman, died 1805. Raising his arms to heaven . . .
I am reaching towards my inheritance.

REV. THOMAS H. GALLAUDET
American teacher of the deaf and dumb, died 1902.
I will go to sleep.

CHRISTIAN GELLERT
German poet, died 1769.
Now, God be praised, only one hour.

RICHARD WATSON GILDER
Poet and editor, died 1909. Writing about Tennyson . . .
He wrote some of his sagest and loveliest things in the last days –
there seems to have been an otherworld light on these latest
utterances. You see him standing serene in the afterglow, await-
ing in tranquility the natural end.

WILLIAM EWART GLADSTONE
*British Prime Minister, died 1898. His last entry
in a diary that spanned seventy years . . .*
I do not enter any interior matters. It is so easy to write, but to
write honestly is nearly impossible.

JOHN GOUGH
*American lawyer, died 1886. Maintaining his
pro-temperance stand till the end . . .*
Young man, keep your record clean.

HENRY W. GRADY
American editor and orator, died 1889.
And the little children cried in the streets.

SIR JAMES GRAHAM
British statesman, died 1861. As he rested after
after a heart attack . . .
Ah! I thought it was over then.

HORACE GREELEY
American publisher and editor, founder of the
New York Daily Tribune, *died 1872.*
It is done.

EDVARD GRIEG
Composer, died 1907.
Well, if it must be so.

ALBRECHT VON HALLER
Physician, died 1777. He checked his own pulse . . .
Now I am dying. The artery ceases to beat.

JONAS HANWAY
British merchant, died 1786.
If you think it will be of service in your practice, or to anyone
who may come after me, I beg you to have my body opened. I
am willing to do as much good as possible.

WILL HAY
British comic, died 1949. A passage in a book he was
reading when he died, and one which was carved
on his gravestone . . .
For each of us there comes a moment when death takes us by the
hand and says – it is time to rest, you are tired, lie down and sleep.

REGINALD HEBER
Clergyman and hymn writer, died 1826. Written on
the back of his sermon on confirmation . . .
Trichinopoly, April 3, 1826.

JOHN HECKEWELDER
Missionary to the Ohio Indians, died 1823.
Golgotha, Gethsemene.

EDWARD HERBERT
Baron Herbert of Cherbury, historian, poet and diplomat,
died 1648. Making an accurate forecast of his death . . .

Then an hour hence he shall depart.

ABRAM S. HEWITT
Industrialist and politician, died 1903. Removed the
oxygen tube from his mouth . . .

And now I am officially dead.

JOHN HILTON
British broadcaster, died 1943. Swallowing a few
drops of tea . . .

That was very good.

LUDWIG HOLTY
German poet, died 1776.

I am very ill. Send for Zimmermann. In fact, I think I'll die today.

WALTER FARQUHAR HOOK
British clergyman, died 1875.

I am old, 78, and very infirm. My contemporaries are passing away and I expect soon to receive my summons. Pray for me.

JULIA WARD HOWE
Composer of 'The Battle Hymn of the Republic,'
died 1910.

God will help me . . . I am so tired!

WILLIAM DEAN HOWELLS
American littérateur, died 1920. Writing about
Henry James . . .

Our walks by day were only in one direction and in one region. We were always going to Fresh Pond, in those days a wandering space of woods and water where people skated in winter and boated in summer.

WILLIAM H. HUDSON
American author, died 1922.

Good-bye.

ISAAC HULL
American admiral, died 1843.

I strike my flag.

DAVID HUME
British philosopher, died 1776. A final letter . . .

I go very fast to decline and last night had a small fever, which I hoped might put a quicker period to this tedious illness; but, unluckily, it has, in a great measure, gone off. I cannot submit to your coming over here on my account, as it is possible for me to see you so small a part of the day; but Dr Black can better inform you concerning the degree of strength which may, from time to time, remain with me. Adieu.

ANNE HYDE
Duchess of York, died 1671.

Truth! Truth!

DOUGLAS JERROLD
Playwright and satirist, died 1857.

I feel like one who is waiting and waited for.

JOHN G. JOHNSON
Lawyer and art collector, died 1917.

Goodnight, I'm going to sleep now.

MAURUS JOKAI
Hungarian novelist, died 1904.

I want to sleep.

AL JOLSON
American singing superstar, died 1950.

This is it. I'm going, I'm going.

JOHN PAUL JONES
American patriot, died 1792. Final paragraph of his will.

I revoke all other testaments or codicils which I may have made before the present, which alone I stand by as containing my last will.

CHRISTIAN JACOB KRAUS
German professor of political science, died 1832.
Dying is different from what I thought.

JEROME LALANDE
Astronomer, died 1807.
Withdraw, I no longer have need of anything.

FELICITE ROBERT DE LAMENNAIS
*Priest and philosopher, died 1854. Watching the sun
streaming through his bedroom window . . .*
Let it come – it is coming for me.

FRANKLIN K. LANE
American Secretary of the Interior, died 1921.
Fragment of a manuscript . . .
But for my heart's content in that new land, I think I'd rather
loaf with Lincoln along a river bank. I know I would understand
him. I would not have to learn who were his enemies, what
theories he was committed to and what against. We could just
talk and open out our minds, and tell our doubts and swap the
longings of our hearts that others never heard of. He wouldn't
try to master me nor make me feel how small I was. I'd dare to
ask him things and know that he felt awkward about them, too.
And I know I would find, I know I would, that he had hit his
shin on those very stumps that had hit me. We'd talk of men a
lot – the kind they call the great. I would not find him scornful.
Yet boys that he knew in New Salem would somehow appear
larger in their souls than some of those that I had called the great.
His wise eyes saw qualities that weighed more than smartness.
Yes, we would sit down where the bank sloped gently to the
great stream and glance at the picture of our people the negroes
being lynched, the miners' civil war, labour's hold-ups, employers' ruthlessness, the subordination of humanity to
industry . . .

PIERRE LAPLACE
Astronomer, died 1827.
What we know is not much, what we do not know is immense.

SIR WILFRED LAURIER
Canadian Prime Minister, died 1919.

It is finished.

FRANZ LEHAR
Composer, died 1948

Now I have finished with all earthly business, and high time too. Yes, yes, my dear child, now comes death.

ELLIS LEWIS
Pennsylvania chief justice, died 1854.

I believe I am dying now.

JOSEPH LIEUTAUD
Doctor to the King of France. Offered conflicting remedies by his fellow doctors . . .

Ah, I shall die well enough without all that!

GEORGE LIPPARD
Died 1854.

Is this death?

☠

KATHERINE MANSFIELD
(Katherine Middleton Murry)
Short story writer, died 1923.

I believe . . . I'm going to die. I love the rain. I want the feeling of it on my face.

CAPTAIN FREDERICK MARRYAT
British novelist of the sea, died 1848. Dictated his last thoughts . . .

After years of casual, and, latterly, months of intense thought, I feel convinced that Christianity is true, and the only religion that can be practised on this earth; that the basis of Christianity is love; and that God is love. To attempt to establish any other creed will only, in the end, be folly. But Christianity must be implanted in the breast of youth; there must be a bias towards it given at an early age. It is now half past nine o'clock. World, adieu!

CHARLES MATHEWS
British comic, died 1836.

I am ready.

CATHERINE DE MEDICI
Consort of Henry II of France, died 1589.

Ah, my God, I am dead!

FELIX MENDELSSOHN
Composer, died 1847

Weary, very weary.

DESIRE JOSEPH MERCIER
Belgian Cardinal, died 1926. After hearing the Profiscere …

Now there is nothing more to be done, except to wait.

PROSPER MÉRIMÉE
French novelist and dramatist, died 1870.

Goodnight now, I want to go to sleep.

HELMUTH VON MOLTKE
*Prussian general, died 1891. Asked 'Uncle Helmuth,
are you ill ?' …*

What ? ?

LOLA MONTEZ
*Adventuress, dancer, mistress of Ludwig I of Bavaria,
died 1861.*

I am very tired.

GOUVERNEUR MORRIS
American politician, died 1816.

Sixty-four years ago it pleased the Almighty to call me into
existence here on this spot, in this very room, and now shall I
complain that he is pleased to call me hence ?

OLIVER MORTON
American politician, died 1877.

I am dying. I am worn out.

ALFRED DE MUSSET
French poet, died 1857.

Sleep! At last I am to sleep.

JOHANN NEANDER
Church historian, died 1850.
I am weary. I will now go to sleep. Goodnight.

SIR ISAAC NEWTON
Philosopher and mathematician, died 1727.
I don't know what I may seem to the world. But as to myself, I seem to have been only a boy playing on the seashore and diverting myself in now and then finding a smoother pebble or prettier shell than the ordinary, whilst the great ocean of truth lay all undiscovered before me.

BARTHOLD GEORGE NIEBUHR
Philologist, died 1831. Noticing that his medicine was reserved only for terminal cases . . .
What essential substance is this ? Am I so far gone ?

HERMANN NOTHNAGEL
Clinician, died 1905. Reported on his own condition . . .
Paroxysms of angina pectoris, with extremely violent pains. Pulse and attacks completely different, sometimes slow, about 56-60, entirely regular, very intense, then again accelerated, 80-90, rather even and regular, finally completely arhythmic, entirely unequal, now palpitating, now slow, with differing intensity. The first sensations of these attacks date several – three or four – years back, in the beginning rather weak, becoming slowly more and more definite. Properly speaking attacks with sharp pains have appeared only within the last five or six days. Written on July 6, 1905, late in the evening, after I had three or four violent attacks.

☠

TITUS OATES
Creator of the 'Popish Plot' of 1678, died 1705.
It is all the same in the end.

☠

JOHN PALMER
British actor, died on stage 1798. Palmer had just delivered this line from his play The Stranger . . .
There is another and a better world.

THEODORE PARKER
Abolitionist, scholar and clergyman, died 1869.
It is all one.

DOROTHY W. PATTISON
'Sister Dora', philanthropist, died 1878.
I have lived alone, let me die alone, let me die alone.

HENRY CHARLES PEERSON
Australian politician.
My life has been faulty, but God will judge me by my intentions.

ST. JOHN PHILBY
Arabist, died 1960.
God, I'm bored!

ORVILLE H. PLATT
US Senator, died 1905.
You know what this means, Doctor, and so do I.

PLOTINUS
Neoplatonic philosopher, died 270 BC.
I am making my last effort to return that which is divine in me
to that which is divine in the universe.

ALEXANDER POPE
British satirist, died 1744.
I am dying, sir, of one hundred good symptoms.

HENRY PURCELL
British composer, died 1695. Final words of his will . . .
And I do hereby constitute and appoint my said loving wife my
sole executrix of this my last will and testament, revoking all
former wills. Witness my hand this day.

JOHN QUICK
British actor, died 1831.
Is this death?

JAMES QUIN
British actor, died 1766.

I could wish this tragic scene were over, but I hope to go through it with becoming modesty.

☠

MAURICE RAVEL
French composer, died 1937. Looking at his bandaged head in a mirror . . .

I look like a Moor.

WALTER REED
American Army bacteriologist, died 1902. Reacting to the news of his promotion to Colonel . . .

I care nothing for that now.

KENNETH REXROTH
20th Century American poet. Remembering his father's last words . . .

He said he was dying of fast women, slow horses, crooked cards and straight whisky.

CARDINAL RICHELIEU
French statesman, died 1642.

I have no enemies save those of the State.

ROB ROY MACGREGOR
Scottish clan chieftain and outlaw, died 1734.

Now all is over. Let the piper play 'Return No More'.

JAMES ROBERTSON
Missionary, died 1794.

I am done out.

JOHN WILMOT, EARL OF ROCHESTER
Poet and libertine, died 1680.

The only objection to the Bible is a bad life.

GEORGE B. RODNEY
British admiral, died 1792.

I am very ill indeed.

SALVATORE ROSA
Italian artist, died 1673.

To judge by what I now endure, the hand of death grasps me strongly.

CLAUDIUS SALMASIUS
French scholar, died 1653.

Oh sirs, mind the world less and God more. Had I but one more year it should be spent in studying David's Psalms and Paul's Epistles.

F. W. SANDERSON
British headmaster, died 1922. Asked if he was not 'too tired' to answer some questions . . .

No . . . No.

FRANZ SCHUBERT
Composer, died 1828.

Here, here is my end.

ADAM SMITH
Economist, died 1790.

I believe we must adjourn the meeting to some other place.

AL SMITH
American politician, died 1944.

Start the Act of Contrition.

CHARLES PROTEUS STEINMETZ
Electrical engineer, died 1923.

All right. I'll lie down.

LAURENCE STERNE
British novelist, died 1768.

Now it has come.

JOHANN STRAUSS
Composer, died 1899. On receiving advice to get some sleep . . .

I will, whatever happens.

August Strindberg
Swedish dramatist, died 1912.

Everything is atoned for.

John M. Synge
Irish dramatist, died 1909.

It is no use fighting death any longer.

☠

Zachary Taylor
American President, died 1850.

I am about to die, I expect the summons soon. I have endeavoured to discharge all my official duties faithfully. I regret nothing, but am sorry that I am about to leave my friends.

William Tennant
Presbyterian divine, died 1777.

I am sensible of the violence of my disorder, and that it is accompanied by symptoms of approaching dissolution. But, blessed be God, I have no wish to live if it should be His will to call me hence.

Baron Edward Thurlow
Lord Chancellor of England, died 1806.

I'll be shot if I don't believe I'm dying!

Horace Traubel
Author and socialist, died 1919.

I am tired, damned tired.

Anthony Trollope
British novelist, died 1882. Final lines of his autobiography . . .

Now I stretch out my hand, and from the further shore I bid adieu to all who have cared to read any among the many words I have written.

John Tyler
President of the United States, died 1862.

I am going. Perhaps it is for the best.

☠

LUCILIO VANINI
Philosopher, burned as a magician.

There is neither God nor devil: for if there were a God, I would pray him to send a thunderbolt on the Council, as all that is unjust and iniquitous; and if there were a devil I would pray him to engulf it in the subterranean regions; but since there is neither one nor the other, there is nothing for me to do.

THORSTEIN VEBLEN
Economist, died 1929. A farewell note . . .

It is also my wish, in case of death, to be cremated, if it can be conveniently done, as expeditiously and inexpensively as may be, without ritual or ceremony of any kind; that my ashes be thrown loose into the sea, or some other sizeable stream running to the sea; that no tombstone, inscription or monument of any name or nature, be set up in my memory or name in any place or at any time; that no obituary, memorial, portrait, or biography of me, nor any letters written to or by me be printed or published, or in any way reproduced, copied or circulated.

WILHELM WAIBLINGER
German poet, died 1830.

Addio!

SAM WARD
Died 1884.

I think I am going to give up the ghost.

JAMES WATT
British engineer, died 1819. To the friends who had gathered at his bedside . . .

I am very sensible of the attachment you show me, and I hasten to thank you for it, as I feel that I am now come to my last illness.

CARL MARIA VON WEBER
Musician, died 1826.

Now let me sleep.

THOMAS WEBSTER
British scholar, died 1824.

Examine it for yourself.

THURLOW WEED
American journalist and politician, died 1882.

I want to go home!

JOSEPH BLANCO WHITE
Author, died 1841.

Now I die.

GEORGE WHITEFIELD
Clergyman, died 1770.

I am dying.

CHRISTOF WIELAND
German dramatist, died 1813.

To sleep – to die.

HORACE WILLIAMS
American philosopher. His nurse asked him his name . . .

Horace Williams.

EDWARD WILSON
*Doctor and explorer, killed 1912. Wilson was lost with
Scott's Antarctic expedition; this letter was left for his wife . . .*

God knows I am sorry to be the cause of sorrow to anyone in the
world, but everyone must die and at every death there must be
some sorrow. All the things I had hoped to do with you after this
Expedition are as nothing now, but there are greater things for
us to do in the world to come. My only regret is leaving you to
struggle through your life alone, but I may be coming to you by
a quicker way. I feel so happy now in having got time to write
to you. One of my notes will surely reach you. Dad's little com-
pass and Mother's little comb are in my pocket. Your little
testament and prayer book will be in my hand or in my breast
pocket when the end comes. All is well.

☠

WILLIAM WOODVILLE
*Died 1805. Advising the carpenter who was measuring
him for his coffin . . .*

I shall not live more than two days, therefore make haste.

FRANCISCO XIMENES DE CISNEROS
Spanish Cardinal, died 1774.

This is death.

ZENO
Stoic philosopher, died 257 BC.

Earth, do you demand me ? I am ready.

COUNT FERDINAND VON ZEPPELIN
Inventor of the airship, died 1917.

I have perfect faith.

JOHN VON ZIMMERMANN
Swiss doctor, died 1795.

I am dying. Leave me alone.

ACROSS THE GREAT DIVIDE

CHARLES ABBOTT
*Lord Chief Justice, died 1832. Addressing an
imaginary jury . . .*
Gentlemen, you are all dismissed.

JOHN ABERNETHY
Surgeon, died 1831.
Is there anybody in the room?

ALEXANDER ADAM
*Schoolmaster, died 1809. Imagining that he was still
teaching his old class . . .*
That Horace was very well said . . . *you* did not do it so well. But
it grows dark, very dark. The boys may dismiss.

JOHN ADAMS
American President, died 1826.
Thomas Jefferson still survives.

WILLIAM AINSWORTH
Editor and historical novelist, died 1882. His last letter . . .
Dr Holman thought me much wasted since I last saw him and
so I am in no doubt. Your affectionate cousin, W. Harrison
Ainsworth.

WILLIAM ALLINGHAM
Poet, died 1889.
I am seeing things that you know nothing of.

EUGENE ARAM
Schoolmaster and murderer, executed 1759. Asked
whether he had anything to say? ...

No.

LUDOVICO ARIOSTO
Italian romantic poet, died 1533.

This is not my home.

DR THOMAS ARNOLD
Headmaster of Rugby School, died 1842. Hearing that
his death was not far off ...

Ah, very well.

GEORGE C. ATCHESON
Died in a plane crash. As the plane plunged into the ocean ...

Well, it can't be helped.

JANE AUSTEN
Author, died 1817. Asked what she required ...

Nothing but death.

MARIE BASHKIRTSEFF
Russian diarist, died 1884. As she watched a candle
go out next to her bed ...

We shall go out together.

LORD BEAVERBROOK
British press magnate, died 1964. His last public statement ...

This is my final word. It is time for me to become an apprentice
once more. I have not settled in which direction. But somewhere,
sometime, soon.

HENRY WARD BEECHER
Divine and religious author, died 1887.

Now comes the mystery.

CLAUDE BERNARD
French physiologist, died 1878. Commenting on a travelling
rug that had been spread over his knees ...

This time it will serve me for the voyage from which there is no
return. The voyage of eternity.

JACOB BOEHM
German mystic, died 1624.
Do you hear the music? Now I go hence.

SIMON BOLIVAR
'The Great Liberator' of Latin America, died 1830.
Dying in exile . . .
Let us go, these people don't want us in this land! Let us go, boys! Take my baggage on board the frigate.

CHARLES BONNET
Swiss naturalist, died 1793. Bonnet believed one of his servants was stealing from him; his wife persuaded one to 'confess' and humour this delusion . . .
So he repents. Let him come in and all will be overlooked.

ANDREW BRADFORD
Publisher of Philadelphia's first newspaper, died 1742.
Oh Lord, forgive the errata!

W. C. BRYANT
American poet, died 1878. Bryant tripped in the street, the blow to his head disorientated him . . .
Whose house is this? What street is this? Would you like to see Miss Fairchild [his niece]?

FRANCIS BUCKLAND
Naturalist and Inspector of Fisheries, died 1880.
I am going on a long journey. I shall see many strange animals on the way. God is so good, so good to the little fishes, I do not believe He would let their Inspector suffer shipwreck at last.

HENRY BUCKLE
British historian, died 1862.
Poor little boys.

CHARLES BURNEY
Father of Fanny Burney, historian of music, died 1796.
All this will soon pass away as a dream.

JOHN BURROUGHS
Naturalist, died 1921.
How far are we from home?

ROBERT BURTON
Divine, died 1640.

Be not solitary, be not idle.

☠

GENERAL PIERRE CAMBRONNE
Led the Old Guard at Waterloo, died 1842.

Ah mademoiselle, man is thought to be something, but he is nothing.

ADMIRAL RICHARD CARTER
British sailor, died 1692.

Fight the ship. Fight the ship as long as she can swim.

JOHN J. CHAPMAN
Essayist, died 1784.

I want to take it away! I want to take it away!
Did he mean the pillow?
No, no! The mute, the mute! I want to play on the open strings!

G. K. CHESTERTON
Essayist, critic, novelist and poet, died 1936.

The issue now is clear: it is between light and darkness and everyone must choose his side.

TALBOT CLIFTON
Explorer, died 1928.

Oh, I offer it.

COLETTE
French novelist, died 1954.

To reach completion is to return to one's starting point. My instinctive bent which takes pleasure in curves and spheres and circles.

ALFRED COOKMAN
American divine, died 1871.

I am sweeping through the gates, washed in the blood of the Lamb!

THOMAS CORYAT
Explorer, died 1617. Dying in delirium at Surat in Persia . . .

Sack, sack! Is there any such thing as sack? Pray you give me some sack!

WILLIAM COWPER
British poet, died 1800.
What does it signify?

DAVID COX
British painter, died 1859.
What does it signify?

STEPHEN CRANE
American author, died 1900.
When you come to the hedge that we must all go over, it isn't so bad. You feel sleepy, you don't care. Just a little dreamy anxiety, which world you're really in, that's all.

MARION CRAWFORD
American novelist, died 1909.
I love to see the reflection of the sun on the bookcase.

ISAPWO MUKSIKA CROWFOOT
Indian chief, died 1890.
A little while and I will be gone from among you. Whither I cannot tell. From nowhere we come, into nowhere we go. What is life? It is the flash of a firefly in the light. It is the breath of the buffalo in the wintertime. It is as the little shadow that runs across the grass and loses itself in the sunset.

CLEMENTINE CUVIER
Daughter of Baron Georges Cuvier.
You know we are sisters for eternity. There is life. It is only there that there is life.

JACQUES DAVID
French painter, died 1825. Checking a print of one of his own paintings . . .
Too dark . . . too light . . . the dimming of the light is not well enough indicated . . . this place is blurred . . . however, I must admit, that is a unique head of Leonidas.

EDOUARD DEKKER
'Multatuli', Dutch radical writer, died 1887. Writing
to his postal chess opponent . . .
That you are still not crushed, I admit, but that will come a little later. And if this is too difficult for you, let it go if you like. The game can wait.

DENIS DIDEROT
French philosopher and critic, died 1784.
The first step towards philosophy is incredulity.

FREDERICK DOUGLASS
Black rights campaigner, died 1895.
Why, what does this mean?

ELEANORA DUSE
Actress, died 1924.
We must stir ourselves. Move on! Work, work! Cover me! Must move on! Must work! Cover me!

☠

THOMAS ALVA EDISON
Pioneer of the telephone, died 1931.
It is very beautiful over there.

☠

JOHANN FAUST
A wandering conjurer, subject of works by Goethe and Marlowe,
died 1541. His death, in Goethe's 'Faust' (1832) seeing
a vision of beauty appear . . .
Ah, stay, thou art so fair.

ROBERT FERGUSSON
Scottish poet, died insane 1774. To a warder . . .
What ails ye? Wherefore sorrow for me, sirs? I am very well cared for here. I do assure you. I want for nothing, but it is cold, it is very cold. You know, I told you, it would come to this at last, yes, I told you so. Oh, do not go yet, mother. I hope to be soon, oh, do not go yet, do not leave me!

KATE FIELD
Lecturer and explorer, died 1896.
The Amherst Eclipse Expedition!

SOLOMON FOOT
US Senator, died 1866.
What, can this be death? Is it come already? I see it, I see it!
The gates are wide open. Beautiful, beautiful.

REAR ADMIRAL ANDREW HULLE FOOTE
US Navy, died 1863.
We will have them, North and South. The coloured people, yes,
we will have them. We must have charity, charity, charity . . .

ARCHIBALD FORBES
*British war correspondent, died 1900. Remembering
the horrors of the Zulu Wars . . .*
Those guns, man, those guns! Don't you hear those guns.

SIR BARTLE FRERE
Colonial official, died 1884.
If they would only read *The Further Correspondence*, they would
surely understand. They must be satisfied.

FRIEDRICH FROEBEL
Educator, died 1852. Asking to be taken out into his garden . . .
My friend, I have peeked at lovely Nature all my life. Permit me
to pass my last hours with this enchanting mistress.

F. J. FURNIVALL
*British scholar, first editor of the Oxford English Dictionary,
died 1910. Asked how he wished to be remembered . . .*
I want the Club.

☠

PIERRE GASSENDI
French metaphysician and philosopher, died 1655.
You see what is man's life.

THOMAS GOFFE
Poet, died 1629. He had been told by one Thomas Thimble
that his wife would break his heart . . .

Oracle, oracle, Tom Thimble.

HENRI GREGOIRE
Bishop of Blois, died 1831. His mind was lost in delirium . . .

Monsieur Baradère, I have been tormented for eight days. I see a whole population of blacks isolated on an island which serves as their refuge. They are going to die of hunger! I was told that some Protestants and Jews came to see me; although they are not of my church, I desire to make acknowledgements of them. Let someone send theological books to Haiti. The poor Haitians! I see that my last hour is come. Do not desert me in my last moments!

☠

MRS HENRIETTA HAMLIN
Missionary in Turkey, died late 19th Century.

What child is this? Is it little Carrie? Yes! It is little Carrie, and the room is full of them.

KASPER HAUSER
Killed mysteriously, 1833. Hauser's enigmatic appearance in Germany fascinated Europe. Some claimed he was the son of the Grand Duke of Baden, put aside to favour a relation. No one ever discovered the truth . . .

I didn't do it myself. Many cats are the sure death of a mouse.

REV. JOHN HENLEY
'Orator Henley', died 1756. He could apparently see some heavenly vision . . .

Stay! Stay! Stay!

O. HENRY
(William S. Porter)
American short story writer, died 1910.

Turn up the lights. I don't want to go home in the dark.

Thomas Hobbes
Political theorist, died 1679.
I am about to take my last voyage. A great leap in the dark.

Charles Hodge
American theologian, died 1878.
My work is done. The pins of the tabernacle are taken out.

A. E. Housman
Classical scholar, died 1936. On hearing a joke as he lay dying . . .
I'll tell that story on the golden floor.

Victor Hugo
French poet, died 1885.
I see the black light!

Vincente Blasco Ibanez
Spanish novelist, died 1928.
My garden, my garden!

Henry James
American novelist, died 1916.
So here it is at last, the distinguished thing.

Don John of Austria
Spanish general, died 1578. He was speaking in a child's high-pitched voice . . .
Aunt, Aunt! My lady Aunt!

Edmund Kean
British actor, died 1833. In a delirium . . .
Give me another horse . . . Howard!

'CHOLLY KNICKERBOCKER'
(Maury Paul) New York gossip columnist, died 1942.
Oh Mother, how beautiful it is.

CHARLES LEE
American Revolutionary General, died 1782.
Delirious . . .
Stand by me, my brave grenadiers.

ROBERT E. LEE
Confederate general in American Civil War, died 1870.
Strike the tent!

CHARLES, PRINCE DE LIGNE
French aristocrat, died 1814. Raving at some unseen horror . . .
Back, thou accursed phantom!

FRANZ LISZT
Composer, died 1886.

Tristan!

GUSTAV MAHLER
Composer, died 1911.

Mozart!

MATTHEW MAURY
Scientist and writer, died 1873.
Bear me through the pass where the laurels bloom. Are my feet
growing cold? Do I drag my anchors? All's well.

GENERAL GEORGE GORDON MEADE
American Civil War commander, died 1872.
I am about crossing a beautiful wide river and the opposite shore
is coming nearer and nearer.

HERMAN MELVILLE
*American author, died 1891. The writer quoted his
own character 'Billy Budd' . . .*
God bless Captain Vere!

JULES MICHELET
French historian, died 1874. His doctor had ordered the
nurse to change his linen . . .

Linen, doctor, you speak of linen. Do you know what linen is? The linen of the peasant, of the worker . . . linen is a great thing, I want to make a book of it.

SILAS WEIR MITCHELL
American neurologist and author, died 1914.
As he died, the doctor relived an emergency operation on a
Civil War battlefield . . .

That leg must come off. Save the leg – lose the life!

DWIGHT MOODY
American evangelist, died 1899.

I see earth receding. Heaven is opening. God is calling me.

☗

LAURENCE OLIPHANT
Journalist, traveller and mystic, died 1888.

More light!

☗

EDWARDS PARK
Educator and scholar, died 1899.

These passages may be found on the following pages.

SIR WILLIAM PARRY
Arctic explorer, died 1855.

The chariots and the horses!

REV. EDWARD PAYSON
Divine, died 1827.

Faith and patience hold out. I feel like a mote in a sunbeam.

LUIGI PIRANDELLO
Italian dramatist, died 1936.

The hearse, the horse, the driver and – enough!

BISHOP PORTEOUS
Died 1808.

Oh, that glorious sun!

☠

THOMAS DE QUINCEY
British writer, died 1859. In his final delirium . . .

Sister, sister, sister.

☠

JOHN RAYMOND
Scholar.

How easy to glide from the work here to the work there.

CHARLES READE
Reformer and dramatist, died 1884.

Amazing, amazing glory! I am having Paul's understanding.

JEAN PAUL RICHTER
German romantic novelist, died 1825.

My beautiful flowers, my lovely flowers.

ROBBIE ROSS
Companion of Oscar Wilde, died 1918. Punning on
Keats' famous farewell lines . . .

Here lies one whose name was written in hot water.

JEAN JACQUES ROUSSEAU
French political theorist, died 1778.

See the sun, whose smiling face calls me, see that immeasurable light. There is God! Yes, God himself, who is opening His arms and inviting me to taste at last that eternal and unchanging joy that I had so long desired.

REV. SAMUEL RUTHERFORD
Divine, died 1779.

If he should slay me ten thousand times, ten thousand times I'll trust him. I feel, I feel, I believe in joy and rejoice. I feed on manna. Oh for arms to embrace him. Oh for a well-tuned harp!

☠

AUGUSTE SAINT-GAUDENS
French sculptor, died 1907. He was watching a sunset . . .
It's very beautiful, but I want to go farther away.

JULES AMI SANDOZ
American pioneer.
The whole damn sandhills is deserted. The cattlemen are broke, the settlers about gone. I got to start all over, ship in a lot of good farmers in the spring, build up, build, build . . .

JOHANN VON SCHILLER
German dramatist and poet, died 1805.
Many things are growing plain and clear to my understanding. One look at the sun . . .

MARY-ANNE SCHIMMELPENNINCK
Author of children's books, died 1856.
Oh, I hear such beautiful voices, and the children are the loudest.

FRIEDRICH VON SCHLEGEL
Literary historian, died 1829.
But the consummate and perfect knowledge . . .

'DUTCH SCHULTZ'
(*Arthur Fleigenheimer*)
New York gangster, shot 1935. Police stenographers recorded the Dutchman's last ravings in an attempt to gain some information. They could make little sense of them . . .
Turn your back to me, please Henry, I am so sick now. The police are getting many complaints. Look out. I want that G-note. Look out for Jimmy Valentine, for he's a friend of mine. Come on, come on, Jim. OK, OK, I am all through. I can't do another thing. Look out mamma. Look out for her. Police, mamma, Helen, please take me out. I will settle the incident. Come on, open the soak duckets; the chimney sweeps. Talk to the sword. Shut up, you got a big mouth! Please help me to get up. Henry! Max! Come over here. French Canadian bean soup. I want to pay. Let them leave me alone.

GEORGE AUGUSTUS SELWYN
Bishop of Lichfield, died 1878.
It is all light.

MLLE LOUISE SERMENT
'The Philosopher'.

Soon the light of the skies
Will be gone from my eyes.
Soon the black night will creep,
Bringing smooth dreamless sleep.
Gone – the struggle and strife
Of the sad dream of life.

WILLIAM SHARP
Scottish poet, wrote as 'Fiona Macleod', died 1905.
Oh, the beautiful 'Green Life' again. Ah, all is well.

JOANNA SOUTHCOTT
*Religious fanatic and mystic, died 1814. Southcott died of
brain disease, still convinced of her supernatural powers,
though when her famous Box of Prophecies was opened in
1927 it was found to contain nothing of interest . . .*
If I have been deceived, doubtless it was the work of a spirit.
Whether the spirit was good or bad I do not know.

SIR HENRY STANLEY
Explorer, died 1904.
Four o'clock. How strange. So that is time. Strange. Enough!

BELLE STARR
*Horse thief and bandit, died 1889. The 'Bandit Queen'
of the Old West, beloved of romantic myth-makers,
perpetuated the illusions on her gravestone . . .*
Shed not for her the bitter tear
Nor give the heart to vain regret.
'Tis but the casket that lies here,
The gem that fills it sparkles yet.

GERTRUDE STEIN
*American writer and patron of the Arts, died 1945.
Stein's last conversation was recorded by Duncan Sutherland . . .*
Just before she died she asked, 'What is the answer?' No answer
came. She laughed and said, 'In that case, what is the question?'

JANE TAYLOR
Author of children's books, died 1823.
Are we not children, all of us?

LORD TENTERDEN
Jurist, died 1832.
Gentlemen of the jury, you will now consider your verdict.

ALFRED, LORD TENNYSON
Poet, died 1892. Whether Tennyson referred to a
package, or something more mysterious, was not established . . .
I have opened it.

SAINT TERESA
Religious reformer and mystic, died 1582.
Over my spirit flash and float in divine radiancy the bright and
glorious visions of the world to which I go.

WILLIAM THACKERAY
British novelist, died 1863.
And my heart throbbed with an exquisite bliss.

THEODORE THOMAS
Orchestra conductor, died 1905.
I have had a beautiful vision, a beautiful vision.

HENRY THOREAU
Radical, ascetic and writer, died 1862. Asked if he had
made his peace with God?
We never quarrelled. Moose . . . Indian . . .

HIDEKO TOJO
Japanese politician and soldier, died 1948.
Oh look, see how the cherry blossoms fall mutely.

LEO NICOLAYEVITCH TOLSTOY
Russian novelist, died 1910.
The truth . . . I care a great deal . . . how they . . .

J. M. W. TURNER
British artist, died 1851.
The Sun is God.

MARK TWAIN

American humorous novelist, died 1910. Twain's
deathbed memorandum . . .

Death, the only immortal, who treats us all alike, whose peace
and whose refuge are for all. The soiled and the pure, the rich
and the poor, the loved and the unloved.

☠

JONAH USTINOV

'Klop', father of Peter Ustinov, died 1962.

I will remember you in my dreams.

☠

DANIEL WEBSTER

American lawyer and politician, died 1852.

Well children, doctor, I trust on this occasion I have said nothing
unworthy of Daniel Webster.

Life – life. Death – death. How curious it is.

SARAH WESLEY

Wife of John Wesley.

Open the gates! Open the gates!

☠

VICTOR YVART

Belgian writer, died 1831.

Nature, how lovely thou art.

☠

FLORENZ ZIEGFELD

American showman and impresario, died 1932.
Dying in his apartment, Ziegfeld imagined himself once more
at a 'Follies' first night . . .

Curtain! Fast music! Light! Ready for the last finale! Great!
The show looks good, the show looks good!

NEARER MY GOD

BISHOP ABBOT
Died 1633.

Come Lord Jesus, come quickly. Finish in me the work that Thou hast begun. Into Thy hands oh Lord I commend my spirit, for Thou hast redeemed me, oh God of truth. Save Thy servant who hopes and confides in Thee alone. Let Thy mercy, oh Lord, be shown unto me. In Thee have I trusted, Oh Lord, let me not be confounded for ever.

MARIE ADELAIDE
*Duchess of Luxembourg. Madame de Maintenon
promised her that she would be with God ...*

Yes, Aunt.

ALBERT, MARGRAVE OF BRANDENBURG
Died 1170.

Lord Jesu!

CARDINAL AMBOISE
French clergyman, died 1510.

I believe.

FISHER AMES
American politician, died 1808.

I have peace of mind. It may arise from stupidity, but I think it is founded on a belief of the gospel. My hope is in the mercy of God.

JAMES ANDREW
Methodist bishop, died 1833.

God bless you all.

EUSEBIUS ANDREWS
Divine, beheaded 1650.
Lord Jesus receive me!

ANGELIQUE ARNAULD
'Mire Angelique', Jansenist reformer and nun, died 1661.
Jesus, oh Jesus, you are my God, my justice, my strength, my all.

EARL OF ARUNDEL
Catholic aristocrat, beheaded 1580.
Jesus, Mary!

ROGER ASCHAM
British humanist and gambler, died 1568.
I desire to die and be with Christ.

CARDINAL D'ASTE
French clergyman.
I wish to die sitting, in tribute to the most worshipful will of my good and precious Jesus.

CARDINAL D'ASTROS
Died 1851.
Neither life, nor death, nor any being can separate us from Him.

☠

DR FREDERICK BAEDEKER
Missionary, died 1906.
I am going in to see the King in all His beauty.

JOHN BANNISTER
British comic, died 1836.
My hope is in Christ.

RICHARD BAXTER
Presbyterian divine, died 1691.
I have pain – there is no arguing against sense – but I have peace.
I have peace! I am almost well.

CARDINAL BEATON
Died 1546.
I am a priest. Fie, fie! All is gone!

Rev. Joseph Beaumont
Died 1699. The vicar collapsed in the pulpit after
announcing the next hymn . . .
Then, while the first Archangel sings
He hides his face beneath His wings.

The Venerable Bede
Historian, died 735.
It is brought to an end. Take my head in your hands for it is very
pleasing to me to sit facing my holy place where I have been used
to pray, so that I may sit and call upon my Father. Gloria Patri et
Filio et Spiritu Sancto.

Bishop Bedell
Died 1642.
I have kept the faith once given to the Saints for which cause I
have also suffered these things, but I am not ashamed for I know
whom I have believed and I am persuaded that he is able to
keep that which I have committed to him against that day.

Bergerus
Councillor to Emperor Maximillian, died 16th Century.
Farewell, oh farewell all earthly things. And welcome heaven.

Charles, Duc de Berry
French aristocrat, died 1820.
Blessed Virgin, have mercy.

Cardinal de Berulle
Died 1629.
I do bless . . . Jesus, Mary, bless, rule and govern.

Johann Bessarion
German humanist, died 1472.
Thou art just, oh Lord, and just are Thy decrees, but Thou art
good and merciful and Thou wilt not recall our failings.

Edward Bickersteth
Evangelist, died 1850.
The Lord bless thee, my child, with overflowing grace, now and
for ever.

JOHN BLACKIE
Translator and scholar, died 1895.

The Psalms of David and the Songs of Burns, but the Psalmist first. Psalms . . . poetry . . .

AMBROSIUS BLAURER
Swabian reformer.

Oh my Lord Jesus, this made you in your great thirst desire nothing, but you were given gall and vinegar.

BISHOP BLOMFIELD
Died 1857.

I am dying.

JOHANN BLUNTSCHLI
Jurist, died 1881.

Glory be to God in the highest. Peace on earth, good will to all men.

HERMAN BOERHAAVE
Dutch doctor, died 1738.

He that loves God ought to think nothing desirable but what is pleasing to the Supreme Goodness.

HENRY, VISCOUNT BOLINGBROKE
Philosopher and politician, died 1751. Letter to
Lord Chesterfield . . .

God who placed me here will do what He pleases with me hereafter and He knows best what to do. May He bless you.

AUGUSTE BOUVIER
Protestant theologian, died 1564.

My God, my God!

ROBERT BOYLE
Chemist, died 1691.

We shall there desire nothing that we have not, except more tongues to sing more praise to Him.

ALDER BRADFORD
Massachusetts politician, died 1843.

Peace!

DAVID BRAINERD
Missionary, died 1747.

I am almost in eternity. I long to be there. The watcher is with me. Why tarry the wheels of his chariot? Lord, now let Thy servant depart in peace.

JOHANN BREITINGER
Swiss critic, died 1776.

Living or dying, we are the Lord's.

FREDERIKA BREMER
(Sweden's Jane Austen) died 1865.

Ah, my child, let us speak of Christ's love – the best, the highest love.

ARTHUR BRISBANE
Journalist, died 1836.

This is the best of all possible worlds.

BISHOP BROOKS OF MASSACHUSETTS
Died 1893.

There is no other life but the eternal.

ELBRIDGE BROOKS
Editor, died 1902.

My head is pillowed on the bosom of the dear Lord.

JOHN BROWN
Scottish preacher, died 1787.

My Christ!

ROBERT BRUCE
Died 1631.

Now God be with you, my dear children. I have breakfasted with you and shall sup with my Lord Jesus Christ.

WILLIAM JENNINGS BRYAN
American politician, died 1925.

With hearts full of gratitude to God.

MARTIN BUCER
Protestant reformer, died 1551. He pointed three
fingers to the sky . . .
He governs and disposes all.

GEORGE BULL
Theologian, died 1710.
Amen.

WILLIAM BULL
Congregationalist minister, died 1814.
Bless the Lord!

JOHN BUNYAN
Religious writer, died 1688. Bunyan quoted the
burial service . . .
Weep not for me but for yourselves. I go to the Father of our
Lord Jesus Christ who will, no doubt, through the mediation of
His blessed Son, receive me, though a sinner. Where I hope that
we, ere long, shall meet to sing the new song and remain ever-
lastingly happy, world without end.

MAJOR-GENERAL ANDREW BURN
British soldier, died 1824. Asked if he would like to see
anyone . . . ?
Nobody, nobody but Jesus Christ. Christ crucified is the stay
of my poor soul.

LADY ISABEL BURTON
Died 1896.
Thank God.

HORACE BUSHNELL
Died 1876.
Well, now we are all going home together and I say, the Lord be
with you and in grace and in peace and love. And that is the way
I have come along home.

SIMEON CALHOUN
Missionary, died 1876.
Were the church of Christ what she should be, twenty years

would not pass away without the story of Christ being uttered in the ear of every living person.

ANTONIO CANOVA
Sculptor, died 1822.
Pure and amiable spirit.

WILLIAM CARSTARES
Divine, died 1715.
I have peace with God through our Lord Jesus Christ.

WILLIAM CAXTON
First British printer, died 1491.
God then give us His grace and find in us such a house that it may please Him to lodge therein, to the end that in this world He keeps us from adversity spiritual and in the end of our days He brings us with Him into His realm of heaven for to be partners of the glory eternal the which grant to us the Holy Trinity. Amen.

THOMAS CHARLES
Preacher, died 1814. Offered a glass of Madeira . . .
Yes, if the Lord pleases.

MATTHIAS CLAUDIUS
Poet, died 1815.
Lead me not into temptation. Deliver me from evil. Goodnight.

THOMAS COBDEN-SANDERSON
Designer and bookbinder, died 1922. Last entry in his diary . . .
Every day, every day my Guide says to me 'Are you ready?'
   And I say to my guide 'I am ready.'
And my Guide says 'March'
And to the end one day more
   I march.
Oh every day, every day,
Am I ever on the ever-diminishing
   way to the end, the end.

SIR EDWARD COKE
Jurist, died 1633.
Thy kingdom come, Thy will be done.

GIOVANNI COLUMBINI
Founder of the Jesuate Order, died 1367.

Father, into Thy hands I commend my spirit.

CHRISTOPHER COLUMBUS
Explorer, died 1506.

Into Thy hand, Oh Lord, I commit my spirit.

JOSIAH CONDER
Author, died 1855.

Amen.

BISHOP COPLESTON
Died 1849.

I expect soon to die and I die in the firm faith of the redemption wrought by God in man through Christ Jesus, assured that all who believe in Him will be saved.

BISHOP COSIN
Died 1672.

Lord.

DR JOHN COZEN
Divine, died 1672.

Lord!

BISHOP CREIGHTON
Died 1901.

God.

HOWARD CROSBY
American scholar, died 1891.

My heart is resting sweetly with Jesus and my hand is in His.

BISHOP CUMMINGS
Died 1876.

Jesus! Precious Saviour!

ERNEST CURTIUS
Archaeologist, died 1896.

As the bird with the day's last gleam
Wearily sings itself asleep.

As it twitters in its dream
Ever fainter comes its peep.
So my songs scarce reach the ear,
Overtaken by my night.
But the loud ones will burst clear
When it comes – another light!

VARINA H. DAVIS
Wife of Jefferson Davis, died 1898.
Oh Lord, in Thee have I trusted. Let me not be confounded.

WENTWORTH DILLON
*Earl of Roscommon, died 1684. His own translation
of the Dies Irae . . .*
My God, my Father and my Friend, do not forsake me in the end.

DUCHESSE DE DONDEAUVILLE
French aristocrat. Asked if she loved God . . .
Yes.

PAUL L. DUNBAR
Poet, died 1906.
Through the valley of the shadow.

MARY BAKER EDDY
American evangelist, died 1910.
God is my life.

RICHARD LOVELL EDGEWORTH
Writer, died 1817.
I die with the soft feeling of gratitude to my friends and submission to the God who made me.

JONATHAN EDWARDS
Divine, died 1758.
Trust in God and you need not fear.

ERASMUS
Humanist, died 1536.
Dear God!

THOMAS ERSKINE OF LINLATHEN
Theologian, died 1639.

You there! To the end. Oh Lord, my God. Jesus, Jesus Christ! Love. The peace of God, for ever and ever, for Jesus' sake, Amen and Amen.

JEREMIAH EVARTS
Missionary, died 1831.

Wonderful, wonderful glory. We cannot understand, we cannot comprehend, wonderful glory, I will praise Him. Who are in the room? Call all in, call all, let a great many come. I wish to give directions, wonderful glory, Jesus reigns.

MARCHESA GIULIETTA FALETTI
Prison reformer.

May the will of God be done in me and by me in time and for eternity.

JOHN FAWCETT
Baptist theologian, died 1817.

Come Lord Jesus, come quickly! Oh receive me to Thy children!

ABBÉ EDGEWORTH DE FIRMONT
Executed 1793. Supposed words to Louis XVI of France as he mounted the scaffold . . .

Son of Saint Louis, ascend to heaven.

JAMES ELROY FLECKER
American poet, died 1915.

Lord, have mercy on my soul.

JOHN FOSTER
Essayist, died 1876.

I commend you to the God of mercy, and very affectionately bid you – Farewell.

SAMUEL FOTHERGILL
Quaker, died 1772.

All is well with me. Through the mercy of God, in Jesus Christ, I am going to a blessed and happy eternity. My troubles are ended. Mourn not for me.

GEORGE FOX
Founder of the Quaker movement, died 1691.

I am glad I was here. Now I am clear. I am fully clear. All is well. The Seed of God reigns over all and over death itself. And though I am weak in body yet the power of God is over all and the Seed reigns over all disorderly spirits.

HENRY WATSON FOX
Missionary, died 1848.

Jesus, Jesus must be first in the heart.

Asked whether he was first in Fox's . . .

Yes He is.

AUGUST FRANCKE
*Scholar and philantropist, died 1727. Asked if Christ
were still with him . . .*

Yes.

JAMES A. FROUDE
Historian, died 1894.

Shall not the Judge of all the earth do right?

ELIZABETH FRY
Prison reformer, died 1845.

Oh dear Lord, help and keep Thy servant.

ANDREW FULLER
*Founder of the American Baptist Missionary Society,
died 1815.*

I have no religious joys, but I have a hope in the strength of which I think I could plunge into eternity.

EDWARD GIBBON
Historian, died 1794.

Mon dieu! Mon dieu!

GEORGE GILFILLAN
Protestant clergyman, died 1878.

I am dying, doctor? . . . the will of the Lord be done . . . Yes, I believe in God, in Christ.

FREDERIC GODET
Swiss theologian, died 1850. To his assembled family . . .
I have carried you in my heart all my life, and I hope it will still
be permitted to do the same up there.

JOHN MASON GOOD
Doctor and writer, died 1827.
Which taketh away the sins of the world.

STEPHEN GRELLET
Quaker missionary, died 1855.
Not my will, but Thine be done.

ROBERT HALDANE
Evangelist, died 1842.
For ever with the Lord. For ever, for ever.

JOHN VINE HALL
Religious writer, died 1860.
Passing away, passing away. Jesus, Jesus! He is, he is! Pray.
Amen!

WILHELM HAUFF
German novelist and poet, died 1827.
Father, into Thy hands I commend my immortal spirit.

FRANCIS HAVERGAL
Poet, died 1879.

He . . .

ROBERT HAWKER
British poet, died 1875.
His banner over me was love.

REV. LEMUEL HAYNES
Divine.
I love my wife, I love my children. But I love my Saviour better
than all.

FATHER ISAAC HECKER
*Founder of the Paulists, died 1888. Insisting on
doing his own blessing . . .*
No, I will.

FELICIA HEMANS
Died 1835.
I feel as if I were sitting with Mary at the feet of my Redeemer,
hearing His voice and learning of Him to be meek and lowly.

EBENEZER HENDERSON
Missionary, died 1858.
My flesh and my heart faileth, but God is the strength of my
heart and my portion for ever.

JAMES HERVEY
Divine, died 1758.
Precious salvation.

HELIUS EOBANUS HESSUS
German humanist, died 1133.
I want to ascend to my Lord.

PETER HEYLIN
Divine, died 1662.
I go to my God and Saviour.

FRANCIS HODGSON
Provost of Eton College, died 1852.
Charming . . . God's mercy.

JAMES HOPE
Physician, died 1841.
I thank God.

WILLIAM HUNTER
Protestant martyr, burned 1555.
Lord, Lord receive my spirit!

REV. EDWARD IRVING
Died 1834.

If I die, I die unto the Lord. Amen.

JOHN ANGELL JAMES
Independent minister, died 1859. To his doctor,
quoting Jesus . . .

Inasmuch as thou hast done it unto one of the least of these, thou hast done it unto Me.

BISHOP JEWELL
Died 1571.

This day let me see the Lord Jesus.

SIR HENRY JONES
Professor of Moral Philosophy, died 1939.

The Lord reigneth, let the earth rejoice.

JOSEPH
Biblical patriarch.

I die. And God will surely visit you and bring you out of the land unto the land which he sware to Abraham, Isaac and Jacob. God will surely visit you and ye shall carry my bones up from hence.

BISHOP KEN
Died 1711.

God's will be done.

JOHANNES KEPLER
Astronomer, died 1630. Asked how he expected
to be saved . . .

Solely by the merits of Jesus Christ, Our Saviour.

CHARLES KINGSLEY
British writer, died 1875. Kingsley quoted from the
Episcopal funeral service . . .

Thou knowest, Oh Lord the secrets of our hearts. Shut not Thy merciful ears to our prayers, but spare us, oh Lord most holy, oh God most mighty, oh holy and merciful Saviour, Thou most worthy judge eternal, suffer us not at our last hour, from any pains of death to fall from Thee.

FRIEDRICH KLOPSTOCK
Religious author, died 1803. Recited the words of his own ode 'der Erbarmer' . . .

Can a woman forget her child that she should not have pity on the fruit of her womb? Yes, she may forget, but I will not forget Thee!

MRS META KLOPSTOCK
Wife of Friedrich Klopstock. To her sister . . .

It is over! The blood of Jesus Christ cleanse thee from all sin!

JOHN KNOX
Protestant reformer, died 1572. Asked whether he had heard prayers . . .

I wish to God you had heard them as I have heard them, and I praise God of that heavenly sound.

WILLIAM H. KRAUSE
Irish divine, died 1852.

I am so restless I can hardly think, but the Lord's hand is not shortened.

☠

JEAN BAPTISTE LACORDAIRE
Died 1861.

My God, open to me!

ADRIENNE LECOUVREUR
Actress, died 1730. Asked by the priest to repent, she pointed to a bust of the Comte de Saxe . . .

There is my universe, my hope my deity.

JOHN LOCKE
Philosopher, died 1704.

Oh, the depths of the riches and the goodness of the knowledge of God.

HENRY LUCE
American magazine entrepreneur, died 1967.

Oh Jesus!

MARY LYON
American educator, died 1849.

I should love to come back to watch over the seminary, but God will take care of it.

CYRUS HALL McCORMICK
Inventor of the mechanical reaper, died 1884.

It's all right, it's all right. I only want heaven.

JOHN McLOUGHLIN
American pioneer, died 1857. Asked 'Comment allez-vous ?'
[literally: How do you go ?], he punned . . .

To God.

RICHARD MANSFIELD
Actor, died 1907.

God is love.

MARGARET OF ANGOULEME
Renaissance writer, died 1549.

Jesus, Jesus, Jesus!

MOTHER MARIANNE
Abbess of Molokai, died 1900.

Now, Sister, to my room.

PERE MARQUETTE
Died 1675.

Jesus, Mary.

MARY, COUNTESS OF WARWICK
Died 1678. To her attendants. . .

Well ladies, if I were but one hour in heaven, I would not again be with you, much as I love you. . .

JOHN F. D. MAURICE
Christian socialist, died 1872.

The knowledge of the love of God, the blessing of God Almighty, the Father, the Son and the Holy Ghost be amongst you – amongst us – and remain with us for ever.

GIUSEPPE MAZZINI
Italian patriot, died 1872.

Yes, yes! I believe in God.

SIR MOSES MONTEFIORE
British magnate, died 1885.

Thank God, thank heaven.

COMTE DE MONTESQUIEU
French political philosopher, died 1755.

I am conscious of the greatness of God and the littleness of Man.

JOHN NEWTON
Divine, once a slaver, died 1807.

I am satisfied with the Lord's will.

MARGARET OGILVY
Mother of James Barrie, died 1895.

God . . . love . . .

MARGARET OLIPHANT
Scottish novelist, died 1897.

I seem to see nothing but God and our Lord.

JOHN OWEN
Nonconformist divine, died 1622. Told by
Rev. William Payne that the first sheet of his 'Meditations
on the Glory of Christ' was being printed . . .

I am glad to hear it. But, oh Brother Payne, the long-wished for day is come at last, in which I shall see that glory in another manner than I have ever done, or was capable of doing in this world.

BLAISE PASCAL
French mathematician and moralist, died 1662.
May God never forsake me.

COVENTRY PATMORE
British poet, died 1896. Embracing his wife . . .
I love you dear, but the Lord is my life and my light.

CAPTAIN J. PATON
Covenanter, beheaded 1684. Last words from the scaffold . . .
Farewell sweet scriptures, preaching, praying, reading, singing and all duties. Welcome, Father, Son and Holy Spirit. I desire to commit my soul to Thee in well-doing. Lord, receive my spirit.

WILLIAM PENN
Founder of Pennsylvania, died 1718.
To be like Christ is to be a Christian.

POPE PIUS IX
Died 1878.
Death wins this time.

JOHN PRESTON
Divine, died 1628.
Blessed be God. Though I change my place I shall not change my company, for I have walked with God while living and now I go to rest with God.

JOSEPH PRIESTLEY
Minister and chemist, died 1804.
I am going to sleep like you, but we shall all awake together and, I trust, to everlasting happiness.

EDWARD PUSEY
High Churchman, died 1882.
My God!

FRANCIS QUARLES
Pamphleteer, died 1644.

What I cannot utter with my mouth, oh Lord, accept from heart and soul.

☠

WILLIAM ROMAINE
British theologian, died 1795.

Holy, holy, holy blessed Lord Jesus. To Thee be endless praise.

PIERRE ROYER-COLLARD
French philosopher, died 1845.

There is nothing solid and substantial in the world but religious ideas.

CHARLES RUSSELL
Lord Russell of Killowen, Judge, died 1900.

My God, have mercy upon me.

REV. THOMAS RUTHERFORD
Divine, died 1771.

He has indeed been a precious Christ to me and now I feel him to be my rock, my strength, my rest, my hope, my joy, my all in all.

☠

LAWRENCE SAUNDERS
Protestant martyr, burnt 1555.

Welcome the cross of Christ. Welcome everlasting life.

ETIENNE SENANCOUR
French romantic novelist, died 1846.

Eternity, be thou my refuge.

ELIZABETH SETON
Founder of the American Sisters of Charity, died 1821.

Soul of Christ sanctify me, body of Christ save me, blood of Christ inebriate me, water out of the side of Christ strengthen me – Jesus, Mary and Joseph.

Mrs Martha Sherwood
British children's author, died 1851.

God is very good. Remember this, my children, that God is love. He that dwelleth in love dwelleth in God, and God in him.

Franz von Sickingen
German nobleman, leader of the Reformation, killed 1523. To his chaplain . . .

I have already confessed my sins to God.

Mrs Jane Lothrop Stanford
Philanthropist and wife of the millionaire, died 1905.

My God forgive my sins.

Sir James Stonehouse
Died 1795.

Precious salvation!

Baron Strathcona and Mount Royal
Canadian administrator, died 1914.

Oh God of Bethel, by whose hand Thy people still are fed.

Simon of Sudbury
Archbishop of Canterbury, killed 1381. After a blow on the neck from one of the John Bull rioters . . .

Ah! It is the hand of God.

Frederick Swartz
Missionary, died 1798.

Had it pleased my Lord to spare me longer I should have been glad. I should have been able to speak yet a word to the sick and the poor. But His will be done. May He in mercy receive me. Into Thy hands I commend my spirit. Thou hast redeemed me, oh Thou faithful God.

Roger B. Taney
American jurist, died 1864.

Lord Jesus, receive my spirit.

TORQUATO TASSO
Courtier and mystic, died 1595.

Lord, into Thy hands I commend my spirit.

BISHOP TAYLOR
Died 1667.

My trust is in God.

EDWARD TAYLOR
American preacher, died 1871. Asked if Jesus was precious? . . .

Why, certainly, certainly.

CATHERINE TEKAKWITHA
'The Lily of the Mohawks', died 1680.

I am leaving you. I am going to die. Remember always what we have done together since we first met. If you change I shall accuse you through the tribunal of God. Take courage, despise the discoursings of those who have not the faith. If they ever try to persuade you to marry, listen only to the Fathers. If you cannot serve God here, go to the Mission at Lorette. Don't give up your mortifications. I shall love you in heaven. I shall pray for you. I shall aid you.

HESTER LYNCH THRALE
Friend of Dr Johnson, died 1821.

I die in the trust and fear of God.

DUDLEY TYNG
Clergyman. Tyng's last words to his father, who asked him if he knew Jesus, provided the keynote for a great hymn . . .

Know him? He is my Saviour and my all. Father, stand up for Jesus!

JAMES USSHER
Archbishop of Armagh, died 1656.

Lord forgive my sins. Especially my sins of omission.

CORNELIUS VANDERBILT
American millionaire, died 1885.
I'll never give up trust in Jesus. How could I let that go.

☠

RICHARD WHATELY
British logician and theologian, died 1863.
Whately backed his chaplain's altered reading of the text,
'Our vile body' from Philippians iii, 21, to 'this body
of our humiliation' . . .
That's right. Not 'Vile'. Nothing that He made is vile.

JONATHAN WILD
Thief and Thief-taker, died 1725. Wild's death-bed
repentance hardly rings true when faced with his record . . .
Lord Jesus receive my soul.

FRANCES WILLARD
Campaigner for temperance, died 1898.
How beautiful to be with God.

JOHN WOOLMAN
Quaker preacher and anti-slavery campaigner, died 1772.
I believe my being here is in the wisdom of Christ. I know not
as to life or death.

☠

BRIGHAM YOUNG
Mormon leader, died 1877.

Amen.

HOLIER THAN THOU

SAINT ACHARD
Died 1170.
No suffering can expiate hate; it is not redeemed by martyrdom. It is a stain that all the blood in us would fail to wash. So I go to join my fathers. Place my body in the sepulchres of our brethren.

SAINT AGATHA
Breasts cut off, 251.
Cruel tyrant, do you not blush to torture this part of my body, you that sucked the breasts of a woman yourself?

SAINT AGATHON
Died 3rd Century.
Show me your charity and speak not to me for I am fully occupied.

SAINT AMBROSE
Died 397. Choosing Bishop Simplicianus as his successor . . .
Old though he be, he is the best of all.

SAINT ANDREW
Apostle, crucified 235.
Oh cross most welcome, most looked for; with a willing mind, joyfully and desirously I come to thee, being the scholar of Him which did hang on thee, because I have always been thy lover and have coveted to embrace thee.

SAINT ANSELM
Died 1109.

Yes, if it be His will I shall obey it willingly. But were He to let me stay with you a little longer till I had resolved a problem about the origin of the soul, I would gladly accept the boon, for I do not know whether anyone will work it out when I am gone. If I could but eat I think I should pick up a little strength. I feel no pain in any part of my body, only I cannot retain nourishment and that exhausts.

SAINT ANTHONY
Died 356.

To Athanasius the bishop give one of my sheepskins and the cloak under me, which was new when he gave it to me and has become old by my use of it, and to Serapion the Bishop give the other sheepskin and do you have the haircloth garment. And for the rest children, farewell, for Anthony is going and is with you no more.

SAINT THOMAS AQUINAS
Died 1274.

I receive Thee, redeeming price of my soul. Out of love for Thee have I studied, watched through many nights and exerted myself. Thee did I preach and teach. I have never said aught against Thee. Nor do I persist stubbornly in my views. If I ever expressed myself erroneously in the sacrament I submit myself to the judgement of the Holy Roman Church, in the obedience of which I now part from this world.

SAINT BERNADETTE SOUBIROUS OF LOURDES
Died 1879.

Blessed Mary Mother of God pray for me a poor sinner. A poor sinner.

SAINT BERNARD
Died 1153.

I know not to which I ought to yield. To the love of my children which urges me to stay here or the love of God which draws me to Him.

SAINT BONIFACE
Killed by having hot lead poured down his throat, 755.
I thank the Lord Jesus, Son of the living God.

SAINT CARLO BORROMEO
Died 1584. Asked when he wished the viaticum . . .
At once.

SAINT JOHN BOSCO
Founder of the Salesian Fathers, died 1888.
Thy will be done.

BUDDHA
Died 483 BC.
Decay is inherent in all component things.

SAINT CATHERINE OF SIENA
Died 1380.
No, I have not sought vain glory. But only the glory and praise of God.

SAINT CECILIA
Killed 230. To Bishop Urbain . . .
I obtained three days delay that I might commend myself and all these to thy beatitude and that thou might consecrate this my house as a church.

SAINT CHRISTODOLE
When deciding where to be buried . . .
My children do not be ungrateful to the desert isle of Patmos, where we have laboured so hard.

SAINT CHRISTOPHER
Killed 3rd Century. A miracle cure that worked . . .
I know O King that I shall be dead on the morrow. When I am dead do you, O tyrant, make a paste of my blood, rub it on your eyes and you shall recover your sight.

SAINT CHRYSOGONUS
Killed 304. To Emperor Diocletian . . .

I adore the One God in heaven and I spurn your proffered dignities as clay.

SAINT COLUMBA
Died 597.

Here I cease. Have peace and love.

SAINT CUTHBERT
Died 687.

For I know that although during my life some have despised me, yet after my death you will see what sort of a man I was and that my doctrine was by no means worthy of contempt.

SAINT CYPRIAN
Killed 258. On hearing his sentence of death . . .

Thanks be to God.

☙

SAINT DOMINIC
Died 1221. When asked where he wanted to be buried . . .

Under the feet of my friars.

☙

SAINT ELIZABETH
Died 1st Century.

The time is already arrived, wherein God has called those that are His friends to the heavenly espousals!

SAINT ELOI
Bishop of Noyon, died 659.

And now, O Christ, I shall render up my last breath in confessing loudly Thy name; receive me in Thy great mercy, and disappoint me not in my hope; open to me the gate of life and render the Prince of Darkness powerless against me. Let Thy clemency protect me, Thy might hedge me, and Thy hand lead me to the place of refreshment and into the tabernacle Thou hast prepared for Thy servants and them that stand in awe of Thee.

SAINT FRANCIS OF ASSISI
Died 1226.

Welcome, sister death.

MAHATMA GANDHI
Assassinated 1948.

Hari Rama! Hari Rama!

SAINT GOAR
Hermit and Patron Saint of the River Rhine, died 575.

Here shall my Saviour be known in all the simplicity of His doctrines. Ah, would that I might witness it, but I have seen these things in a vision. But I faint! I am weary! My earthly journey is finished. Receive my blessing. Go and be kind to one another.

SAINT MARIA GORETTI
(The Martyr of Purity), killed 1902. Stabbed, aged 11, while resisting the advances of a 19 year old youth . . .

May God forgive him; I want him in heaven.

SAINT IGNATIUS
Thrown to the lions, 110 AD.

Let me enjoy these beasts, whom I wish much more cruel than they are; and if they will not attempt me, I will provoke and draw them by force. I am God's wheat and I am ground by the teeth of wild beasts that I may be found pure bread for Christ.

JAMES THE APOSTLE
Brother of John, crucified 43 AD. Kissing his fellow martyr . . .

Peace be to thee, brother.

SAINT JAMES
Stoned to death, 44 AD.

O Lord God, Father I beseech Thee to forgive them, for they know not what they do.

SAINT JAMES THE DISMEMBERED
Killed 421.

O Lord of lords, Lord of the living and the dead, give ear to me who am half dead. I have no fingers to hold out to Thee, O Lord, nor hands to stretch forth to Thee. My feet are cut off and my knees demolished, wherefore I cannot bend the knee to Thee, and I am like to a house that is about to fall because its columns are taken away. Hear me, O Lord Jesus Christ, and deliver my soul from its prison!

SAINT JEAN BAPTISTE DE LA SALLE
Died 1719. When asked if he accepted with joy
his sufferings . . .

Yes. I adore in all things the designs of God in my regard.

SAINT JEROME
Burnt 1416.

Bring thy torch hither. Do thine office before my face. Had I feared death I might have avoided it.

JESUS OF NAZARETH
Crucified 33 AD.

It is finished.

SAINT JOAN OF ARC
Burnt 1431.

Ah Rouen, I have great fear that you are going to suffer by my death. Jesus, Jesus!

SAINT JOHN THE ABBOT
Died 813.

Never have I done my own will, and never have I taught others to do what I had not first done myself!

SAINT JOHN THE ALMONER
Died 616.

I thank Thee, O my God, that Thy mercy has granted the desire of my weakness, which was that at my death I should possess naught but a single penny. And now this penny, too, can be given to the poor!

SAINT JOHN OF THE CROSS
Died 1591.
Into Thy hands, O Lord, I commend my spirit.

SAINT JOHN CHRYSOSTOM
Killed 407.
Glory be to God in all things.

SAINT JOHN THE EVANGELIST
Died 104.
Thou hast invited me to Thy table, Lord; and behold I come, thanking Thee for having invited me, for Thou knowest that I have desired it with all my heart.

SAINT LAWRENCE
Roasted 3rd Century.
This side is roasted enough, turn up, oh tyrant great, assay whether roasted or raw thou thinkest the better meat.

SAINT LEGER
Executed 678. As four swordsmen were leading him away to be beheaded . . .
There is no need to weary yourselves longer, brothers! Do here the bidding of him that sent you!

SAINT IGNATIUS LOYOLA
Died 1556.
Tell him that my hour has come and that I ask his benediction. Tell him that if I go to a place where my prayers are of any avail, as I trust, I shall not fail to pray for him, as I have unfailingly, even when I had most occasion to pray for myself.

SAINT LUCY
Died c.300.

I make known to you that peace is restored to the Church! This very day Maximian has died, and Diocletian has been driven from the throne. And just as God has bestowed my sister Agatha upon the city of Catania as its protectress, so He has this moment entitled me to be the patroness of the city of Syracuse.

☠

SAINT MARGARET
Died 1093. Her last letter . . .

I am of noble birth, and was called Margaret in the world; but in order safely to cross the sea of temptations, I called myself Pelagius, and was taken for a man. I did this not for a lie and a deception, as my deeds have shown. From the false accusation I have gained virtue, and have done penance albeit I was innocent. Now I ask that the holy sisters may bury me, whom men have not known; and that my death may show forth the innocence of my life, when women acknowledge the virginity of one whom slanderers accused as an adulterer.

SAINT MARGARET OF ANTIOCH
Executed 304. To the executioner . . .

Brother, draw thy sword now, and strike!

SAINT MARK THE EVANGELIST
Died 75 AD.

Into Thy Hands I commend my spirit.

SAINT MARTIN OF TOURS
Died c.370. Seeing the Devil near him . . .

Why standest thou here, horrible beast? Thou hast no share in me. Abraham's bosom is receiving me.

MOHAMMED
Died 632.

Oh Allah, be it so.

SAINT MONICA
Mother of Saint Augustine, died 387.
Lay this body wherever it may be. Let no care of it disturb you:
this only I ask of you that you should remember me at the altar
of the Lord wherever you may be.

SAINT OSWALD
Killed at the battle of Maserfield, 642.
Lord have mercy on their souls.

SAINT PANCRATIUS
Killed 1st Century. Aged 14, to the Emperor Diocletian . . .
In body I am a child, but I bear a man's heart: and by grace of
my Master Jesus Christ, thy threats seem as vain to me as this
idol which stands before me. And as for the gods whom thou
desirest me to adore, they are naught but imposters, who sully
the women of their own household, and spare not their own kin.
If thine own slaves today behaved as these gods, thou wouldst
be in haste to put them to death. And it wonders me much that
thou dost not blush to adore such gods!

SAINT PAUL
Died 67 AD. Written in 2nd Epistle to Timothy . . .
Do thy diligence to come before winter. Eubulus greeteth thee,
and Pudens, and Linus, and Claudia, and all the brethren. The
Lord Jesus Christ be with thy spirit. Grace be with you. Amen.

SAINT PAULINUS
Bishop of Nola, died 431.
Thy word is a lantern unto my feet, and a light unto my paths.

SAINT PELAGIA
Died 300.
Hast thou a bishop ? . . . Let him pray the Lord for me, for he is
a true apostle of Christ.

PEMBO
The Hermit.

Thank God that not a day of my life has been spent in idleness. Never have I eaten bread that I have not earned. I do not recall any bitter speech that I have made for which I ought to repent now.

SAINT PERPETUA
Killed in arena by cow 203.

Continue firm in the faith, love one another and don't be scandalized by our sufferings.

SAINT PETER
Crucified 67 AD. To his wife as he was led out to die . . .

Oh thou, remember the Lord Jesus Christ.

SAINT PETER MARTYR
Died 16th Century.

Lord, into Thy hands I commend my spirit.

SAINT POLYCARP
Burnt 166. Refusing to be nailed to the stake . . .

He who gives me the power will grant me to remain in the flames without the security you will give by the nails.

SAINT PRISCA
Killed 250.

My courage and my mind are so firmly founded upon the firm stone of My Lord Jesus Christ that no assault can move me. Your words are but wind, your promises are but rain, your menaces are passing floods, and however hardly these things hurtle at the foundation of my courage, they cannot change me.

SAINT PROTASIUS
Executed 352.

I bear thee no anger, count, for I know that thou art blind in thy heart, but rather do I pity thee, for thou knowest not what thou dost. Cease not to torture me, that I may share with my brother the good countenance of our Master.

☠

SAINT SAVINA
Died 311.

O Lord, who hast ever preserved me in chastity, suffer me not longer to be wearied with journeying! Command me not to go beyond this place! Let my body here find rest! I commend to Thee my servant, who has borne so much for me, and let me be worthy to see my brother in Thy kingdom, whom I have not seen here!

SAINT SAVINIANUS
Killed 275.

Fear not to strike me down; and do ye bear away some drops of my blood to the emperor, that he may receive his sight, and acknowledge the power of God.

SAINT SECUNDUS
*Killed 119. When boiling pitch and resin was poured
into his mouth . . .*

How sweet are Thy words to my palate! more than honey to my mouth.

SIXTUS
Bishop, killed 258. Addressing Saint Lawrence.

Cease weeping, you will soon follow me!

SAINT STEPHEN
Killed 1038.

Lord lay not this sin to their charge.

SAINT THEODORA
*Executed 867. Spoken to the child that she was falsely accused
of being the father of when disguised as a monk . . .*

Sweet my son, the end of my life approaches, and I leave thee to God, who shall be thy Father and thy Helper. Sweetest son, persevere in fasting and prayer, and serve thy brethren devoutly.

SAINT THEODORE
Died 690.

With my Christ I was, and am, and will be.

SAINT THOMAS THE APOSTLE
Died 1st Century.

I adore, but not this metal; I adore, but not this graven image; I adore my Master Jesus Christ in Whose name I command thee, demon of this idol, to destroy it forthwith!

SAINT VINCENT DE PAUL
Died 1680.

Jesus.

SAINT FRANCIS XAVIER
Died 1552.

In Thee, O Lord, have I hoped, let me never be confounded!

THE KING IS DEAD

ABIMELECH
King of Judea.

Draw thy sword and slay me; that men say not of me 'A woman slew him'.

AGESILAUS
Died 361 BC.

If I have done any honourable exploit, that is my monument. But if I have done none, then all your statues will signify nothing.

AGIS
King of Sparta, strangled 240 BC.

Weep not for me.

ALBERT
Prince Consort, died 1861. A private farewell . . .

Good little woman.

And a public one . . .

I have had wealth, rank and power, but if these were all, how wretched I should be. Rock of ages cleft for me; Let me hide myself in thee.

ALBERT I
King of Belgium, killed in climbing accident, 1934.
To his companions . . .

If I feel in good form I shall take the difficult way up. If I do not, I shall take the easy one. I shall join you in an hour.

ALEXANDER I
Czar of Russia, died 1825.

What a beautiful day.

ALEXANDER II
Czar of Russia, assassinated 1881.

I am sweeping through the gates, washed in the blood of the lamb.

ALEXANDER THE GREAT
King of Macedon, died 323 BC.

To the strongest!

ALEXANDER
King of Judea, died 78 BC.

Fear not true Pharisees, but greatly fear painted Pharisees.

ALEXANDER VI
Pope, Roderigo Borgia, died 1503.

I come. It is right. Wait a minute.

ALFONSO XIII
King of Spain, died 1941.

Spain, My God!

ALI PASHA
'The Lion of Janina', assassinated 1822.

Go my friend, dispatch poor Vasiliky, that these dogs may not profane her beauteous form.

ANDRONICUS I
Roman Emperor of Comneni Dynasty, assassinated 1185.

Lord have mercy on me! Wilt thou break a bruised reed?

ANNE OF AUSTRIA
Died 1666.

M. de Montaigu, consider what I owe to God, the favour He has shown to me and the great indulgence for which I am beholden to Him.

ANNE
Queen of England, died 1714. While handing the staff of the Treasury to Lord Shrewsbury . . .

Use it for the good of my people.

ANTONINUS PIUS
Roman Emperor, died 161.

Tranquility.

ARTAGERSES
King of Persia, died 424 BC. To Cyrus the Younger

Oh most unjust and senseless of men, who are the disgrace of the honoured name of Cyrus, are you come here leading the wicked Greeks on a wicked journey to plunder the good things of the Persians, and this with the intention of slaying your Lord and brother, the master of ten thousand times ten thousand servants that are better men than you, as you shall see this instant. For you shall lose your head here before you look upon the face of the King.

ATTICUS
Titus Pomponius, died 132 BC.

I have determined on ceasing to feed the disease, as by the food and drink I have taken during the last few days I have prolonged life only so as to increase my pains, without hope of recovery. I therefore entreat you, in the first place to approve my resolution, and in the next, not to labour in vain trying to dissuade me from executing it.

AUGUSTUS
Roman Emperor, died 14 AD.

Forty young men are carrying me off.

MARCUS AURELIUS
Roman Emperor, died 180.

Go to the rising sun, for I am setting. Think more of death than of me.

AURUNGZEBE
Emperor of Hindustan, died 1707.

Soul of my soul, now I am going alone. I grieve for your help-lessness. But what is the use. Every torture that I have inflicted, every sin that I have committed, every wrong that I have done I carry the consequences with me. Strange that I came with nothing into the world and now go away with this stupendous caravan of sin; wherever I look I see only God. I have greatly sinned and I know not what torment awaits me. Let not Muslims be slain and the reproach fall upon my useless head. I commit you and your sons to God's care and bid you farewell. Your sick mother, Udaipur, would fain die with me. Peace.

BABAR
First Mogul Emperor, died 1530. His prayer for the life of his son was answered when he, not Humayan, died . . .

Oh God, if a life may be exchanged for a life, I, Babar, give my life and my being for Humayan.

BEATRIX
Grand Duchess of Bavaria, died 1447.

Noble prince, dear brother, it is proper that you should know that we fell ill last Monday and though we had hopes of getting the better of our infirmity, we notice that the weakness and sickness is going from bad to worse. We beg you in all friendliness to send one or two of your councillors here so that if God Almighty calls us, your brotherly affection may know what sort of departure we made.

CAMBYSES
King of Persia, died 521 BC.

I charge you all that you do not tamely allow the kingdom to go back to the Medes. Recover it one way or another, by force or fraud. By fraud if it is by fraud that they have seized it, by force if force has helped them in their enterprise. Do this and then may your land bring you forth fruit abundantly and your wives bear children and your herds increase and freedom be your portion for ever. But do it not, make no brave struggle to regain the kingdom and then may my curse be on you and may the opposite of all these things happen to you and not only so, but may you one and all perish at last by such a fate as mine.

CAROLINE
Queen and wife of George II of England, died 1737.

Pray louder that I may hear.

CAROLINE
Princess of Brunswick and wife of George IV of England.
I would spare you the affliction of seeing me die. Pray . . .

CATHERINE OF ARAGON
Wife of Henry VIII of England, died 1536.
Lord into Thy hands I commend my spirit.

CHARLEMAGNE
Died 814.
Into Thy hands, Oh Lord, I commend my spirit.

CHARLES I
King of England, executed 1649.
I die a Christian, according to the profession of the Church of England, as I found it left me by my father. I needed not to have come here; and therefore I tell you, and I pray God it may not be laid to your charge, that I am the Martyr of the People.

CHARLES II
King of England, died 1685. Thinking of his mistress, Nell Gwynn . . .
Let not poor Nelly starve.

CHARLES V
King of France, died 1380.
I find that Kings are happy but in this that they have the power of doing good.

CHARLES VIII
King of France, died 1498.
I hope never again to commit a mortal sin, not even a venial one, if I can help it.

CHARLES IX
King of France, died 1574.
Ah my nurse, my dearest nurse, what blood and murders. I have had but wicked counsel. Oh my God forgive me all that and so it please Thee, have mercy on me.

CHARLES XII
King of Sweden, killed 1718.
Don't be afraid.

CHARLOTTE AUGUSTA
Princess of Wales, died 1817. Calling for Baron Stockmar . . .
They have made me tipsy. Stocky, Stocky!

CHARLOTTE SOPHIA
Wife of George III of England, died 1818.
Told 'There is a better life' . . .
Very true.

CHARMION
Maid of Cleopatra, suicide 30 BC. Asked how
Cleopatra had died . . .
Extremely well, and as became the descendant of many kings.

CHRISTINA
Queen of Sweden, died 1689. Dictating the inscription
on her gravestone . . .
Queen Christina lived LXIII years.

CLEOPATRA
Queen of Egypt, suicide 30 BC. On finding the asp
in a bowl of fruit . . .
So here it is!

CYRUS THE GREAT
King of Persia, died 529 BC.
Remember my last saying: show kindness to your friends then
you shall have it in your power to chastise your enemies. Goodbye my dear sons, bid your mother goodbye for me. And all my
friends, who are here or far away, goodbye.

CYRUS THE YOUNGER
King of Persia, killed 401 BC.
Clear the way, villains, clear the way!

DARIUS III
King of Persia, died 330 BC.
But Alexander, whose kindness to my mother, my wife and my
children, I hope the Gods will recompense, will doubtless thank
you for your humanity to me. Tell him therefore in token of
my acknowledgement, I give him this right hand.

DIDIUS JULIANUS
Roman Emperor, killed 193.
What harm have I done ? Have I put anybody to death ?

EDMUND
Saint and King of East Anglia, killed for refusing to abjure his religion 870.
Jesus, Jesus!

EDWARD I
King of England, died 1307.
Carry my bones before you on your march. For the rebels will not be able to endure the sight of me, alive or dead.

EDWARD
The Black Prince, died 1327.
I thank Thee, O Lord, for all Thy benefits. With all my power I ask for Thy mercy that Thou wilt forgive me for all the sins that I, in my wrongdoing, have committed against Thee. And I ask with my whole heart the grace of pardon from all men whom I have knowingly or unwittingly offended.

EDWARD III
King of England, died 1377.
Jesu.

EDWARD VI
King of England, died 1553.
Lord take my spirit.

EDWARD VII
King of England, died 1910.
No, I shall not give in. I shall go on. I shall work to the end.

EDWARD VIII
King of England, on his abdication 1936. Official Proclamation of the Abdication . . .
I Edward VIII, of Great Britain, Ireland, and the British Dominions beyond the seas, King, Emperor of India, do hereby declare My irrevocable determination to renounce the throne for Myself and My descendants, and My desire that effect

should be given to this Instrument of Abdication immediately. In token whereof I have hereunto set My hand this 10th day of December 1936, in the presence of witnesses whose signatures are subscribed.

ELIZABETH I
Queen of England, died 1603. To Robert Cecil . . .
Must! Is must a word to be addressed to princes? Little man, little man! Thy father, if he had been alive, durst not have used that word. All my possessions for one moment of time.

ELIZABETH CHRISTINE
Wife of Frederick the Great, died 1797.
I know you will not forget me.

'MADAME' ELIZABETH
Sister of Louis XVI, guillotined 1794.
In the name of modesty, cover my bosom.

EPAMINONDAS
King of Thebes, killed 362 BC.
Now is the time to die. The victories of Leuctra and Mantinea are daughters enough to keep my name alive.

FAROUK
King of Egypt, deposed 1952.
There will soon be only five Kings left: the Kings of England, Diamonds, Hearts, Spades and Clubs.

FRANZ FERDINAND
Archduke of Austria, killed 1914. His assassination at Sarajevo started the First World War . . .
Sophie, don't die, live for the children.

FRANZ JOSEPH
Emperor of Holy Roman Empire, died 1916.
God preserve the Emperor!

FREDERICK THE GREAT
King of Prussia, died 1786.

I am tired of ruling over slaves. We are over the mountain, we shall go better now.

FREDERICK WILLIAM
King of Prussia, died 1740. In reply to the priest's words 'Naked came I out of my mother's womb and naked shall I return' . . .

No, not quite naked, I shall have my uniform on.

FREDERICK V
King of Denmark, died 1776.

It is a great consolation to me in my last hour that I have never wilfully offended anyone and that there is not a drop of blood on my hands.

FREDERICK III
King of Germany, died 1888. To his daughter . . .

Remain as noble and good as you have been in the past. This is the last wish of your dying father.

GALBA
Servius Selpicius, Roman Emperor, killed 69 AD.

What's all this comrades? I am yours and you are mine. Strike, if it be for the good of Rome!

GEORGE IV
King of England, died 1830. To his page Sir Walter Waller . . .

Wally, what is this? It is death, my boy. They have deceived me.

GEORGE V
King of England, died 1936. To his Privy Councillors while having difficulty signing his initials . . .

Gentlemen, I am sorry for keeping you waiting like this. I am unable to concentrate.

His patriotic farewell was . . .

How is the Empire?

But popular tradition claims . . .

Bugger Bognor!

GIANGER

Son of Solyman the Magnificent of Turkey, suicide.
To Solyman, who had killed his son Mustapha
and offered Gianger his brother's spoils . . .

Fie of thee, thou impious and wretched dog, traitor, murderer, I cannot call thee father; take the treasure, the horse and armour of Mustapha to thyself.

GUSTAVUS ADOLPHUS II

King of Sweden, killed 1632. On the battlefield of Lutzen
to the Duke of Lauenberg . . .

I have enough, save thyself brother.

Traditionally . . .

I seal with my blood my religion and the liberties of Germany.

HADRIAN

Roman Emperor, died 138.

O blithe little soul, thou, flitting away,
Guest and comrade of this my clay,
Whither now goest thou, to what place
Bare and ghastly and without grace?
Nor, as thy wont was, joke and play.

HAROUN AL-RASHID

Caliph and patron of the Arts, died 809.

Sahl, remember in a moment like this what the poet has said: 'Descended from a race so great, I firmly bear the hardest fate.'

HENRI IV

King of France, assassinated 1610.

It is nothing.

HENRIETTA ANNE

Duchess of Orleans, died 1670.
Asked by the abbé: 'Madame, you believe in God? You hope
in God? You love God?' . . .

With all my heart.

HENRY IV
King of Germany and Holy Roman Emperor,
died 1106.

O how unhappy I am who squandered such great treasures in vain; how happy I could have been if I had given these things to the poor! But I swear before the eye of the All-Knowing that all my efforts have been for the advancement of my church.

HENRY II
King of England, died 1189.

Shame, shame on a conquered king.

HENRY IV
King of England, died 1413. When told that the chamber in which he was sick was called Jerusalem . . .

Lauds be given to the Father of Heaven, for now I know that I shall die here in this chamber, according to the prophecy of me declared, that I should depart this life in Jerusalem.

HENRY V
King of England, died 1422.

Into Thy hands, O Lord . . .

HENRY VIII
King of England, died 1547.

Monks! Monks! Monks!

HENRY PRINCE OF WALES
Son of James I, died 1612.

I would say somewhat, but I cannot utter it.

CATHERINE HOWARD
Wife of Henry VIII, executed 1542.

I die a Queen, but I would rather die the wife of Culpepper. God have mercy on my soul. Good people, I beg you pray for me.

HUMBERT I
King of Italy, assassinated 1900.

It is nothing . . .

ISABELLA
Queen of Spain, died 1504.

Do not weep for me, nor waste your time in fruitless prayers for my recovery, but pray rather for the salvation of my soul.

JAMES II
King of England, died 1701. To Louis XIV who visited his deathbed . . .

Grateful; in peace.

JAMES V
King of Scotland, died 1542.

The Devil do with it! It will end as it began, it came with a lass and it will go with a lass.

JEHORAM
King of Judea, assassinated 849 BC.

There is treachery, O Ahaziah.

JOHN
King of England, died 1216.

I commit my soul to God and my body to Saint Alstane.

JOSEPH II
Holy Roman Emperor, died 1790.

Let my epitaph be: Here lies Joseph, who was unsuccessful in all his undertakings.

JOSEPHINE
Empress, died 1814.

Napoleon! Elba! Marie Louise!

JUGURTHA
Died in freezing underground cell 104 BC.

Oh Hercules, how cold your bath is!

JULIAN
Roman Emperor, died 363.

You have conquered, Galilean.

JULIUS CAESAR
Roman Emperor, assassinated 44 BC.

Et tu Brute?

DAVID KALAKAUA
*King of the Hawaiian Islands, died 1891. He had
his dying message recorded . . .*

Tell my people I tried to restore our Gods, our way of life . . .

ABDUR RAHMAN KHAN
Amir of Afghanistan, died 1901.

My spirit will remain in Afghanistan, though my soul shall go to
God. My last words to you, my son and successor, are never
trust the Russians.

KONRADIN
King of Sweden, executed 1268.

Oh my mother, how deep will be thy sorrow at the news of
today.

PRINCESSE DE LAMBALLE
*Torn to pieces, 1792. Asked by French Revolutionary
mob to cry, 'Vive la nation!' . . .*

Fie on the horror.

LEOPOLD I
King of Belgium, died 1865.

Don't leave me.

LEOPOLD II
King of Belgium, died 1909.

I am hot.

LOTHAR I
King of the Franks, died 885.

What manner of king is He above who thus doeth to death such
great kings?

LOUIS I
King of France, died 840.
Out, out!

LOUIS IX
King of France, St. Louis, died 1270.
I will enter now into the house of the Lord.

LOUIS XIII
King of France, died 1643.
Dinet! Thoughts arise which trouble me. Well, my God, I consent with all my heart.

LOUIS XIV
King of France, died 1715.
Why weep you? Did you think I should live for ever. I thought dying was harder.

LOUIS XV
King of France, died 1774. Referring to the text of his
public apology to his subjects . . .
Repeat those words, Monsieur Almoner, repeat them.

LOUIS XVI
King of France, guillotined 1793.
I shall drink the cup to the last dregs.

LOUIS XVII
Ten year old son of Louis XVI, died in prison 1795.
I have something to tell you.
I suffer much less. The music is so beautiful.
Listen, listen, in the midst of all those voices
I recognize my mother's!

LOUIS XVIII
Died 1824. Trying to rise from his bed . . .
A king should die standing up.

LOUIS I DE BOURBON-CONDÉ
Killed at the battle of Jarnac, 1686. To D'Argence,
who told him, 'Hide your face' . . .
Ah, D'Argence, D'Argence! you will not be able to save me.

LOUIS II DE BOURBON-CONDÉ
Son of Louis I.

In Thy justice free me.

LOUIS THE DAUPHIN
Son of Louis XV, died 1765. Taking the hand of the
Bishop of Verdun . . .

Lay it on my heart; you have never left it . . .
When the doctor took his pulse . . .
Ah! take the bishop's. What fortitude he has!

MADAME LOUISE
Daughter of Louis XV, died 1800.

Hurry! At a gallop! To Paradise!

LOUISE
Queen of Prussia, died 1820.

I am a Queen but I have no power to move my arms.

MARGARET OF AUSTRIA
Regent of the Netherlands, died 1530.
Letter to her nephew, the future Charles V . . .

I have made you my universal and sole heir, recommending you
to fulfil the charges in my will.

I leave you your countries over here which, during your absence,
I have not only kept as you left them to me at your departure,
but have greatly increased them, and restore to you the government of the same, of which I believe to have loyally acquitted
myself, in such a way as I hope for divine reward, satisfaction
from you, monseigneur, and the goodwill of your subjects;
particularly recommending to you peace, especially with the
Kings of France and England.

And to end, monseigneur, I beg of you for the love you have
been pleased to bear this poor body, that you will remember the
salvation of the soul, and the recommendation of my poor vassals
and servants.

Bidding you the last adieu, to whom I pray, monseigneur, and
give you prosperity and a long life. From Malines, the last day of
November 1530.

Your very humble aunt, Margaret.

MARGARET
Queen of Scotland, died 1445.

Fin de la vie! Qu'on ne m'en parle plus.
(Death. Don't talk to me about it any more.)

MARGARET OF VALOIS
Died 1594.

Farewell and remember me.

MARIA THERESA OF AUSTRIA
Died 1780.

I could sleep, but must not give way to it. Death is so near, he must not be allowed to steal upon me unawares. For fifteen years I have been making ready for him, and must meet him awake.

MARIA THERESA OF FRANCE
Died 1682. It was raining outside ...

Yes, it is indeed frightful weather for a journey as long as the one before me.

MARIE ANTOINETTE
Guillotined 1793. Having tripped over the executioner's foot ...

Monsieur, I beg your pardon. I did not do it on purpose.

MARY
Queen of England, died 1558.

When I am dead and opened, you shall find 'Calais' lying in my heart.

MARY II
*Queen of England, died 1694. To Archbishop Tillotson
who broke down while praying for her ...*

My Lord, why do you not go on? I am not afraid to die.

MARY QUEEN OF SCOTS
Executed 1587.

Do not cry, I have prayed for you. In You, Lord, I have faith, and You shall protect me for ever. Into Thy hands, O Lord, I commend my spirit.

MAXIMILIAN
Emperor of Mexico, died 1867. His wife's name ...

Lotte!

MONTEZUMA II
Last Aztec Emperor, died 1520. Forgiving his old
enemy Cortes . . .
For all my misfortunes, Malinche, I bear you no ill will.

JOACHIM MURAT
'The King of Naples', shot 1815.
Soldiers, do your duty. Aim for the heart but spare the face. I
have too often faced death to fear it.

☠

NAPOLEON II
Duke of Reichstadt, died 1832.
Call my mother! Call my mother! Take the table away. I don't
need anything any more . . . Poultices.

NAPOLEON III
Died 1873. In exile . . .
Were you at Sedan?

☠

OSCAR
King of Sweden, died 1907.
Don't let them shut the theatres for me.

MARCUS SALVIUS OTHO
Roman Emperor, suicide by falling on his sword,
69 AD. To one of his freedmen . . .
Go then and show yourself to the soldiers, lest they should cut
you to pieces for being accessory to my death.

☠

PERICLES OF ATHENS
Died 429 BC.
No Athenian, through my means, ever wore mourning.

PRINCE PETER
Brother of Prince Henry the Navigator, died 15th Century.
Oh, body of mine! I feel that you can do not more; and you my

spirit, why should you tarry here? Fight on, comrades! And you, you villains, do your worst!

PETER THE GREAT
Czar of Russia, died 1725. In writing . . .
Give back all to . . .

PETER III
Czar of Russia, strangled on the orders of his wife,
Catherine the Great, 1792.
It was not enough to prevent me reigning over Sweden and to tear from my head the crown of Russia! They must have my life besides!

PHILIP II
King of Spain, died 1598.
I die like a good Catholic. In faith and obedience to the Holy Roman Church.

PHILIP III
King of Spain, died 1621.
Oh would to God I had never reigned. Oh that those years in my kingdom I had lived a solitary life in the wilderness. Oh that I had lived alone with God. How much more secure should I have died. With how much more confidence should I have gone to the throne of God; what doth all my glory profit but that I have so much the more torment in my death.

RICHARD I
King of England, killed in skirmish by one
Bertrand de Gourdon 1199.
Youth, I forgive thee. Take off his chains, give him 100 shillings and let him go.

RICHARD III
King of England, killed 1485.
I will die King of England, I will not budge a foot! Treason! Treason!

RUDOLF OF HAPSBURG
Crown Prince of Austria, suicide pact with
Mary Vetsera 1889. Letter to his wife . . .

Dear Stephanie, You are freed henceforward from the torment of my presence. Be happy, in your own way. Be good to the poor little girl who is the only thing I leave behind. Give my last greetings to all my acquaintances, especially Bombelles, Spindler Latour, Nowo, Gisela, Leopold, etc, etc. I face death calmly; death alone can save my good name. With warmest love from your affectionate Rudolf.

SALADIN
Died 1193. On hearing the passage, 'He is God,
than whom there is no other God, who knoweth the unseen
and the seen, the Compassionate, the Merciful' . . .

True.

SAUL
King of Israel, died c.1000 BC.

Stand, I pray thee, upon me, and slay me; for anguish is come upon me, because my life is yet whole in me.

SEPTIMUS SEVERUS
Roman Emperor, died 211.

Little urn, you will soon hold all that will remain of him whom the world could not contain.

STANISLAUS I
King of Poland, died of burns from his cloak
catching fire 1766.

You gave it me to warm me, but it has kept me too hot.

TAMBERLAINE
Died 1405.

Never yet has death been frightened away by screaming.

THEODORIC THE GOTH
Died 526. Disappearing on a strange coal black steed . . .
I am ill-mounted. This must be the foul fiend on which I ride.
Yet will I return, if God wills and Holy Mary.

TITUS
Roman Emperor, died 81 AD.
My life is taken from me though I have done nothing to deserve
it. For there is no action of mine which I should repent but one.

TZU-HSI
Chinese Empress, died 1908.
Never again allow a woman to hold the supreme power in the
State. It is against the house-law of our dynasty and should be
forbidden. Be careful not to allow eunuchs to meddle in government matters. The Ming dynasty was brought to ruin by
eunuchs, and its fate should be a warning to my people.

VESPASIAN
Roman Emperor, died 79 AD.
Dear me, I must be turning into a god.

MARY VETSERA
Suicide pact with Rudolf of Hapsburg, 1889.
Letter to Marie Larisch . . .
Dear Marie, Forgive me all the trouble I have caused. I thank
you so much for everything you have done for me. If life becomes hard for you, and I fear it will after what we have done,
follow us. It is the best thing you can do. Your Mary.

VICTOR EMMANUEL II
King of Italy, died 1878.
How much longer will it last? I have some important things to
attend to.

VICTORIA
Queen of England, died 1901.
Oh that peace may come.
Bertie!

VITELLIUS
Roman Emperor, executed 69 AD. To executioner . . .
Yet I was once your Emperor.

WILLIAM THE CONQUEROR
Died 1087.
I commend myself to the blessed Lady Mary, hoping by Her intercessions to be reconciled to Her most dear Son, Our Lord Jesus Christ.

WILLIAM II
King of England, killed in shooting accident 1100.
To Walter Tirel, who shot, but not the deer . . .
Shoot, Walter, shoot; as if it were the devil.

WILLIAM III
King of England, died 1702.
Can this last long?

WILLIAM OF ORANGE
Assassinated, 1584.
May God have mercy upon my soul and upon this poor people.

WILLIAM THE SILENT
Founder of Dutch Republic. Asked 'Do you trust your
soul to Jesus Christ?' . . .
Yes.

DULCE ET DECORUM

SIR RALPH ABERCROMBY
*Died in battle 1801. Finding that a soldier had given
up his blanket to put under his wounded body . . .*
Only a soldier's blanket? Make haste and return it to him at once!

ANAXABIUS
Greek soldier, killed in an ambush.
Men, it is good for me to die on this spot where honour bids me, but you hurry and save yourselves before the enemy can close with us.

GENERAL LEWIS ARMISTEAD
American Civil War leader, killed 1863.
Give them the cold steel, men!

GENERAL GEORGE BAYARD
*American Civil War leader, killed at the battle of
Fredericksburg 1862.*
My black mare and sorrel horse I give to you, father. There are about $60 in my pocket book. There are papers in my trunk to be turned over to the Quarter-Master's department to settle. One more goodbye, beloved father, mother, sisters all. Ever yours . . .

BREVET-BRIGADIER-GENERAL LEWIS BENEDICT
*American Civil War leader, killed at the battle of
Pleasant Hill 1864. Giving his last order . . .*
Colonel, rally your men and advance as soon as possible.

COLONEL G. E. BENSON
*British officer in the Boer War, killed at
Bakenlaagte 1899. Benson specialized in night marches and
surprise attacks. He died with 161 out of a force of 178 men . . .*
We shall do no more night marching. It is all day now. Goodbye
and God bless you.

MARCUS JUNIUS BRUTUS
Roman general, killed at the battle of Phillippi 42 BC.
Oh wretched valour thou wert but a name, and yet I worshipped
thee as real indeed. But now it seems thou wert but fortune's
slave.

MARSHAL ROBERT BUGEAUD DE LA PICONNERIE
French general and imperialist, killed 1849.
It is all over with me.

MAJOR HENRY WARD CAMP
*American Civil War leader, killed at the battle of
Richmond 1865.*
Come on boys! Come on!

GENERAL JEAN CHAMPIONNET
*French soldier, died 1800. Dying in bed, he regretted
surviving all his battles . . .*
My friends, take care to console my mother. Would that I had
been able to die like Joubert.

GENERAL AUGUSTE COLBERT
French general, killed 1809. To an aide . . .
You are then very much afraid of dying today?

GENERAL GEORGE CUSTER
*Killed with his men at the battle
of the Little Big Horn, 1876. His last message, penned by
Adjutant Lieutenant W. W. Cooke . . .*
Benteen – come on – Big Village – be quick – bring packs.

Admiral George Dewey
American sailor, died 1917.

Gentlemen, the battle is done. The victory is ours!

Dieneces
Greek warrior. Hearing that the Medean archers were so many that their arrows would darken the sky . . .

Our Trachinian friend brings excellent tidings. If the Medes darken the sun we shall have our fight in the shade.

Colonel Charles Dreux
American Civil War leader, killed at the battle of Newport News.

Steady boys, steady!

Captain George Duff
British sailor, killed at the battle of Trafalgar 1805. Last letter to his wife . . .

My dearest Sophia, I have just had time to tell you that we are going into action with the Combined Fleets. I hope and trust in God that we shall all behave as becomes us and that I may yet have the happiness of taking my beloved wife and children in my arms. Norwich [who had witnessed his father's death] is quite well and happy. I have, however, ordered him off the quarter deck. Yours ever and most truly, Geo. Duff.

Viscount Dundee
Killed at the battle of Killiecrankie 1689. Asked how the battle went and was told 'Well for King James, bad for you' . . .

If it goes well for him it matters the less for me.

Colonel Henry Egbert
Killed during the American invasion of Manila 1899.

Goodbye General. I'm done. I'm too old.

EUCLES
*Greek soldier, killed 490 BC. Eucles had brought with
his last breath the famous message of victory
from the battle of Marathon when a tiny Greek force
defeated the Persians . . .*

Rejoice, we rejoice!

WING COMMANDER PADDY FINUCANE
*Killed in the Battle of Britain 1940. His plane was
shot down over the Channel . . .*

This is it, chaps.

GENERAL CHARLES 'CHINESE' GORDON
Killed at Khartoum 1885.

Where is the Mahdi?

LIEUTENANT BRYANT GRAY
American Civil War soldier.

Forward! March!

LIEUTENANT-COLONEL JOHN GREBLE
*American Civil War officer, killed at the battle of
County Creek 1861.*

Sergeant, take command! Go ahead!

BERTRAND DU GUESCLIN
'The Eagle of Brittany', died 1380.

Remember that your business is only with those that carry arms.
The churchmen, the poor, the women and children are not your
enemies. I commend to the King my wife, my brother . . .
farewell . . . I am at an end.

WILLIAM, DUKE OF HAMILTON
Killed at the battle of Worcester 1651.
*Hamilton was killed fighting for Charles II, although he had
opposed Charles I . . .*

I believe that though in the last hour of the day I have entered
into my Master's service, yet I shall receive my penny.

SIR HENRY HAVELOCK
Killed at the Siege of Lucknow 1857.
Come, my son, and see in what peace a Christian can die.

GENERAL JEAN HUMBERT
French soldier, died 1921.
I die far from my country, too far, alas! To rest one day in the cemetery of my village, beside my poor parents – there I should have wished to die. Ah, my friends . . . let the will of God . . .

GENERAL THOMAS 'STONEWALL' JACKSON
American Civil War leader, killed in error by his own troops at the battle of Chancellorsville 1863.
Let us cross over the river and sit in the shade of the trees.

ALBERT S. JOHNSTON
American Civil War general, killed 1862. Asked if he was wounded? . . .
Yes. And I fear seriously.

THEODOR KOERNER
German patriot and poet, killed in battle 1813.
Referring to his wounds . . .
There I have one but it doesn't matter.

SIR WILLIAM DE LANCEY
Killed at the battle of Waterloo, 1815.
Magdalene, my love, the spirits.

CAPTAIN JAMES LAWRENCE
American sailor, killed 1813. Lawrence commanded the USS Chesapeake *against the* HMS Shannon . . .
Don't give up the ship.

MARSHAL DE MONCEY, DUC DE CONEGLIANO
Soldier in French Revolutionary and Napoleonic armies, died 1842.

Let everyone fulfil and close his course like me.

MARQUIS DE MONTCALM
Killed in battle 1759. Told that he was about to die . . .

So much the better. I shall not then live to see the surrender of Quebec.

SIMON DE MONTFORT
British aristocrat, killed at the battle of Evesham 1265.
To his supporters . . .

Commend your souls to God, for our bodies are the foe's.

CAPTAIN LEWIS NOLAN
Killed at The Charge of the Light Brigade 1854.
Nolan took the fatal message to Lord Lucan. When Lucan seemed unwilling to obey it, Nolan urged him to charge . . .

There are the enemy, my Lord, and there are the guns!

CHARLES PEGUY
French writer, killed at the first battle of the Marne 1914.

Keep firing.

RITTMEISTER MANFRED FREIHERR VON RICHTHOFEN
'The Red Baron', German air ace, shot down 1918.
To his mechanics . . .

Don't you think I'll be back.

LIEUTENANT ALOYSIUS SCHMITT
American Navy chaplain, killed at Pearl Harbour 1941.
Schmitt was chaplain of the USS Oklahoma, bombed by the Japanese. He insisted on being last through the porthole to safety, and his shoulders stuck . . .

Go ahead boys, I'm all right.

COUNT VON SCHWERIN
Prussian soldier, killed 1757. Killed by a cannonball . . .
Let all brave Prussians follow me!

GENERAL SEDGEWICK
American Civil War commander, killed at the
battle of Spotsylvania 1864. Looking foolishly over the parapet
at the enemy lines . . .
They couldn't hit an elephant at this dist . . .

SIR PHILIP SIDNEY
British soldier, killed at the battle of Zutphen 1586. Passing
his water bottle to another wounded man . . .
Thy necessity is yet greater than mine.

SIMONIDES
Glorifying the battle of Thermopylae 480 BC.
Go stranger and to Lacedaemon tell
That here, obedient to her laws, we fell.

GENERAL J. E. B. STUART
American Civil War soldier, killed at the battle of
Yellow Tavern 1864.
I am resigned, if it be God's will.

GENERAL PENN SYMONS
British general in the Boer War, killed 1899.
Symons ignored subordinates' warnings when he stood
on a rampart to survey the scene . . .
I am severely – mortally – wounded in the stomach.

TECUMSEH
Indian chief, killed 1813.
Brother warriors, we are about to enter an engagement from
which I will not return. My body will remain on the field of
battle.

W. BARRETT TRAVIS
Commander of the Alamo, killed there 1836.

I am besieged by one thousand or more of the Mexicans under Santa Anna. I have sustained a continuous bombardment for twenty-four hours and have not lost a man. The enemy have demanded a surrender and I have answered the summons with a cannon shot and our flag still waves proudly from the walls.

LIEUTENANT COMMANDER SAKUMA TSUHMU
Japanese sailor, drowned in submarine 1910. Note found in the submarine . . .

12.30 I feel great pain in breathing. I thought I had blown out gasoline, but I have been intoxicated by gasoline. Commander Nakano . . . It is now 12.40 . . .

VICOMTE DE TURENNE
French soldier, killed at the battle of Salzback 1675.

I did not mean to be killed today.

'MAD ANTHONY' WAYNE
American Revolutionary soldier, killed 1796.

This is the end. I am dying. I can't bear up much longer. Bury me here on the hill by the flagpole.

GENERAL JAMES WOLFE
British soldier, killed in Canada 1759.

Go one of you, my lads, with all speed to Colonel Burton and tell him to march Webb's regiment down to the St Charles River and cut off the retreat of the fugitives from the bridge. Now, God be praised, I die happy.

MY COUNTRY, TIS OF THEE

John Adams
*American President, died 1876. Suggesting his
own epitaph . . .*

Here lies John Adams – who took upon himself the responsibility of peace with France in the year 1800.

Dr John Adams
*American clergyman, died 1862. Final entry in his
diary, saddened by the outbreak of Civil War . . .*

This day I enter my ninety-first year. The year just closed has been one of trial and deep solicitude. My country, oh my country! I do not expect to see peace restored during the short remainder of my stay, but I am earnestly looking forward to the everlasting rest which remaineth to the people of God. God reigns. He will accomplish all his purposes. Amen and Amen.

Anonymous Vietcong Soldier

It is the duty of our generation to die for our country.

Seigneur de Bayard
*'Chevalier sans peur et sans reproche', killed at the
battle of Romagnano 1524.*

Let me die facing the enemy.

Count Otto von Bismarck
German statesman, died 1898.

I do not want a lying official epitaph. Write on my tomb that I was the faithful servant of my master, the Emperor Wilhelm, King of Prussia.

When his daughter wiped his brow . . .
Thank you my child.

ROBERT BLUM
Socialist, shot 1848. He refused the traditional blindfold . . .
I want to look death in the eye. I die for freedom. May my country remember me. I am ready. Let there be no mistake and no delay.

NAPOLEON BONAPARTE
Emperor of France, died 1821.
France! Army! Head of the Army! Josephine!

JOHN WILKES BOOTH
Assassin of Abraham Lincoln, shot 1865.
Tell my mother that I died for my country. I thought I did it for the best. Useless! Useless!

MARCOS BOZZARI
Greek patriot, died 1823.
Oh, to die for liberty is a pleasure and not a pain!

GENERAL KARL BRANDT
Nazi war criminal, hanged 1946.
It is no shame to stand on this scaffold. I served my fatherland as others before me.

ROBERT THE BRUCE
King of Scotland, died 1329. To Sir James Douglas . . .
I will that as soon as I shall be dead, you take my heart from my body and have it well embalmed. You will also take as much money from my treasury as shall appear to you sufficient to perform your journey as well as for all those more whom you shall choose to take with you in your train and you will then deposit your charge at the Holy Sepulchre where our Lord was buried. Gallant knight, I thank you. You promise it me then . . . Thanks be to God for I shall now die in peace, since I know that the most valiant, accomplished knight of my kingdom will perform that for me which I am unable to perform for myself.

JAMES BUCHANAN
American President, died 1868.

Whatever the result may be, I shall carry to my grave the consciousness that I at least meant well for my country.

ARTHUR BUCKMINSTER FULLER
Union chaplain, killed at the battle of
Fredericksburg 1862. Fuller grabbed a musket and
asked his company commander . . .

Captain, I must do something for my country. What shall I do?

JOHN C. CALHOUN
American politician, died 1850.

The South, the poor South! God knows what will become of her.

CALLICRATES
Greek general, died at the battle of Platea 148 BC.

I grieve not because I have to die for my country, but because I have not lifted my arm against the enemy or done any deed worthy of me, much as I have desired to achieve something.

LUIS DE CAMOENS
Portuguese poet, died 1580.

So I shall conclude my life and all will see how I was so attached to my country that I was not satisfied to die in it, but to die with it.

GEORGE CANNING
British Prime Minister, died 1827.

Spain and Portugal.

EDITH CAVELL
British nurse, shot for spying 1915.

I realize that patriotism is not enough. I must have no hatred or bitterness towards anyone.

CAMILLO CAVOUR
Italian patriot, died 1861.

Italy is made – all is safe!

JACQUES CAZOTTE
French author, guillotined 1792.
I die as I have lived. Faithful to God and my king.

GEORGES CLEMENCEAU
French premier, died 1929.
I wish to be buried standing – facing Germany.

AUGUSTIN COCHIN
French academic, died 1916.
The Republic has been killed by her own children. The odious 1793, the foolish 1848. 1870 has carried her to her grave. She was killed by Robespierre, by Marat and then by all the word-mongers who have dealt in plots, in debts and foolish actions and who have three times ascended this chariot of the people.

ANTHONY COLLINS
Essayist, died 1729.
I have always endeavoured to the best of my ability to serve God, my King and my country. I go to the place God has designed for those who love Him.

CRANTOR
Greek philosopher, died 275 BC.
Sweet in some corner of native soil to rest.

LEON CZOGOLSZ
Assassin of President McKinley, hanged 1901.
I killed the President because he was the enemy of the good people, the good working people. I am not sorry for my crime.

RICHARD HARDING DAVIS
American war correspondent, died 1916.
His final communiqué . . .
That France and her Allies succeed should be the hope and prayer of every rightful American. The fight they are waging is for the things the real unhyphenated American is supposed to hold most high and most dear. Incidentally they are fighting his fight, for their success will later save him, unprepared as he is to defend himself from a humiliating and terrible thrashing.

And every word and act of his now that helps the Allies is a blow against frightfulness, against despotism and on behalf of a broader civilization, a nobler freedom and a much more pleasant world in which to live.

SIR JAMES DOUGLAS
*'The Black Douglas', died 1330. Douglas set off with
the Bruce's heart to Jerusalem, but was killed
by the Moors in Andalusia. As he died he threw the box
containing the heart in front of him, towards the Holy Land . . .*
Now pass thee onward as thou wast wont, and Douglas will follow thee or die.

MARCUS DRUSUS
Roman citizen, died 109 BC.
Will the Republic again find a citizen like me?

☠

DUC D'ENGHIEN
Shot 1804.
Let's go my friends, I die for my King and for France.

☠

HANS FRANK
Nazi war criminal, hanged 1946.
A thousand years will pass and the guilt of Germany will not be erased.

☠

GIUSEPPE GARIBALDI
*Italian patriot, died 1882. In fact he was talking about
two birds that came to his window rather than the
more noble concept of the people of Italy . . .*
Feed them when I am gone.

GOPAL GODSE AND NARAYAN APAL
Assassins of Gandhi, hanged 1948.
India united!

SAMUEL GOMPERS
American labour leader, died 1924.

God bless our American institutions, they grow better day by day.

JOHN CARTERET, EARL GRANVILLE
*British statesman, died 1763. On seeing a draft of
the Treaty of Paris . . .*

It has been the most glorious war and it is now the most honourable peace.

SIR RICHARD GRENVILLE
Elizabethan sailor, killed 1591.

Here I die, Richard Grenville, with a joyful and quiet mind, for that I have ended my life as a good soldier ought to, who has fought for his country, Queen, religion and honour. Wherefore my soul most joyfully departeth out of this body . . . but the others of my company have done as traitors and dogs, for which they shall be reproached all their lives and leave a shameful name for ever.

JAMES GUTHRIE
Presbyterian divine, hanged 1661.

The covenants, the covenants shall yet be Scotland's reviving!

NATHAN HALE
Shot by the British as a spy 1776.

What a pity it is that we can die but once to serve our country.

PHILIP HAMERTON
Essayist, died 1894.

If I indulge my imagination in dreaming about a country where justice and right would always surely prevail, where the weak would never be oppressed, nor an honest man incur any penalty for his honesty – a country where no animal would ever be ill-treated or killed, otherwise than in mercy – that is truly ideal dreaming because, however far I travel, I shall not find such a country in the world, and there is not any record of such a country in the authentic history of mankind.

PATRICK HAMILTON
Scottish martyr, killed 1528.

How long, Lord, will darkness overwhelm this kingdom? How long wilt Thou suffer this tyranny of men? Lord Jesus, receive my spirit!

JOHN HAMPDEN
Opponent of Charles I, killed at the battle of Chalgrove Field, 1643.

Oh Lord save my country! Oh Lord be merciful to ...

LAZARE HOCHE
French revolutionary general, died 1797.

Goodbye my friends, goodbye. Tell the government to keep a sharp eye in the direction of Belgium. Goodbye my friends.

GENERAL HERMAN HOEFFLE
Nazi war criminal, hanged 1945.

Dear Germany.

SAM HOUSTON
Texas patriot, died 1863.

Texas, Texas, Margaret ...

GENERAL AUGUSTIN DE ITURBIDE
Emperor of Mexico, shot 1824.

I am no traitor! Such a stain will never attach to my children or to their descendants.

HELEN HUNT JACKSON
American novelist, died 1885. Letter to President Cleveland ...

Dear Sir, From my deathbed I send you message of heartfelt thanks for what you have already done for the Indians. I ask you to read my *Century of Dishonour*. I am dying happier in the belief that it is your hand that is destined to strike the first steady blow toward lifting this burden of infamy from our country and righting the wrongs of the Indian race. With respect and gratitude, Helen Jackson.

JACOB
Biblical patriarch.

I am to be gathered unto my people. Bury me with my fathers in the cave that is in the field of Ephron the Hittite, in the cave that is in the field of Machpeleh, which is before Mamrex, in the land of Canaan which Abraham bought with the field of Ephron the Hittite for a possession of a burying place. There they buried Abraham and Sarah his wife, there they buried Isaac and Rebecca his wife and there I buried Leah. The purchase of the field and of the cave that is therein was from the children of Heth.

THOMAS JEFFERSON
American President, died 1826. Dying on
Independence Day . . .

Is it the Fourth? I resign my soul to God and my daughter to my country.

LOUIS KOSSUTH
Hungarian patriot, died 1914. He died outside Hungary,
in Turin, and complained to his sister . . .

It grieves me that I have to perish in exile.
She told him that he was
'the most popular Hungarian' . . .
Only your vanity holds this.

PIERRE LAVAL
France's collaborationist Premier, shot 1945.

Vive la France!

SIR HENRY LAWRENCE
Indian administrator, died 1857. Choosing his epitaph . . .

'Here lies Henry Lawrence who tried to do his duty.' This text I should like: 'To the Lord our God belong mercies and forgivenesses, though we have rebelled against Him.' Is it not in Daniel? It was on my dear wife's tomb.

CARL LODY
German spy, shot 1914. Last letter to his family . . .

My Dear Ones, I have trusted in God and He has decided. My hour has come, and I must start on the journey through the Dark Valley like so many of my comrades in this terrible war of nations. May my life be offered as a humble offering on the altar of the Fatherland. A hero's death on the battlefield is certainly finer, but such is not to be my lot and I die here in the enemy's country silent and unknown, but the consciousness that I die in the service of the Fatherland makes death easy. The Supreme Court Martial in London has sentenced me to die for military conspiracy. Tomorrow I shall be shot in the Tower. I have had just judges and I shall die as an officer, not as a spy. Farewell, God bless you, 'Hans'.

FRANCISCO LOPEZ
Paraguayan dictator, died 1870.

I die with my country!

MAO TSE TUNG
Chairman of China, died 1976. Two versions of Mao's last instructions exist, their different interpretations call for opposing theories of China's future . . .

Act according to the principles laid down.
Act in accordance with past principles.

JOSE MARTI
Cuban patriot, died 1895. An unfinished letter . . .

There are some affections which involve such delicate points of honour . . .

COUNT METTERNICH
Austrian statesman, died 1859.

I was a rock of order.

DRAZA MIHAJLOVIC
Yugoslav freedom fighter, shot 1946.

I found myself in a whirl of events and intrigues. I found Destiny was merciless to me when it threw me into the most difficult whirlwinds. I wanted much, I began much – the whirlwind, the whirlwind, carried me and my work away.

LORD HORATIO NELSON
British admiral, killed at the battle of Trafalgar, 1805.
Thank God I have done my duty.

WILLIAM PITT THE ELDER
British statesman, died 1778. To his son . . .
Go my son, whither your country calls you. Let her engross all your attentions. Spare not a moment which is due to her service in weeping over an old man who will soon be no more.

WILLIAM PITT THE YOUNGER
British Prime Minister, died 1806. There are several versions of Pitt's last words. All of them, including the less grandiose, but most likely, are well supported . . .
Oh my country, how I leave thee.
Oh my country how I love thee.
My country, oh my country.
I think I could eat one of Bellamy's veal pies.

'BILL THE BUTCHER' POOLE
American gang leader, killed 1855. This deathbed repentance of the leader of New York's Bowery Boys inspired many melodramas which climaxed on a tableau of The Butcher wrapped in the Stars and Stripes . . .
Goodbye boys, I die a true American!

ETIENNE PORCARO
Italian patriot, hanged.
Oh my people, your deliverer dies today!

MANUEL QUEZON
Philippine statesman, died 1945. Hearing that American troops had landed in Dutch New Guinea . . .
Just 600 miles!

RED JACKET
Chief of the Seneca Indians, died 1830.

Bury me among my people. I do not wish to rise among pale faces.

JOACHIM VON RIBBENTROP
Nazi war criminal, hanged 1946.

God save Germany! My last wish is that Germany rediscover her unity and that an alliance is made between East and West and that peace reign on earth.

PATRICK SARSFIELD
*Earl of Lucan, Irish soldier, killed fighting for France
at the battle of Landen 1693.*

Would to God this was shed for Ireland.

ROBERT FALCON SCOTT
Antarctic explorer, killed 1912. Scott's last note to the public . . .

Had we lived, I should have had a tale to tell of the hardihood, endurance and courage of my companions which would have stirred the heart of every Englishman. These rough notes and our dead bodies must tell the tale.

STEFAN STAMBOULOFF
Bulgarian politician, died 1895.

God preserve Bulgaria!

COUNT KLAUS VON STAUFFENBERG
Plotter against Hitler, executed 1944.

God save our sacred Germany!

SUN-YAT-SEN
Liberator of China, died 1925.

Peace, struggle, save China.

GETULLIO VARGAS
President of Brazil, suicide 1954.

I fought against the looting of the people. I have fought bare-breasted. The hatred, infamy and calumny did not beat down my spirit. I gave you my life! Now I offer my death. Nothing remains. Serenely I take the first step on the road to eternity and I leave life to enter history.

NOAH WEBSTER
American lexicographer, died 1843.
I have struggled with many difficulties. Some I have been able to overcome and by some I have been overcome. I have made many mistakes but I love my country and have laboured for the youth of my country, and I trust no precept of mine has taught any dear youth to sin.

WILLIAM WINDOM
American politician, died 1891. His last speech . . .
Give us direct and ample transportation facilities under the American flag, and controlled by American citizens. A currency sound in quality and adequate in quantity. An international bank to facilitate exchanges and a system of reciprocity carefully adjusted within the lines of protection – and not only will our foreign commerce again invade every sea, but every American industry will be quickened and our whole people feel the impulse of a new and enduring prosperity.

JOHN ZISKA
Czechoslovak patriot, died 1424.
Make my skin into drumheads for the Bohemian cause!

THE TOUGH GET GOING

LOUIS AGASSIZ
Naturalist, died 1910.

The play is finished.

SIR ANDREW AGNEW
Died 1771.

Did the doctor really say I was not to get up? If they said so I won't get up, but I feel well. No. I will keep the pillows as the doctors left them.

JOSEPH BEN AKIBA
Jewish patriot, flayed alive 32 AD. Killed in the Bar Kocha rebellion, he died adamant in his belief in one God . . .

One!

ETHAN ALLEN
American Revolutionary General, died 1789. When he was told 'I fear the angels are waiting for you' . . .

Waiting are they, waiting are they? Well let 'em wait!

MARK ANTONY
Roman general, suicide 30 BC.

You must not pity me in this last turn of fate. You should rather be happy in the remembrance of our love and in the recollection that of all men I was once the most powerful and how at the end not dishonourable – a Roman by a Roman vanquished.

ARCHIMEDES
Greek mathematician, killed 212 BC. To the invading soldiers who killed him . . .

Stand away, fellow, from my diagram!

ARRIA
*Wife of Caecinus Paetus, suicide 42 AD. Killed
herself to give her husband the courage to obey the Emperor's
command to do the same . . .*
It is not painful, Paetus.

ARIZONA 'MA' BARKER
*American bank robber, killed 1935. To her sons, ordering
the start of their fatal shootout with the FBI . . .*
All right! Go ahead!

CHARLES DE BEDOYERE
*French Count, killed 1815. When being shot, for
treachery, he pointed to his heart . . .*
This is what you must not miss.

BILLY THE KID
*(William Bonney) Outlaw, killed 1881. To his killer,
Pat Garratt . . .*
Who's there?

GUSTAVUS VAUGHN BROOKE
Drowned in shipwreck, 1866. Refusing to enter the lifeboat . . .
No, no! Goodbye. Should you survive, give my last farewell to
the people of Melbourne.

GIORDANO BRUNO
Heretic, burnt to death 1600. To Judge . . .
You are more afraid to pronounce my sentence than I am to
receive it.

I die a martyr and willingly. My soul shall mount up with the
smoke to Paradise.

ROBERT O'HARA BURKE
*Explorer, died from starvation 1861.
Died while attempting the first European crossing of
Australia, leaving this last note . . .*
I hope we shall be done justice to. We have fulfilled our task but
we have been abandoned. We have not been followed up as we
expected. And the depot party abandoned their post. King
behaved nobly. He stayed with me to the last and placed the
pistol in my hand, leaving me lying on the surface as I wished.

LORD GEORGE BYRON
Poet, died 1824.

The damned doctors have drenched me so that I can scarcely stand. I want to sleep now. Shall I sue for mercy? Come, come, no weakness. Let me be a man to the last.

KIT CARSON
Western trapper, died 1868.

Adios, compadre!

MARCUS TULLIUS CICERO
Roman author, killed 43 BC. To the soldier who killed him . . .

Here veteran – if you think it right, strike.

IKE CLANTON
*Rancher, shot 1881. Killed by the Earp Brothers at
the Gunfight at the OK Corral . . .*

God, God, won't somebody give me some more cartridges for a last shot . . .

BUFFALO BILL CODY
Western folk-hero, died 1917.

Well, let's forget about it and play High Five. I wish Johnny would come.

JOEL COLLINS
Outlaw and member of the Sam Bass gang, killed 1877.

I'm going down with my six-guns.

BERNARD COY
*American murderer, killed 1946. While attempting to
escape from Alcatraz, seconds before guards shot him down . . .*

It don't matter, I figure I licked the Rock anyway.

FRANCIS 'TWO GUN' CROWLEY
*American murderer and bank robber, died in the
electric chair 1931. Captured after 'The Siege of W.90th St'
and sentenced to death by electrocution . . .*

You sons of bitches. Give my love to Mother.

THE DECEMBERISTS
Russian Revolutionaries, massacred 1825. Before they
were mown down by a cannon in St Petersburg . . .
Yes we shall die, but it will be a fine death.

GENERAL E. DELGADO
Executed in Honduras by firing squad, 1886.
We are ready. Soldiers fire!

VINCENT 'THE SCHEMER' DRUCCI
Gangster, killed 1927. To the policeman who shot him
in a struggle . . .
I'll take you and your tool! I'll fix you!

FRANCISCO FERRER
Spanish revolutionary and educator, killed 1909. To
the soldiers . . .
I desire to be shot standing, without a bandage over my eyes.
To the school children . . .
Look well, my children, it is not your fault. I am innocent. Long
live the School.

ADOLF FISCHER
Haymarket rioter, died by hanging 1881.
This is the happiest moment of my life!

CHARLES 'PRETTY BOY' FLOYD
Bankrobber, killed 1934. Trapped by FBI agents in
Ohio field . . .
Who the hell tipped you off. I'm Floyd alright. You got me this
time.

ERROLL FLYNN
Film star, died 1959. Statement shortly before his death . . .
I've had a hell of a lot of fun and I've enjoyed every minute of it.

JACK 'THREE FINGERED' GARCIA
Bandit, killed 1853.
I will throw up my hands for no gringo dog.

GARY GILMORE
American murderer, shot 1977. Gilmore asked for death
by a firing squad, thus paving the way for the
possible restoration of the death penalty in American states . . .
Let's do it.

and told the Priest . . .
Dominus vobiscum.

FRANK GUSENBERG
Gangster, killed 1929. He survived the St Valentine's
Day Massacre for two hours . . .
Nobody shot me. I ain't no copper.

PRINCE HAMLET
'Hamlet' by William Shakespeare.
The rest is silence.

JOHN WESLEY HARDIN
Outlaw, killed 1895. Shot while playing dice in
Acme Saloon, El Paso . . .
Four sixes to beat!

WILLIAM MICAJAH 'BIG' HARPE
American desperado and killer, lynched 1799.
The giant bandit wreaked havoc along the frontier until he
fell, blown off his horse by a troop of frontiersmen.
Mortally wounded, he lived for a while as they sawed at
his neck with their long knives . . .
You are a God-damned rough butcher, but cut on and be
damned!

WILD BILL HICKOK
Western folk-hero, killed 1876. His last letter home . . .
Agnes darling, if such should be we never meet again, while
firing my last shot I will gently breathe the name of my wife –
Agnes – and with wishes even for my enemies, I will make the
plunge and try to swim to the other shore.

ANDREAS HOFER
Tyrolean patriot, killed 1810. Refusing to kneel in
front of the firing squad . . .

I stand in the presence of my Creator and standing I will render back my account to God who gave it. Fire!

DOC HOLLIDAY
Gambler and gunfighter, died 1885. When someone
took his boots off . . .

Dammit! Put them back on. This is funny.

WILLIAM HOTMAN
Hero of American Revolution, killed 1781. The British
were about to blow up a Revolutionary fort and all within it.
Hotman put out the fuse with his dying wounds . . .

We will endeavour to crawl to this line, we will completely wet the powder with our blood; thus will we, with the life that remains in us, save the fort and the magazine and perhaps a few of our comrades who are only wounded.

SOLYMAN ILLEPPY
Turkish assassin of General Kleber, impaled 1800.

That is good.

ISAIAH
Prophet, sawed to death 660 BC.

Go ye to the country of Tyre and Sidon for the Lord has mixed the cup for me alone.

GEORGE JACKSON
Black Power campaigner, killed 1972.
His last letter, to the editor at Bantam Books, two months
before being killed in Soledad prison . . .

I paraphrase Castro on trial after Moncada: I warn you gentlemen, I have only just begun!

JESSE JAMES
*Train robber, shot 1882. Standing on a chair, he was
adjusting a picture as his killer came in . . .*
That picture is crooked.

WILLIAM JONES
Gambler, died 1877. Gambler's eulogy, recited at his funeral . . .
O when I die, just bury me
In a box-back coat and hat.
Put a twenty-dollar gold piece on my watch chain
To let the Lord know I'm standing pat.

BLACK JACK KETCHUM
Bankrobber and killer, died by hanging 1901.
I'll be in hell before you're finished breakfast, boys . . . Let her
rip!

SIR GEORGE LISLE
English Royalist, executed 1648.
Oh how many do I see here about me, whose lives I have shed in
hot blood: and now must mine be taken away in cold blood most
barbarously! Sure the like was never heard of among the Goths
and Vandals, or the veriest barbarians in the world in any age.
But what dare not those rebels and traitors do, that have im-
prisoned, and could willingly cut the throat of their King? for
whose deliverance from his enemies and peace to this distracted
kingdom, these my last prayers shall be presented. Now then
rebels and traitors, do your worst to me . . . Jesus.

HARVEY LOGAN, 'KID CURRY'
*American outlaw, killed 1903. The toughest of the
legendary 'Wild Bunch' was already mortally wounded by
lawmen when he killed himself with his own gun. Asked
by a fellow outlaw 'Are you hit', he replied . . .*
Yes. And I'm going to end it here.

SIR CHARLES LUCAS
English Royalist, shot 1648.
Soldiers – fire!

CHARLES 'LUCKY' LUCIANO
Gangster, died of heart attack 1962.

Marty ...

MACBETH
'Macbeth' by William Shakespeare.

Lay on Macduff, and damned be him that first cries 'Hold enough'.

JUDAS MACCABAEUS
Jewish patriot, died 160 BC.

If our time be come, let us die manfully for our brethren, and let us not stain our honour.

THOMAS B. MORAN
Pickpocket, died 1971.

I've never forgiven that smart-alecky reporter who named me 'Butterfingers' – to me it's not funny.

JOAQUIN MURRIETA
Californian desperado, killed 1853.

It is enough. Shoot no more. The job is finished. I am dead.

JOHN OATES
Member of Scott's last expedition to the Antarctic, killed 1912.

I am just going outside and I may be some time.

BONNIE PARKER
Bank robber, killed 1934. The last verse of her final poem, 'The Story of Suicide Sal' ...

Some day they will go down together
And they will bury them side by side
To a few it means grief
To the law it's relief
But it's death to Bonnie and Clyde.

CHARLES PEACE
Murderer, died by hanging 1879.
What is the scaffold ? A short cut to heaven.

☠

ARNOLD ROTHSTEIN
Gangster and financial genius, killed 1928.
When asked who shot him . . .
Me mudder did it!

SAN QUENTIN PRISON DEATH ROW
Traditional joke:
I'd like a little bicarb, Warden, because I'm gonna have some gas.

☠

EDWARD 'DEATH VALLEY SCOTTY' SCOTT
Recluse, died 1954.
I got four things to live by: don't say nothin' that will hurt anybody; don't give advice – nobody will take it anyway; don't complain; don't explain.

CAPTAIN E. J. SMITH
Captain of the SS Titanic, drowned 1912.
Declining to be helped into a lifeboat to which he
had just swum with a child.
Let me go.

MRS ISADORE STRAUS
Passenger on the SS Titanic, drowned 1912.
Refusing to take a lifeboat which would have parted
her from her husband . . .
We have been together for forty years, and we will not separate now.

☠

PLACIDO VALDES
Cuban slave rebellion leader, shot 1844.
Here, fire here!

VICTIMS OF CIRCUMSTANCE

VITTORIA ACCORAMBONI DUCHESS OF BRACCIANO
Stabbed 1585.

Jesus! I pardon you.

ALBERT ANASTASIA
American gangster, killed 1957. Shot in a barber's chair . . .

Haircut!

ANAXARCHUS
Greek philosopher, pounded to death with pestles,
4th Century BC.

Pound, pound the pouch containing Anaxarchus. You pound not Anaxarchus.

SAINT THOMAS A BECKET
Assassinated 1170. Killed to satisfy King Henry II's
anger, in Canterbury Cathedral . . .

I am prepared to die for Christ and His Church. I charge you in the name of the Almighty not to hurt any other person here, for none of them has been concerned in the late transactions.

In vain you menace me. If all the swords in England were brandishing over my head, your terrors did not move me.

COUNT BERNADOTTE
Pioneer of the United Nations, assassinated 1948.
Acknowledging wishes of 'Good Luck' . . .

I'll need it!

REV. JOHN BEWGILL
English Clergyman, drowned.

Oh dear, dear, dear me. We are dead.

☠

GASPARD DE COLIGNY
Huguenot leader, killed 1572. First victim of the
St Bartholemew's Day Massacre ...

Young man, you ought to consider my age and infirmity, but you will not make my life any shorter.

MICHAEL COLLINS
Irish patriot, killed 1921. His comment on signing the
Irish Treaty, 1921; he was assassinated soon after ...

I am signing my death warrant.

☠

A. P. DOSTIE
Anti-slavery campaigner, killed by a mob.

I am dying. I die for the cause of liberty. Let the good work go on.

DANIEL DRAPER
Methodist minister, drowned in shipwreck.

We may all make the port of Heaven. Oh God, may those that are not converted be converted now, hundreds of them. In a few moments we must all appear before Our Great Judge. Let us prepare to meet Him. Rock of ages cleft for me ...

ANTHONY J. DREXEL III
American socialite, shot himself 1893. While
demonstrating a new pistol ...

Here's one you've never seen before ...

JEAN E. DURANTI
President of Toulouse parliament under Henri III,
killed by mob 1589. To his wife ...

Adieu, my beloved; what God has granted me: life, goods, honours, I am presently to be stripped of. Death is the end, but not the punishment of life; innocent of the charges imputed me, my soul is to appear at the tribunal of the sovereign Judge. Trust in Him; He will always help you.

To the mob . . .

Yes, here I am. But what crime have I committed, what is wrong, O people, I am guilty of in your eyes? Lord God, receive my soul. Do not blame them for this wrong, for they know not what they do.

☠

ELIZABETH
Empress of Austria, stabbed 1898.
Why, what has happened?

☠

CHARLES FROHMAN
Drowned 1915. When the SS Lusitania was torpedoed by a German submarine . . .
Why fear death? It is the most beautiful adventure in life.

MARGARET FULLER
Transcendentalist, drowned in shipwreck 1850.
I see nothing but death before me; I shall never reach the shore.

☠

EVARISTE GALOIS
Mathematician, killed in a duel 1832.
Don't cry, I need all my courage to die at 20.

JAMES GARFIELD
American President, assassinated 1881.
The people my trust.

☠

ALEXANDER HAMILTON
American politician, killed in a duel with Aaron Burr 1804.
Remember, my Eliza, you are a Christian.

PRINCE HIROBUMI ITO
Japanese statesman, assassinated 1909. When told the identity of his assailant . . .

The fellow is a fool.

ELBERT HUBBARD
Drowned 1915. Going down on the SS Lusitania, torpedoed by a German submarine . . .

Well, Jack, they have got us. They are a damned sight worse than I thought they were.

💀

TERRY KATH
Rock musician, killed 1978. Playing Russian roulette with a loaded pistol . . .

Don't worry, it's not loaded.

JOHN FITZGERALD KENNEDY
American President, assassinated 1963. On insisting on visiting Dallas . . .

If someone is going to kill me, they will kill me.

JEAN BAPTISTE KLEBER
Napolean's commander in Egypt, stabbed 1880.

I have been assassinated!

💀

LEO X
Pope, poisoned 1521.

I have been murdered. No remedy can prevent my speedy death.

RICHARD A. LOEB
Child murderer, killed in prison 1936. He was slashed 56 times with a razor in the prison shower by a fellow inmate, James Day, whom he had tried to seduce . . .

I think I'm going to make it. . .

HUEY P. LONG
Governor of Louisiana, assassinated 1935.

I wonder why he shot me?

💀

WILLIAM McKINLEY
American President, assassinated 1901.
We are all going, we are all going, we are all going . . . oh dear!

MALCOLM X
(Malcom Little) Black Muslim leader, killed 1966.
Let's cool it brothers . . .

JOHN MARSH
Pioneer, killed 1868. To Mexican robbers . . .
Do you want to kill me?

FATHER BASIL MATURIN
*Drowned 1915. Lost on the SS Lusitania after handing
over a little child as the last boat was lowered . . .*
Find its mother.

THOMAS MOLENEUX
*Constable of Chester in reign of Richard II,
killed 14th Century. Caught by his enemies refreshing himself
in a river, his request was not granted . . .*
Suffer me to come up and let me fight either with thee or some
other, and die like a man.

AIRSHIP HINDENBERG
*German airship crashed 1937. Radio journalist
Herbert Morrison reporting the disaster live to his audience . . .*
It's burst into flames! Oh my . . . it's burning, bursting into
flames! . . . oh the humanity and all the passengers!

NADIR SHAH
Indian Prince, assassinated 1747.
Thou dog!

SPENCER PERCEVAL
British Prime Minister, assassinated 1812.
Murder!

DAVID GRAHAM PHILLIPS
American novelist, shot by a paranoiac 1911.
I could have won against two bullets but not against six.

FRANCISCO PIZZARO
Conqueror of Peru, assassinated 1541.
Jesu!

☻

VIRGINIA RAPPE
Hollywood starlet, killed 1921. Good time girl, she tangled fatally with Hollywood comic Fatty Arbuckle . . .
I'm dying, I'm dying – he hurt me!

ERNST ROEHM
Head of the Nazi SA, killed 1934. Roehm, and all the other SA leaders were killed on Hitler's orders in a mass purge . . .
If I am to be killed, let Adolf do it himself.

ALEXANDER RUTHVEN
Gowrie conspirator against James VI of Scotland, stabbed 1600.
Alas! I had na wyte (blame) of it!

☻

MARIE FRANCOIS SADI CARNOT
President of France, assassinated 1894. To those who were trying to save him . . .
I am very touched by your presence and I thank you for what you are doing for me.

LOUIS MICHEL LEPELLETIER DE SAINT-FARGEAU
French politician, killed 1793. Assassinated on the eve of the execution of Louis XVI . . .
I am cold.

GALEAZZO SFORZA, DUKE OF MILAN
Assassinated 1476.
Oh God!

JOSEPH SMITH
Mormon martyr, killed by a mob 1844.
That's right brother Taylor, parry them off as well as you can.

CARL 'ALFALFA' SWITZER
Star of the 'Our Gang' film series, shot 1959.
His youthful stardom far behind him, Switzer was drunk in
a bar, so was the man who shot him . . .
I want that fifty bucks you owe me and I want it now!

LEON TROTSKY
Leader of the Russian Revolution, assassinated 1940.
On the way to hospital . . .
I feel here that this time they have succeeded.

GEORGE VILLIERS, DUKE OF BUCKINGHAM
Favourite of James I, assassinated 1628.
God's wounds, the villain has killed me!

JOHN DE WITT
Dutch statesman, killed by a mob 1672.
To the angry mob . . .
What are you doing? This is not what you wanted.

CORNELIUS DE WITT
Dutch official and brother of John, killed by same mob
1672. To the angry mob . . .
What do you want me to do? Where do you want me to go?

GALLOWS HUMOUR

AGESISTRATA
Mother of Agis of Sparta, hanged 3rd Century BC.
I trust it may redound to the good of Sparta.

JOHN ANDRE
Shot as a British spy by the Americans, 1780.
I am reconciled to my death, but I detest the mode. It will be but a momentary pang. I pray you to bear witness that I met my fate like a brave man.

ARCHIBALD, 8TH EARL OF ARGYLL
Beheaded 1661.
I die not only a protestant, but with a heart-hatred of Popery, Prelacy and all superstitions whatsoever.

9TH EARL OF ARGYLL
Beheaded 1685.
Lord Jesus receive me into Thy glory.

MAJOR HERBERT ARMSTRONG
Hanged. Armstrong was condemned for the murder of his wife, Katherine . . .
I am coming Katie!

BENEDICT ARNOLD
Dying in exile 1801.
Let me die in the old uniform in which I fought my battles for freedom. May God forgive me for putting on any other.

ANTHONY BABINGTON

*Beheaded 1586. Babington had attempted to
assassinate Queen Elizabeth I . . .*

The murder of the Queen has been represented to me as a deed
lawful and meritorious. I die a firm Catholic.

JEAN SYLVAIN BAILLY

*First Mayor of Revolutionary Paris, guillotined 1793.
A bystander noticed that Bailly was trembling on the scaffold . . .*

Only from cold, my friend.

JAMES BAINHAM

Heretic, burnt 1532.

Oh ye papists! Behold, ye look for miracles – here now ye may
see a miracle. For in this fire I feel no more pain than if I were
in a bed of down, but it is to me as a bed of roses.

VASCO NUNEZ DE BALBOA

Conqueror of the Indies, beheaded 1517.

This is false. I have always served my king loyally and sought to
add to his domains.

CHEVALIER DE LA BARRE

Beheaded. He died for mutilating a crucifix . . .

I did not think they would put a young gentleman to death for
such a trifle.

JEREBOAM BEAUCHAMP

*Hanged 1826. Beauchamp and his wife were both
due to die but she alone succeeded in their suicide pact. He
went to the gallows clutching her dead body . . .*

Farewell, child of sorrow! For you have I lived, and for you I
die!

JOHN BELLINGHAM

The assassin of Spencer Perceval, hanged 1812.

I thank God for having enabled me to meet my fate with so much
fortitude and resignation.

DUC DE LANZON DE BIRON

Guillotined 1793. Telling the executioner to wait . . .

I beg a thousand pardons, my friend, but permit me to finish
this last dozen of oysters.

On the scaffold . . .
I have been false to my God, my order and my King. I die full of
faith and repentance.

JOHN BRADFORD
Burnt 1555.
Be of good comfort, brother, for we shall have a merry supper
with the Lord this night. If there be any way to heaven on
horseback or in fiery chariots, this is it.

WILLIAM BRERETON
Beheaded 1536. He was executed with Anne Boleyn . . .
I have deserved to die if it were one thousand deaths. But the
cause wherefore I die, judge it not. But if you judge, judge the
best.

JOHN BROWN
Anti-slavery fanatic, hanged 1859. To his executioner . . .
Don't keep me waiting longer than necessary.

BART CARITATIVO
*Gassed 1958. A houseboy in California, he murdered
his employers for their money . . .*
God bless you all, God bless you all.

BEATRICE CENCI
Murderer, beheaded 1599.

Jesus! Mary!

HENRY DE TALEYRAND DE CHALAIS
Beheaded 1626. To his executioner . . .
Do not keep me in suspense.

GERALD CHAPMAN
*Swindler, conman and murderer, hanged 1926.
Chapman was a real-life 'Raffles' until he blundered and
killed a cop . . .*
Death itself isn't dreadful, but hanging seems an awkward way
of entering the adventure.

ANDRÉ CHENIER
French romantic, poet, guillotined 1794. He was still
composing poetry on the scaffold.
Le sommeil du tombeau pressera ma paupiere.

CHEROKEE BILL
Outlaw, hanged 1896.
The quicker this thing's over the better.
Asked if he had anything to say . . .
No. I came here to die. Not make a speech.

JACQUES CLEMENT
Executed 1589. Clement, who attempted the murder of
Henri III of France was asked 'Dare you look an angry King
in the face?' . . .
Yes, yes, yes! And kill him too!

WILLIAM COLLINGBOURN
Hanged, drawn and quartered 15th Century.
Collingbourn allegedly muttered this complaint as the
executioner tore out his heart; the whole
execution took an hour . . .
Lord Jesus, yet more trouble.

CHARLOTTE CORDAY
Assassin of Marat, guillotined 1793. Gazing at the guillotine . . .
I have a right to be curious, I have never seen one before. It is
the toilette of death, but it leads to immortality.

WILLIAM CORDER
Murderer, hanged 1828. Corder had killed Maria Marten,
a murder that fascinated all England . . .
I am justly sentenced and may God forgive me.

THOMAS CRANMER
Burnt 1555. Cranmer recanted his protestant views,
then repudiated his statement. At the stake he tortured himself
physically and mentally with this moment of weakness . . .
This hand having sinned in signing the writing must be the first
to suffer punishment. This hand hath offended.

NEIL CREAM
*Murderer, hanged 1892. Did Cream try to confess
to the 'Jack the Ripper' killings? . . .*

I'm Jack . . .

HARVEY HAWLEY CRIPPEN
Poisoner, hanged 1910.

In this farewell letter to the world, written as I face eternity, I
say that Ethel le Neve loved me as few women love men and
that her innocence of any crime, save that of yielding to the
dictates of her heart, is absolute. My last prayer will be that God
will protect her and keep her safe from harm and allow her to
join me in eternity.

THOMAS CROMWELL
Secretary to Henry VIII, beheaded 1540.

The devil is ready to seduce us and I have been seduced, but
bear me witness that I die in the Catholic faith of the Holy
Church and I heartily desire you to pray for the King's grace,
that he may long live with you in health and prosperity, and
after him that his son Edward, that goodly imp, may long reign
over you, and once again I desire you to pray for me, that as
long as life remaineth in this flesh I wander nothing in my faith.

ANACHARSIS CLOOTZ
'Orator of the Human Race', guillotined 1794.

In the name of the earth, in the name of humanity, do not
confuse me with your memory of these common fellows. No
patched up peace!

BOOD CRUMPTON
Outlaw, hanged 1875.

Men, the next time you lift a glass of whisky, I want you to look
into the bottom of the glass and see if there isn't a hangman's
noose in it, like the one here.

☻

GEORGES DANTON
Leader of the French Revolution, guillotined 1794.

Show my head to the people – it is worth it.

ROBERT DEVEREUX, EARL OF ESSEX
Beheaded 1601.

In humility and obedience to Thy commandment, in obedience to Thy ordinance and to Thy good pleasure, Oh God, I prostrate myself to my deserved punishment. Lord be merciful to Thy prostrate servant. Lord, into Thy hands I commend my spirit.

SIR EVERARD DIGBY
Hanged, drawn and quartered 1605. As the executioner exposed Digby's heart with the cry of 'Here is the heart of a traitor!', his victim replied . . .

Thou liest!

REV. WILLIAM DODD
Forger, hanged 1777. Dodd persuaded the executioner to drag on his legs to speed up the process of strangulation . . .

Come to me.

ETIENNE DOLET
Heretic, burnt 1546.

This is not doleful for Dolet, but it means dole for the people.

JEAN-FRANCOIS DUCOS
Guillotined 1793. To the executioner who was cutting off his hair . . .

I hope that the edge of your guillotine is sharper than your scissors.

JOHN DUDLEY, DUKE OF NORTHUMBERLAND
Beheaded 1553.

I have deserved one thousand deaths.

THEO DURRANT
Sex killer, hanged 1898. Sunday school superintendent and church librarian, Durrant loved necrophilia . . .

Don't put that rope on, boy, till I talk.

COUNT LAMORAL EGMONT
Dutch freedom fighter, beheaded 1568.
Lord, into Thy hands I commend my spirit.

ROBERT EMMETT
Irish patriot, hanged 1803.
Not . . .

GEORGE ENGEL
One of Haymarket Rioters in Chicago, hanged 1881.
Hurray for Anarchy!

☠

LAWRENCE, EARL FERRERS
*Murderer, hanged 1760. Ferrers, an aristocratic
psychopath, who should have been confined and not killed, was
the only nobleman to suffer hanging rather than
the usual beheading . . .*
I freely forgive you as I do all mankind and I hope myself to be
forgiven.

ALBERT FISH
*Child molester, murderer and cannibal,
electrocuted 1936. Sixty-six year old Fish killed and
butchered scores of youngsters.
He fixed his own electrodes in the death cell . . .*
What a thrill that will be if I have to die in the electric chair. It
will be the supreme thrill. The only one I haven't tried.

SUBRIUS FLAVUS
*Conspirator against Emperor Nero, beheaded 67 AD.
Told to offer his neck resolutely . . .*
I wish that your stroke may be as resolute.

FRANCIS FONTON
*Forger, hanged. Declared on the scaffold that it was
best for God to lead him home . . .*
By a way I know not.

SAM FOOY
*Murderer, hanged 1875. Fooy told the assembled press
of a dream he had on the night before his execution . . .*

When the drop came I felt no pain. I just fell asleep and woke up in the beautiful garden. It had running waters and stars were dancing on the waves.

HENRY GARNETT
Executed for his part in the Gunpowder Plot 1605.
Imprint the cross on my heart . . . Mary, mother of grace.

SIR JOHN GATES
Beheaded 1553. To his executioner . . .
I forgive thee with all my heart. I will see how meet the block is for my neck. I pray thee strike not yet, for I have a few prayers to say, and that done, strike on God's name, good leave have thou.

HARVEY GLATMAN
Rapist and murderer, gassed 1959. Glatman was a rope
fetishist who tied up his victims first . . .
It's better this way. I knew this is the way it would be.

BARBARA GRAHAM
Murderer, gassed 1955. Graham killed for money;
she asked for a blindfold at San Quentin to avoid looking
at the obligatory witnesses . . .
I don't want to have to look at people.

URBAIN GRANDIER
Executed for causing religious mania in Loudun, burnt 1634.
My God, by the light I wait for you . . . My God, forgive my enemies.

JUDD GRAY
Murderer, electrocuted, 1928. Gray had helped
Ruth Snyder do away with her husband . . .
I am ready to go. I have nothing to fear.

LADY JANE GREY
Beheaded 1554.
I die in peace with all people. God save the Queen.

CHARLES JULIUS GUITEAU
Assassin of President Garfield, hanged 1882.
Glory hallelujah! I'm going to the Lordy!

☙

JAMES HACKMAN
Murdered Martha Ray, mistress of Lord Sandwich,
because she refused to marry him, hanged 1779.
Note scribbled to a friend . . .
Farewell for ever in this world. I die a sincere Christian and
penitent, and everything I hope that you can wish me. Would it
prevent my example's having any bad effect if the world should
know how I abhor my former ideas of suicide, my crime . . .
will be the best judge. Of her fame I charge you to be careful.
My poor sister will . . .

JACOB S. HARDEN
Minister who murdered his wife, hanged.
God have mercy upon me! Lord Jesus save me in heaven.

GENERAL THOMAS HARRISON
Regicide, hanged, drawn and quartered 1660.
He hath covered my head many times in the day of battle. By
God I have leaped over a wall, by God I have run through a
troop, and by my God I will go through this death and He will
make it easy for me. Now into Thy hands, Oh Lord Jesus, I
commit my spirit.

NEVILLE HEATH
Murderer, hanged 1946. Asking for a last whisky . . .
Ah . . . you might make that a double.

RICHARD EUGENE HICKOK
Murderer, hanged 1965. One of the two youths who
killed a Mid-West family for their non-existent fortune . . .
I just wanna say I hold no hard feelings. You people are sending
me to a better world than this ever was.

RAHIM HINGORO
Murderer, hanged. Follower of Pir Pigaro, leader of
the fanatical Hur sect in India . . .
Praise Pigaro!

JOHN HOLLOWAY
Murderer, hanged 1807. 40,000 Londoners flocked to
Holloway's execution, dozens died in the stampede . . .
I am innocent, innocent by God! Innocent, innocent, innocent!
Gentlemen, no verdict, no verdict, no verdict! Gentlemen!
Innocent, innocent, innocent!

BISHOP HOOPER
Burnt 1555.
If you love my soul, away with it!

FATHER JOHN HOUGHTON
Hanged, drawn and quartered 1535. Houghton
refused to accept Henry VIII's rejection of Catholicism and
died for his beliefs. As the executioner prepared to
tear out his heart . . .
Good Jesu, what will you do with my heart?

WILLIAM HOWARD, VISCOUNT STAFFORD
Beheaded 1680. To the executioner . . .
I do forgive you.

JOHN HUSS
Protestant reformer, burnt 1415. Watching a peasant
add more fuel to the fire . . .
Oh sancta simplicitas!

JAMES INGS
Member of the 'Cato Street Conspiracy' hanged 1820.
Oh give me death or give me liberty!

KALIAYEV
Russian anarchist revolutionary, hanged 1905. He
refused a crucifix on the scaffold . . .
I already told you that I am finished with life and am prepared
for death. I consider my death as the supreme protest against a
world of blood and tears.

HERMANN VON KATTE
Executed 1730. Von Katte was charged with conspiracy
with Frederick the Great, when the Emperor
was still the Crown Prince . . .
Death is sweet for a Prince I love so well.

NED KELLY
Australian desperado, hanged 1880.
Such is life.

KUSAKABE
Japanese revolutionary, executed. Repeated Chinese
verse on his way to execution . . .
It is better to be a crystal
   and be broken,
Than to remain perfect like a tile
   upon the housetop.

JOHN LAMBERT
Martyr, burnt 1538.
None but Christ, none but Christ.

HENRI LANDRU
The French 'Bluebeard', guillotined 1922. Landru had
done away with a number of hapless 'wives' . . .
Ah well, it is not the first time that an innocent man has been
condemned.

HUGH LATIMER
Protestant martyr, burnt 1555.
Be of good comfort, Master Ridley, and play the man. We shall
this day light such a candle, by God's grace, in England, as I
trust shall never be put out.

ARCHBISHOP LAUD
Supporter of King Charles I, beheaded 1645.
Lord, receive my soul.

JOHN DOYLE LEE
'Official assassin' of the Mormon Church, shot 1857.
Lee and a gang of other renegades used their
membership of the Church to prey on wagon trains. He was
killed for massacring the 123 adults in one such train,
sparing only their seventeen children. A last letter . . .

I hope to meet the bullets with manly courage. I declare my innocence. I have done nothing wrong. I have a reward in heaven and my conscience does not accuse me. This to me is a consolation. I place more value upon it than I would upon an eulogy without merit. If my work be finished on earth, I ask God in heaven, in the name of his son Jesus Christ, to receive my spirit and to allow me to meet my loved ones who have gone beyond the veil . . . with whom I parted in sorrow but shall meet in joy. I bid you farewell. Be true to each other. Live faithful before God that we may meet in the mansion God has prepared for his servants. Remember the last words of your most true friend on earth, and let them sink into your aching hearts. I leave my blessing with you. Farewell.

CAPTAIN LIGHTFOOT
(Michael Martin)
American highwayman, hanged 1822. To the hangman . . .

Whenever you're ready.

WILLIAM P. LONGLEY
Gunfighter and killer, hanged 1877. Longley was
obsessed with the mythical Old South. He killed in the
name of the defunct Confederacy . . .

I deserve this fate. It is a debt I owe for a wild and reckless life. So long, everybody!

ALVARO DE LUNA
Favourite of King John II of Castile, beheaded 1453.
After being shown the post and hook which would display
his remains . . .

It does not matter what they do with my body and head after my death.

MacCail

Scottish covenanter, tortured to death 1668.

Farewell moon and stars, farewell world and time, farewell weak and frail body. Welcome eternity, welcome angels and saints, welcome saviour of the world, welcome God, the judge of all.

James Macpherson

Hanged 1700. Macpherson composed his own funeral oration which he sang, accompanying himself on the violin.

I've spent my time in rioting
Debauched my health and strength.
I squandered fast as pillage came,
And fell to shame at length.
But dauntingly and wantonly and rantingly I'll go
I'll play the tune and dance it roun'
Beneath the gallows tree.

Marc, Chevalier de Montreal

Beheaded. Reached up to make sure that the executioner would put the axe through the right part of his neck . . .

You are not putting it in the right place.

Marcus of Arethusa

Marcus was covered in honey, hoisted up in a basket and stung to death by bees . . .

How I am advanced, despising you that are upon the earth.

Mata Hari

(Gertrude Margaret Zelle)

Spy, shot 1917. The quintessential glamorous spy, Mata Hari went smiling to her death . . .

Thank you, monsieur.

James, Duke of Monmouth

Beheaded 1685.

Prithee, let me feel the axe. I fear it is not sharp enough. Do not hack me as you did my Lord Russell.

Duc Henri II de Montmorency

Beheaded 1632. Cardinal Richelieu had the Duke killed for rebellion against him . . .

Give a good stroke. Sweet Saviour, receive my soul.

JAMES GRAHAM, EARL OF MONTROSE
Supporter of Charles I, hanged 1650.
May God have mercy upon this afflicted Kingdom.

THOMAS MORE
British statesman, beheaded 1535. More refused to sacrifice
his beliefs despite all of Henry VIII's laws . . .
Pluck up thy spirits man, and do not be afraid to do thine office.
My neck is very short, take heed therefore, do not strike awry,
for saving of thine honesty.

FRA MORIALE
Italian adventurer, hanged. Shouted to the crowds . . .
I die for your poverty and my wealth!

HERMAN MUDGETT
America's most prolific murderer, hanged 1896.
Mudgett was executed for the killings of at least two
hundred women. He lured them to their deaths by
promising marriage and then obtaining their insurance
payments. He pleaded innocence till the end . . .
As God is my witness I was responsible for the death of only two
women. I didn't kill Minnie Williams. Minnie killed her . . .!

BENITO MUSSOLINI
Duce of Italy, shot 1945.
But, but, Mr Colonel . . .

EARLE NELSON
Mass murderer, hanged 1927. Sex killer with a bible
in his hand, Nelson oozed sanctimonious sentiments as he
raped and strangled his way across America . . .
I am innocent. I stand innocent before God and man. I forgive
those who have wronged me and I ask forgiveness of those whom
I have injured. God have mercy!

MARSHAL NEY
French soldier, shot 1815.
Don't you know, sir, that a soldier does not fear death? I protest
against my condemnation. My honour . . .

John Noyes
Protestant martyr, burnt 1555.

We shall not lose our lives in this fire, but change them for a better. And for coals have pearls.

Girolamo Olgiatti
Assassin of Galeazzo Sforza, executed 1476.

My death is untimely, my fame eternal, the memory of the deed will last for aye.

Duc d'Orleans
French aristocrat, executed 1793. The executioner tried to take off the Duke's boots . . .

You can do that more easily to my dead body. Come – be quick!

Johann Philipp Palm
Book dealer, shot 1806. Palm issued a pamphlet attacking Napoleon. The Emperor had him shot. He wrote to his family . . .

To you, my dear wife, I say a thousand thanks for your love. Trust in God and do not forget me. I have nothing in the world to say but farewell, you and the children. God bless you and them. My regards to Mr and Mrs Schwagerin and all my friends, whom I thank for their goodness and love. Once more, farewell. Yonder, we shall meet again. Your husband and children's father, Johann Palm. Braunau, in prison, August 26, 1806, a half hour before my death.

William Palmer
Poisoner, hanged 1856. Stepping on to the gallows . . .

Are you sure it's safe?

Carl Panzram
Mass murderer, hanged 1930. In a letter to the Society for the Abolition of Capital Punishment who were campaigning to save him from death . . .

I do not believe that being hanged by the neck until dead is a barbaric or inhuman punishment. I look forward to that as a real pleasure and a big relief to me . . . when my last hour comes I will dance out of my dungeon and on to the scaffold with a smile on my face and happiness in my heart . . . the only thanks that you and your kind will ever get from me for your efforts is that I wish you all had one neck and I had my hands on it.

Asked if he had anything to say, Panzram, who admitted to his killings and resolutely refused any form of repentance, replied . . .

Yes. Hurry it up, you Hoosier bastard! I could hang a dozen men while you're fooling around.

ALBERT PARSONS
Hanged 1881. One of the 'Haymarket Rioters' . . .
Let the voice of the people be heard!

ANTHONY PEERSON
Martyr, burnt 1555. He pulled the straw around his legs and put a bundle of it on his head . . .
This is God's hat. Now I am dressed like a true soldier of Christ, by whose merits only I trust to enter into His joy.

COLONEL JOHN PENRUDDOCK
Supporter of Charles I, beheaded 1655. Kissing the axe . . .
I am like to have a sharp passage of it, but my Saviour hath sweetened it unto me. If I would have been so unworthy as others have been, I suppose I might by a lie have saved my life, which I scorn to purchase at such a rate. I defy temptations and them that gave them me. Glory to be to God on high, on earth peace, good will towards men, and the Lord have mercy upon my poor soul. Amen.

COUNT PESTEL
Russian revolutionary, hanged 1826. The first attempt to hang him broke the rope . . .
Stupid country, where they do not even know how to hang.

HUGH PETERS
Hanged, drawn and quartered 1660. The executioner was mocking him as he waited by the scaffold . . .
Friend, you do not well to trample on a dying man.

PHOCION
Athenian statesman, executed 317 BC.

No resentment.

☠

GENERAL ALFREDO QUIJANO
Mexican revolutionary, shot 1927. Asking the
firing squad to move closer . . .

Still a little closer.

To the watching newsmen . . .

Goodbye, goodbye.

☠

SIR WALTER RALEIGH
Elizabethan adventurer, beheaded 1618.

'Tis a sharp remedy, but a sure one for all ills.

FRANCOIS RAVAILLAC
Assassin of Henri IV of France, executed 1510.
Ravaillac swore that he was the sole assassin, thus entitling
himself to the solace of religion, as well as the rack,
the pincers, boiling oil and being torn apart by four horses . . .

I receive absolution on that condition.

NICHOLAS RIDLEY
Protestant martyr, burnt 1555. The wood piled around
him was too green to burn well . . .

Let the fire come unto me! I cannot burn! Lord have mercy
upon me!

MAXIMILLIEN DE ROBESPIERRE
French revolutionary leader, guillotined 1794.

Thank you, sir.

JAMES W. RODGERS
American criminal, shot 1960. Asked if he had any
last requests . . .

Why yes – a bulletproof vest!

REV. JOHN ROGERS
Protestant martyr, burnt 1555.

Lord, receive my soul.

Madame Roland
Jacobin leader, guillotined 1793. To an old man who
was frightened of his death . . .
Go first. At least I can spare you the pain of seeing my blood flow.

Ethel Rosenberg
Electrocuted for alleged spying 1953.
We are the first victims of American fascism.

Julius Rosenberg
Electrocuted for alleged spying 1953. In his petition
to President Eisenhower . . .
We are innocent. That is the whole truth. To forsake this truth is to pay too high a price even for the priceless gift of life. For life thus purchased we could not live out in dignity.

Bartolomeo Sacco
Hanged for alleged anarchism, 1927.
If it had not been for these things I might live out my life talking at street corners to scorning men. I might have died unmarked, a failure, unknown. Now we are not a failure. This is our career and our triumph. Never in our full life could we hope to do such work for tolerance, for justice and for man's understanding of man.

Caserio Santo-Ironimo
Assassin of French President Sadi-Carnot, guillotined 1894.
Courage comrades! Long live anarchy!

Girolamo Savonarola
Hanged and burnt for heresy 1498.
The Lord hath suffered so much for me.

Lieutenant Schmidt
Shot as a spy.
My death will consummate everything and my cause, crowned by my death, will emerge irreproachable and perfect.

MICHAEL SERVETUS
Protestant martyr, burnt 1553. The green wood
burnt too slowly . . .
Jesus, son of the eternal God have mercy on me.

JACK SHEPPARD
Thief, hanged 1724.
Of two virtues have I ever cherished an honest pride. Never have I stooped to friendship with Jonathan Wild or with any of his detestable thief-takers, and though an undutiful son, I never damned my mother's eyes.

PERRY EDWARD SMITH
Murderer, hanged 1965. With Eugene Hickok, Smith
killed the mid-Western Clutter family for no apparent
reason except for their not having a cache of money . . .
I think it's a hell of a thing to take a life in this manner. I don't believe in capital punishment, morally or legally. Maybe I had something to contribute, something . . . It would be meaningless to apologize for what I did. But I do. I apologize.

RUTH SNYDER
Murderer, electrocuted 1928. Snyder's crime was a
simple enough 'eternal triangle' situation, but she gained
special notoriety when a Daily News *cameraman*
snapped her death agony with his hidden camera . . .
Oh Father, forgive them for they know not what they do . . . Father, forgive me! Oh Father, forgive me! Father, forgive them, Father forgive them . . .

HENRY BEAUFORT, DUKE OF SOMERSET
Beheaded 1552.
Lord Jesus save me.

HENRY SPENCER
Murderer, hanged 1914. Spencer, who killed a rich
spinster, claimed to have repented and found God, but he
cracked on the scaffold . . .
What I got to say is that I'm innocent of the murder of Allison Rexroat. I never killed her! It's a lie! You're all dirty bastards! You got no right! I never touched her! So help me God, I never harmed a hair on her head! So help me God!

August Spies
Hanged 1881. One of the 'Haymarket Rioters' . . .

There will come a time when our silence will be more powerful than the voices you strangle today.

Earl of Stafford
Beheaded 1680.

This block will be my pillow and I shall repose there well without pain, grief, or fear.

Charlie Starkweather
Mass murderer, electrocuted 1959. Asked if he would donate his eyes to medicine . . .

Hell no! No-one ever did anything for me. Why in hell should I do anything for anyone else.

Earl of Strafford
Supporter of Charles I, beheaded 1641.

I do as cheerfully put off my doublet at this time as ever I did when I went to bed.

Jack Straw
Leader of the 'Peasants' Revolt', hanged 1381.
He confessed on the gallows . . .

Against that same day that Wat Tyler was killed, we proposed that evening, because the poor people of London seemed to favour us, to set fire in four corners of the city and so to have burnt it, and to have divided the riches at our pleasures amongst us.

Julius Streicher
Nazi war criminal, hanged 1946.

Heil Hitler!

Fritz Suckel
Nazi war criminal, hanged 1946.

I pay my respects to American officers and American soldiers, but not to American justice.

Mary Surratt
Conspirator to assassinate President Lincoln, hanged 1865.

Please don't let me fall.

☠

REV. ROWLAND TAYLOR
Burnt 1555. Pointing out that he would be burnt
rather than buried . . .
I shall this day deceive the worms in Hadley churchyard.

MARTIN GEORGE THORN
Murderer, electrocuted 1897. Thorn killed his
landlady's ex-lover. She got twenty years and
he was executed . . .
I have no fear. I am not afraid. I am positive God will forgive me.

LEON TORAL
Assassin of President Obregon, executed.
Long live . . .

ROGER 'TERRIBLE' TOUHY
Bootlegger, shot 1959. Touhy fell foul of
the Chicago mobs, killed after serving a seventeen year
jail sentence . . .
I've been expecting it. The bastards never forget.

WILLIAM TYNDALE
Protestant martyr, strangled at the stake 1536.
Lord, open the King of England's eyes!

💀

WILBUR UNDERHILL
Bankrobber 'The Tri-State Terror', shot by police 1934.
Tell the boys I'm coming home.

💀

NICCOLO VANZETTI
Hanged for alleged anarchy 1927.
I am so convinced to be right that if you execute me two times,
and if I could be reborn those other two times, I would live
again to do what I have already.

💀

PAUL VERGNIAUD
Jacobin, guillotined 1794.

Death before dishonour.

MENDY WEISS
Murderer, electrocuted 1944.

All I want to say is I'm innocent. I'm here on a framed up case.
Give my love to my family and everything.

CHARLES WHITMAN
*Mass murderer, shot by police 1966. Whitman took
over the tower of Texas University campus and shot forty-six
people, sixteen of whom died. He left a note . . .*

Life is not worth living.

CAPTAIN HENRY WIRZ
*Commander of the Andersonville prison camp for
Union prisoners, hanged 1866.*

This is too tight, loosen it a little. I am innocent. I will have to
die sometime. I will die like a man. My hopes are in the future.

GEORGE WISHART
Martyr, burnt 1546.

I shall suffer this with a glad heart. Behold and consider my
visage. You shall not see me change colour. I fear not this fire.

SIR THOMAS WYATT
*Led a protestant rebellion against Queen Mary,
beheaded 1554. Referring to a confession he had
made under duress . . .*

That which I said then, I said. But that which I say now is true.

JOSEPH ZANGARA
*Attempted to assassinate Franklin D. Roosevelt, electrocuted
1933. Zangara fired at Roosevelt as a protest against
the Depression; he killed Mayor Cermak of Chicago instead . . .*

Goodbye. Adios to the world.

EMILIANO ZAPATA
Mexican freedom fighter, killed 1919.

Better fighting death than a slave's life!

WHAT, ME WORRY?

JIM AVERILL
*American brothel-keeper, lynched 1888. To the
enraged cowboys who had strung a rope around his neck* . . .
Stop your fooling, fellows!

CATHERINE BEECHER
*American feminist, died 1878.
An unwittingly final telegram* . . .
I hope to be in Phil. in about ten days. I am stronger than for
years, but take no new responsibilities.

LUDWIG VAN BEETHOVEN
Composer, died 1827.
I shall hear in heaven!

ANEURIN BEVAN
*British socialist politician, died 1960. Commenting
to a friend on his plans for the future* . . .
I want to live because there are one or two things I want to do.

THOMAS BLOOD
Adventurer, died 1680.
I do not fear death.

DAVID BOGUE
*Divine, died 1825.
Told that a visitor had just arrived* . . .
Is he?

NICHOLAS BOILEAU
French critic and poet, died 1711.

It is a great consolation to a dying poet to have never written anything against morality.

To a playwright who was offering
him his latest work . . .

Do you wish to hasten my last hour?

HORATIO BOTTOMLEY
Super-patriot and charlatan, died 1933. Despite his
successes during the Great War, Bottomley died in poverty . . .

Goodbye and God bless you. I'll see you again tomorrow.

CHEVALIER DE BOUFFLERS
French poet, died 1815.

My friend, I believe that I sleep.

CLARA BOW
Film star, died 1965. For all her early success,
Clara Bow's contract lapsed without renewal by her
company, Paramount. Her 'trip' was in fact to the
mental home where she died . . .

I've been working hard for years and I need a rest. So I'm figuring on going to Europe for a year or more when my contract expires.

BRASIDAS
Spartan general, killed in battle 422 BC.

These men do not mean to face us. See how their heads and spears are shaking. Such behaviour always shows that an army is going to run away. Open the gates as I ordered and let us attack them boldly at once.

BERTOLD BRECHT
German playwright, died 1956. Commenting on his
58th birthday, a few months before his death . . .

At least one knows that death will be easy. A slight knock at the window pane, then . . .

BEAU BRUMMEL
Social arbiter, died 1840. Told that he should pray . . .

I do try.

GEORGE BUCHANAN
Scottish scholar, died 1582. Showing how little
he cared for the fate of his mortal remains ...

It matters little to me, for if I am once dead, they may bury me or not bury me as they please. They may leave my corpse to rot where I die if they wish.

BENJAMIN BUTLER
American Attorney General, died 1858.

I have peace, perfect peace.

BISHOP BUTLER
Clergyman, died 1752. The prelate was referring to
John vi. 37 ...

I have often read and thought of that scripture, but never till this moment did I feel its full power, and now I die happy.

DONN BYRNE
American novelist, killed 1928.
Byrne failed to return from his drive ...

I think I'll go for a drive before dinner. Anyone come along?

FRANCESCA CABRINI
'Mother' Cabrini, died 1917. Asked what she wanted for lunch? ...

Bring me anything you like. If I don't take it I may take something else.

CALIGULA
Emperor of Rome, killed 41AD.

I am still alive!

SIR HENRY CAMPBELL-BANNERMAN
British Prime Minister, died 1908.

This is not the end of me.

GIACOMO CASANOVA DA SEINGALT
Lover and adventurer, died 1798.

I have lived as a philosopher, I die as a Christian.

MARCUS PORCIUS CATO
The Younger, suicide 46 BC.

Now I am master of myself.

ROBERT CHAMBERS
Publisher, died 1871. Asked how he felt . . .

Quite comfortable, quite happy, nothing more.

CHANG TZU
Chinese philosopher, died 4th Century BC.

Above ground I shall be food for the kites. Below I shall be food for mole-crickets and ants. Why rob one to feed the other?

CHRYSIPPUS
Greek philosopher, died 207 BC. After an ass had eaten his store of figs . . .

Now give the ass a drink of pure wine to wash down the figs.

ELIZABETH CHUDLEIGH
Society beauty, died 1788.

I will lie down on the couch. I can sleep and after that I shall be entirely recovered.

JOSEPH CONRAD
British author, died 1924.

You, Jess. I am better this morning. I can always get a rise out of you.

BENJAMIN CONSTANT
French philosopher and orator, died 1830. Taking a break from correcting proofs . . .

The rest tomorrow.

NOEL COWARD
British dramatist, died 1976.
To Cole Lesley, his lifelong companion . . .

Goodnight my darlings, I'll see you tomorrow.

PEARL CRAIGIE
American novelist, died 1906. Final telegram . . .

Excellent journey. Crowded train. Reached here by nine. Fondest love Pearl.

JAMES CROLL

Scottish scientist, died 1890. Teetotal all his life,
Croll asked for spirits on his deathbed . . .

I'll take a wee drop of that. I don't think there's much fear of
me learning to drink now.

BING CROSBY

American singer, died 1977.

That was a great game of golf, fellers.

Invited to write his own epitaph by a fanzine . . .

He was an average guy who could carry a tune.

WILLIAM CULLEN

Physician, died 1790.

I wish I had the power of writing for then I would describe to
you how pleasant a thing it is to die.

E. E. CUMMINGS

American poet, died 1962. His wife told him to stop
chopping wood on such a hot day . . .

I'm going to stop now, but I'm going to sharpen the axe before
I put it up, dear.

☠

CHARLES DARWIN

Scientist, died 1882.

I am not in the least afraid to die.

THOMAS DAVIS

Irish poet, died 1845.

In four days I hope to be able to look at light business for a short
time.

MARY DELANY

Literary hostess and letter-writer, died 1788. She was reluctant
to accept the use of a remedy that, rightly, she suspected . . .

I have always had a presentiment that if bark were to be given it
would be my death. You know I have at times a great defluxion
on my lungs – it will stop that, and my lungs with it. Oh, I was
never reckoned obstinate and I will not die so.

DEMONAX
Greek philosopher, died 150.
Draw the curtain, the farce is over.
> *Asked if he cared that his corpse might be exposed*
> *to wild animals . . .*
I can see nothing out of the way in it if even in death I am going to be of service to living things.

JACK 'LEGS' DIAMOND
Gangster, shot 1931. His perennial, delusory boast . . .
The bullet hasn't been made that can kill me.

BENJAMIN DISRAELI
British Prime Minister, died 1881.
I had rather live, but I am not afraid to die.

ALFRED I. DUPONT
American millionaire, died 1902.
Thank you doctors, thank you nurses. I'll be all right in a few days.

☠

JEANNE EAGELS
American actress, died 1929.
I'm going to Dr Caldwell's for one of my regular treatments.

JOSEPH B. EASTMAN
American bureaucrat, died 1944.
I am glad to say that I seem to be making good progress, and from all prognostications I shall be back in circulation again before too long.

LORD CHANCELLOR ELDON
British jurist, died 1838. Told that the weather was fine . . .
It matters not to me, where I am going, whether the weather here is hot or cold.

HAVELOCK ELLIS
Pioneer sexologist, died 1939.
You must go to bed, you are so tired and I feel better. Perhaps I may sleep a little. I shall ring if I need you.

EUGENE, PRINCE OF SAVOY
Austrian general, died 1736.
Postponing a conference till the next day . . .
That is enough for today. We will reserve the rest for tomorrow
– if I live that long.

EDWARD EVERETT
Orator, died 1865. In a letter to his daughter . . .
I have turned the corner, and as soon as I can get a little appetite,
shake off my carking cough, and get the kidneys to resume their
action, and subdue the numbness of my limbs, and get the better
of my neuralgic pain in the left shoulder, I hope to do nicely.

DOUGLAS FAIRBANKS, SR
Film star, died 1939.
I've never felt better.

LEO FERRERA
*Belgian anthropologist. Reassuring those
concerned for him . . .*
It is nothing. A little dizziness.

REGINALD FESSENDEN
Electrical engineer, died 1932.
That was a nice little party. I am sure this summer is helping me
with all the rest and sunshine and the sunshine lamps. I ought
to be able to find out something that will be helpful not only to
me, but to others.

JOHANN FICHTE
German philosopher, died 1814.
Never mind that. I need no more medicine. I feel that I am
cured.

MILLARD FILLMORE
American President, died 1874.
The nourishment is palatable.

F. SCOTT FITZGERALD
American novelist, died 1940. When Sheila Graham asked
him if he wanted Hershey Bars from Schwab's drug-store
in Hollywood . . .
Good enough, they'll be fine.

JOHN FLAVEL
Nonconformist clergyman, died 1691.
I know that it will be well with me.

☠

MRS DAVID GARRICK
Wife of the actor, died 1822. Offered a cup of tea
by a maid . . .
Put it down, hussy! Do you think I cannot help myself?

CHARLIER DE GERSON
'The Most Christian Doctor', died 1429.
Now God dost thou let thy servant depart in peace. The soul that
is accompanied to divinity by the prayers of three hundred
children may advance with humble hope into the presence of
their Father and their God.

CARDINAL JAMES GIBBONS
Died 1521.
I have had a good day.

SIR WILLIAM SCHWENCK GILBERT
Librettist, died 1911. Gilbert suffered a heart attack
when he tried to rescue a girl from drowning on his estate . . .
Put your hands on my shoulders and don't struggle.

EARL GODWIN
Died 1053. Edward the Confessor accused him of
murdering his brother. Godwin choked on the testing
piece of bread . . .
So might I safely swallow this morsel of bread, as I am guiltless
of the deed.

ROBERT GRIMSTON
British sportsman, died 1884.

I don't think I shall join you at dinner, but I will punish your dinner for you. I will have a bit of your fish.

FRANCOIS GUIZOT
French historian, died 1874. To his daughter who said
'We shall meet again, my father' . . .

No one is more convinced of that than I am.

☠

EARL DOUGLAS HAIG
British general, died 1928. His final appointment . . .

I hope to see you on Tuesday at 10.30 a.m.

EDWARD EVERETT HALE
Author, died 1909. Last entry in journal . . .

It was a lovely day and I spent all the time on the deck from half-past ten till five. Had a very good night.

JOHN HANCOCK
Signatory of American Declaration of Independence, died 1793.

I shall look forward to a pleasant time.

FRANZ JOSEPH HAYDN
Composer, died 1809.

Cheer up children, I'm all right.

RUTHERFORD B. HAYES
American President, died 1893.
Welcoming the chance to see his wife again . . .

I know that I'm going where Lucy is.

HEINRICH HEINE
German poet, died 1856.

God will pardon me – it is His profession.

MYRON T. HERRICK
American ambassador to France, died 1929. After
doctors told him he would be 'all right'. . .

Do you really think so? Well, I will do my best.

RICHARD HILLARY
Writer on flight, killed in a crash. Asked over the
intercom 'Are you happy?'...
Moderately, I am continuing to orbit.

PAUL VON HINDENBURG
German Chancellor, died 1934. 'Friend Hein' was
Claudius Matthias' pet name for death ...
It is all right, Sauerbruch, now tell Friend Hein he can come in.

GUSTAV HOLST
Composer, died 1934. A last note ...
And I wish myself the joy of your Fellowship at Whitsuntide.

HARRY HOPKINS
American statesmen, died 1946.
Writing to Winston Churchill ...
Do give my love to Clemmie and Sarah [Churchill's wife and
daughter], all of whom I shall hope to see before you go back,
but I want to have a good talk with you over the state of world
affairs, to say nothing of our private lives.

JOHN HENRY HOPKINS
Episcopal Bishop of Vermont, died 1868.
I feel easier.

REV. SAMUEL HOPKINS
Divine, died 1837.
My anchor is well cast and my ship, though weatherbeaten, will
out-ride the storm.

BISHOP HOUGH
Died 1743.
We part to meet again, I hope in endless joys.

JOHN HOWARD
Quaker leader, died 1790.
Suffer no pomp at my funeral, nor monumental inscription where
I am laid. Lay me quietly in the earth and put a sundial over my
grave and let me be forgotten.

WILLIAM HUTTON
Geologist, died 1815. Asked if he sat comfortably? . . .
Oh yes.

THOMAS HUXLEY
Scientist and philosopher, died 1895.
At present I don't feel like sending in my cheques! And without
being over-sanguine, I rather incline to think that my natural
toughness will get the best of it. Albuminiria or otherwise. Ever
your faithful friend . . .

☠

ROBERT INGERSOLL
Militant atheist, died 1899. Asked how he felt? . . .
Oh, better.

☠

REV. SYLVESTER JUDD
Unitarian and author, died 1853.
Cover me up warm. Keep my utterance clear. I'm doing well.

ANNE JUDSON
Wife of missionary Adironam Judson, died 1826.
I feel quite well. Only very weak.

☠

GEORGE S. KAUFMAN
American dramatist and wit, died 1961.
I'm not afraid any more.

JOHN PHILIP KEMBLE
Actor, died 1823. Reassuring his wife . . .
Don't be alarmed my dear, I have had a slight attack of apoplexy.

COL. J. HOWARD KITCHING
Officer in the army of the Potomac.
To his sister, just before his operation . . .
It will be over in a few minutes, darling, and we will have such
a nice talk about it afterward!

RICHARD KNIBB
Missionary, died 1845. To his congregation in Jamaica . . .
The service is over, you may go. All is well.

HENRY LABOUCHERE
British politician, died 1869.
As a lamp flared at his bedside . . .
Flames ? Not yet, I think.

MARQUIS DE LAFAYETTE
French fighter in American Revolution, died 1834.
Commenting on the inevitability of death . . .
What do you expect ? Life is like the flame of a lamp – when
there is no more oil . . . zest! It goes out and all is over.

KENESAW MOUNTAIN LANDIS
American judge, died 1944. Asked his nurse to give out
an optimistic message to callers . . .
The Judge is doing all right.

T. E. LAWRENCE
'Lawrence of Arabia', killed 1935.
The last telegram from 'Aircraftsman Shaw' . . .
Lunch Tuesday wet fine cottage one mile Bovington Camp
Shaw.

ABRAHAM LINCOLN
American President, assassinated 1865. Replying to his
wife who asked whether the theatre audience would laugh
at their holding hands in their box . . .
They won't think anything about it.

JAKE LINGLE
Chicago newspaperman, killed 1930. Lingle, an intimate
of many gangsters, paid dearly for this boast. It was
presumed Al Capone had him executed . . .
I fix the price of beer in this town.

HENRY CABOT LODGE
American diplomat, died 1924. Letter to President Coolidge ...
The doctors promise prompt recovery. I shall be back in Washington well and strong and I trust that I shall be able to be of some service to you when I get there.

JACK LONDON
American author, died 1916. Telegram ...
I leave California Wednesday following. Daddy.

☠

THOMAS BABINGTON MACAULAY, 1ST BARON MACAULAY
British historian, died 1859.
I shall retire early. I am very tired.

GENERAL GEORGE B. McCLELLAN
American soldier, died 1885. Sent word to his wife ...
Tell her I am better now.

GENERAL FRANCIS MARION
American soldier, died 1795.
Thank God I can lay my hand upon my heart and say that since I came to man's estate I have never intentionally done wrong to anyone.

HARRIET MARTINEAU
Writer and social reformer, died 1876.
I have had a noble share of life and I do not ask for any other life. I see no reason why the existence of Harriet Martineau should be perpetuated.

MEHER BABA
Guru, died 1969. The Baba's last words in 1925 preceded a lifetime of silence before his actual death ...
Don't worry, be happy.

MICHELANGELO BUONARROTI
Sculptor, died 1564.
My soul I resign to God, my body to the earth, my worldly goods to my next of kin.

MARY RUSSELL MITFORD
British novelist, died 1855. Her last letter . . .

Today I am better, but if you wish for another cheerful evening with your old friend, there is no time to be lost.

MOLIERE
(Jean-Baptiste Poquelin)
French dramatist, died 1673.

There is no need to be frightened. You have seen me spit more blood than that and to spare. Nevertheless, go and ask my wife to come up to me.

BLAIR MOODY
US Senator

I feel better.

H. H. MUNRO
'Saki' British author, killed 1916.
In trying to save a soldier's life he lost his own . . .

Put that bloody cigarette out!

HUGO MUNSTERBERG
Psychologist, died 1916.

By spring we shall have peace.

☠

RAMON MARIA NARVAEZ
Spanish patriot, died 1868. To his confessor . . .

I do not have to forgive my enemies, because I killed them all.

SIR WILLIAM ROBERTSON NICHOLL
Died 1923.

I believe everything I have written about immortality.

☠

WILLIAM O'BRIEN
Irish nationalist, died 1864.

Well, the night is so long and dreary, I think I will wait up a little longer.

WILFRED OWEN

British poet, killed 1918.

To one of the troops he commanded . . .

Well done, you are doing that very well, my boy.

VISCOUNT PALMERSTON

British Prime Minister, died 1865.

Told by his doctor he was dying . . .

Die, my dear doctor – that's the last thing I shall do!

GRAM PARSONS

American rock musician, killed 1972.

Warned that his drug use would prove fatal . . .

Death is a warm cloak, and old friend. I regard death as something that comes up on a roulette wheel every once in a while.

BORIS PASTERNAK

Russian novelist, died 1959.

Goodbye . . . why am I haemorrhaging?

ANNA PAVLOVA

Prima ballerina, died 1931.

Get my 'Swan' costume ready.

SIR ROBERT PEEL

British Prime Minister, killed 1850. Saying goodbye to his wife as he set out for a ride which proved fatal . . .

Julia, you are not going without wishing me goodbye, or saying those sweet words 'God bless you'.

MAX PLOWMAN

British poet, died 1941.

Last letter to one of his magazine editors . . .

Good wishes to you very sincerely. Do come and see us here some day – even tho' we are bunged up at the moment. And let me know if the enclosed needs revision. Yours ever, Max P.

PRESTON B. PLUMB

US Senator, died 1891. Letter to his former secretary . . .

Dear Frank, Please come to my room tomorrow about ten o'clock. Yours truly, P.B.P.

BEATRIX POTTER
Author and illustrator of children's books, died 1943.
Her last letter . . .
Dear Joe Moscrop, Still some strength in me. I write a line to shake you by the hand – our friendship has been entirely pleasant. I am very ill with bronchitis. With best wishes for the New Year . . .

FREDERICK REMINGTON
Painter, died 1909. Before an operation on his appendix
from which he did not recover . . .
Cut her loose, doc!

PIERRE RENOIR
French artist, died 1919.
I am still progressing.

STEPHEN REYNOLDS
British essayist. Telegram . . .
Reference my letter of last night. Have got influenza myself now. Stop. Pretty sure unable to come to London next week.

COMTE HENRI DE SAINT-SIMON
Socialist reformer, died 1825.
The future belongs to us. In order to do great things one must be enthusiastic.

MORITZ VON SCHWIND
German artist, died 1871. Aked how he felt ? . . .
Excellent!

SIR WALTER SCOTT
British novelist, died 1832.
I have written nothing which on my deathbed I should wish blotted. God bless you all, I feel myself again.

BISHOP SMALRIDGE
Divine, died 1719.
God be thanked I have had a very good night.

JOHN SUTTER
American pioneer, died 1880.
Next year, next year they will surely . . .

SOFIA SOYMANOV SVETCHINE
Russian writer, died 1857.
It will soon be time for Mass. They must raise me.

SIR RIGBY SWIFT
Judge, died 1937. A final letter . . .
My dear Chief, Your most kind and sympathetic letter has been a wonderful tonic and already I feel much better. Yours very faithfully, Rigby Swift.

☠

TALLEYRAND
*French statesman, died 1838. Hearing that the
Archbishop of Paris had offered his own life rather than
see Talleyrand die . . .*
He can find a better use for it.

EDWARD THRING
Schoolmaster, died 1887. Last entry in his diary . . .
And now to bed. Sermon finished and a blessed feeling of Sunday coming.

SS TITANIC
Sunk 1912. Last SOS . . .
Have struck iceberg. Badly damaged. Rush aid.

☠

RUDOLF VALENTINO
Film star, died 1926.
Don't pull down the blinds. I feel fine. I want the sunlight to greet me!

☠

RICHARD WAGNER
German composer, died 1883.

I am fond of them, of the inferior beings of the abyss, of those who are full of longing.

ARCHBISHOP WARHAM
Died 1532. On being told that he still had some £30 in cash . . .

That is enough to last until I get to heaven.

CHARLES WARNER
Author, died 1900. To his hosts at the house
in which he was staying . . .

I am not well and should like to lie down. Will you call me in ten minutes. Thank you, you are very kind. In ten minutes, remember.

MARY WEBB
British rural author, died 1927. Told that everyone
would gather for tea in the afternoon . . .

That will be nice.

DUKE OF WELLINGTON
British soldier, died 1852.

Do you know where the apothecary lives? Then send and let him know that I should like to see him. I don't feel quite well and I will lie still till he comes.

H. G. WELLS
British novelist and reformer, died 1946. To his nurse . . .

Go away. I'm all right.

HENRY KIRKE WHITE
British poet, died 1806. Letter to his brother from
Cambridge, where White died of overwork . . .

Our lectures begin on Friday, but I do not attend them until I am better. I have not written to my mother, nor shall I while I remain unwell. You will tell her, as a reason, that our lectures begin on Friday. I know she will be uneasy, if she do not hear from me, and still more so if I tell her I am ill. I cannot write any more at present, than that I am your truly affectionate brother, H. K. White.

JACK B. YEATS
Painter, brother of W. B. Yeats, died 1957. To a friend . . .
Remember, you have promised me a sitting in the morning.

WILLIAM BUTLER YEATS
Poet, died 1939. A last letter . . .
In two or three weeks – I am now idle that I may rest after writing much verse – I will begin to write my most fundamental thoughts and the arrangement of thought which I am convinced will complete my studies. I am happy and I think full of an energy I had despaired of. It seems to me that I have found what I wanted. When I try to put all into a phrase I say 'Man can embody truth, but he cannot know it'. I must embody it in the completion of my life. The abstract is not life and everywhere drags out its contradictions. You can refute Hegel, but not the Saint or the Song of Sixpence.

EMILE ZOLA
French novelist, died 1902.
I feel sick. My head is splitting. No, don't you see the dog is sick too. We are both ill. It must be something we have eaten. It will pass away. Let us not bother them.

ULRICH ZWINGLI
Protestant divine, killed 1531.
What does it matter ? They may kill the body, but they cannot kill the soul.

TOP OF
THE WORLD

PIETRO ARETINO
Italian comic dramatist, died 1556.
After receiving Extreme Unction . . .
Keep the rats away now that I'm all greased up.

JOHN J. AUDUBON
American ornithologist, died 1851.
I have enjoyed a world which though wicked enough in all conscience, is perhaps as good as worlds unknown.

FRANCIS BACON
Philosopher, author and lawyer, died 1626.
My name and memory I leave to man's charitable speeches, to foreign nations and to the next age.

MAJOR NORMAN BAESELL
American Air Force, killed 1944. Baesell flew bandleader
Glenn Miller to France on the flight that
vanished over the Channel . . .
What's the matter Miller, do you want to live for ever?

WALTER BAGEHOT
Banker, economist, constitutional historian, died 1877.
Let me have my own fidgets.

ELIAS BALDWIN
American gambler.
By God, I'm not licked yet!

JOHN BARRYMORE
American actor, died 1942. Interviewed during his
final illness . . .
Die? I should say not, dear fellow. No Barrymore would allow
such a conventional thing to happen to him.

LIONEL BARRYMORE
American actor, died 1954.
Invited to contribute his own epitaph to a fanzine . . .
Well, I've played everything but a harp.

HENRY WARD BEECHER
Religious author, died 1849.
Asked by his doctor whether he could raise his arm? . . .
Well, high enough to hit you, Doctor!

LYMAN BEECHER
Divine, died 1863.
I have fought a good fight. I have finished my course. I have kept
the faith, henceforth there is laid up for me a crown which God
the righteous judge will give me at that day. That is my testimony. Write it down. That is my testimony.

DOMINIQUE BOUHOURS
Grammarian, died 1702.
I am about to, or, I am going to die. Either expression is used.

ROBERT BUCHANAN
Poet and novelist, died 1901.
I should like to have a good spin down Regent Street.

DON RODRIGO CALDERON
Spanish courtier, executed 1621.
His death gave rise to the Spanish proverb:
to be haughtier than Don Rodrigo on the scaffold . . .
All my life I have carried myself gracefully.

SIR WINSTON CHURCHILL
British Prime Minister, died 1965.
Interviewed on his 75th birthday, Churchill's

sentiments were probably unchanged on his death . . .
I am ready to meet my Maker. Whether my Maker is prepared
for the ordeal of meeting me is another matter.

ANDREW COMBE
Phrenologist, died 1847.

Happy, happy!

JOHN COPLEY
British artist, died 1815.
Happy, happy, supremely happy.

GEORGE CRABBE
British poet, died 1832.
All is well at last. You must make an entertainment. God bless
you, God bless you!

BRUCE CUMMINGS
Biologist, died 1919.
My horizon has cleared. My thoughts are tinged with sweetness
and I am content.

BARON GEORGES CUVIER
Zoologist, died 1832. To his nurse, who was applying leeches . . .
Nurse, it was I who discovered that leeches have red blood.
*To his daughter, who was drinking
a glass of lemonade he had refused . . .*
It is delightful to see those whom I love still able to swallow.

ARCHBISHOP ELECTOR KARL VON DALBERG
Died 1817.
Love! Life! God's will!

RENE DESCARTES
French mathematician and philosopher, died 1650.
My soul, thou has long been held captive. The hour has now
come for thee to quit thy prison, to leave the trammels of this
body. Then to this separation with joy and courage!

JOHN DONNE
British poet, died 1631.

I were miserable if I might not die. Thy Kingdom come, Thy Will be done.

NORMAN DOUGLAS
British author, died 1952.

Love, love, love!

SAMUEL DREW
Divine, died 1833.
Told 'Today you will be with Christ' ...
Yes, my good sir, I trust that I will.

JOSEPH DUNCAN
American educator and politician, died 1844.
Ever precious, ever precious.

☗

GENERAL WILLIAM EATON
American soldier, died 1811.
Asked if he wanted his head raised to see the sunrise? ...
Yes sir, I thank you.

REV. NATHANIEL EMMONS
Divine, died 1840.

I am ready.

JOHN ERICSSON
Inventor and engineer, died 1889

I am resting. This rest is more magnificent, more beautiful than words can tell.

RALPH ERSKINE
Scottish poet, died 1752.

I shall be for ever a debtor to free grace. Victory, victory, victory!

WILLIAM ETTY
British artist, died 1849
Wonderful, wonderful this death.

☗

MARSHAL FERDINAND FOCH
French soldier, died 1929.

Let us go!

BERNARD DE FONTENELLE
French scholar, died 1757. Aged one hundred,
de Fontenelle's words are an understatement ...
I feel nothing except a certain difficulty in continuing to exist.

JOHANN FORSTER
Polish naturalist, died 1798.
This is a beautiful world.

STEPHEN F. FOSTER
Texan patriot, died 1836.
Texas recognized! Archer told me so. Did you see it in the papers?

CHARLES JAMES FOX
British politician, died 1806.
I die happy.

THEODORE FRELINGHUYSEN
American politician and educator, died 1862.
All peace, more than ever before.

THOMAS GAINSBOROUGH
British artist, died 1788.
We are all going to heaven and Van Dyck is of the party.

SIR SAMUEL GARTH
Doctor and poet, died 1718. To his doctors ...
Dear gentlemen, let me die a natural death.
After receiving the Last Rites ...
I am going on a long journey, they have greased my boots already.

HENRY GEORGE
American writer, died 1897.
Yes, yes, yes!

ANDRE GIDE
French novelist, died 1951.

C'est bien.

GEORGE GISSING
British novelist, died 1903.

Patience, patience . . . God's will be done.

SIR EDMUND GOSSE
Biographer and critic, died 1928.
Gosse died on the operating table, this is his last letter . . .

You will think of me in this hour with sympathy and hope. There seems good reason to think I will survive the shock. In any case I am perfectly calm, and able to enjoy the love which has accompanied me through such long years and surrounds me still.

HENRY GRATTAN
Irish statesman, died 1820.

I am perfectly resigned. I am surrounded by my family. I have served my country. I have reliance upon God and I am not afraid of the Devil.

ROBERT GRAY
Bishop of Cape Town, died 1872. Told that to take
Holy Communion 'tomorrow' would be too late . . .

Well, dear fellow, I am ready when you like.

☠

JAMES ALEXANDER HALDANE
First Congregational minister in Scotland, died 1857.
Told by his wife 'You are going to Jesus,
how happy you will be soon' . . .

Oh, yes.

RADCLYFFE HALL
British author, died 1963.

What a life; but such as it is, I offer it to God.

JEAN FRANCOIS LA HARPE
French dramatist, died 1803.

I am grateful to divine mercy for having left me sufficient recollection to feel how consoling these prayers are for the dying.

WILLIAM H. HARVEY
Botanist, died 1866.

Yes, it has been a pleasant world to me.

WILLIAM HAZLITT
Critic and essayist, died 1830.

Well, I have had a happy life.

ALEXANDER HENDERSON
Moderator of Glasgow Assembly, died 1646.
His written declaration that he was . . .

. . . most of all obliged to the grace and goodness of God, for calling
me to believe the promises of the Gospel, and for exalting me
to be a preacher of them to others, and to be a willing, though
weak instrument in this great and wonderful work of Reformation, which I beseech the Lord to bring to a happy conclusion.

THOMAS HENDRICKS
American Vice President, died 1885.

At rest at last. Now I am free from pain.

MATTHEW HENRY
Theologian and translator, died 1714.

A life spent in the service of God and in communion with Him
is the most comfortable and pleasant life anyone can live in the
world.

PATRICK HENRY
American patriot, died 1799.

Be thankful for the kind God who allows me to go this painlessly.

GEORGE HERBERT
Composer of hymns, died 1632.

I am now ready to die. Lord, forsake me not, now for my
strength faileth me, but grant me mercy for the merits of Jesus.
And now Lord, receive my soul.

SIDNEY HERBERT, LORD HERBERT OF LEA
British statesman, died 1861.

Well, this is the end. I have had a life of great happiness. A short
one, perhaps, but an active one. I have not done all I wished, but
I have tried to do my best.

URELI CORELLI HILL
Founder of New York Philharmonic Orchestra,
suicide 1875. His note read . . .
Ha ha! I go, the sooner the better!

EUGENE A. HOFFMAN
Theologian, died 1902. Saying goodbye to his favourite
retreat . . .
Goodbye, Matapedia.

RICHARD HOOKER
Theologian, died 1600.
My days are past as a shadow that returns not.

THOMAS HOOKER
Founding Father, died 1647. Told 'You are going
to receive the reward of all your labours' . . .
Brother, I am going to receive mercy.

GERARD MANLEY HOPKINS
Poet, died 1889.
I am so happy, so happy.

FRIEDRICH HUMBOLDT
German traveller and scientist, died 1859.
How grand is the sunlight. It seems to beckon earth to heaven.

LEIGH HUNT
Essayist and critic, died 1859.
Deep dream of peace.

SELINA, COUNTESS OF HUNTINGDON
Philanthropist, died 1791.
My work is done. I have nothing to do but go to my Father.

COLONEL JOHN HUTCHINSON
Puritan leader, died 1664.
'Tis as I would have it, 'tis where I would have it.

☻

ALEXANDER ILITCHEWSKI
Russian writer. His life's quest was for a perfect love,
on finding it he seems to have died of joy . . .
I have found at last the object of my love!

HENRY JAMES, SR
Philosopher, died 1882.
I stick by Almighty God. He alone is. All else is death. Don't call this dying – I am just entering on life.

WILLIAM JAMES
American philosopher, died 1910.
It's so good to get home!

REV. JACOB J. JANEWAY
Divine, died 1674.
I am tired of eating, I want to go home!

TOM L. JOHNSON
American politician, died 1911.
It's all right. I'm so happy.

HENRY A. JONES
Dramatist, died 1929.
Told that 'Gertie' would be back . . .
I'm so glad.

JOHN JORTIN
Ecclesiastic and historian, died 1770.
Refusing some food that was offered him . . .
No thank you, I have had enough of everything.

IMMANUEL KANT
German philosopher, died 1804.
It is enough.

ANGELICA KAUFMANN
*Artist, died 1807. Stopping her cousin who had begun
to read her a hymn for the dying . . .*

No, Johann, I will not hear that. Read me the 'Hymn for the Sick' on page 128.

MICHAEL C. KERR
American politician, died 1876.

I stand upon my record.

REGINALD DE KOVEN
American composer, died 1920. Final telegram . . .

House sold out for Friday night, box office *Vox Dei* hurrah!

ROBERT M. LAFOLLETTE
American politician, died 1925.

I am at peace with all the world, but there is still a lot of work I could do. I don't know how the people will feel towards me, but I shall take to the grave my love for them which has sustained me through life.

LUCY LARCOM
Author and educator, died 1893.

Freedom!

NINON DE LENCLOS
Wit, beauty and literary hostess, died 1705.

Let no vain hope . . .
  at the core,
I'm ripe for death . . .
  business here . . .

SINCLAIR LEWIS
American novelist, died 1951.

I am happy. God bless you all.

THEOPHILUS LINDSEY
*Divine, died 1805. Asked if he lived by the maxim
'Whatever is, is right'? . . .*

No. Whatever is, is best.

HAMILTON W. MABIE
American editor and essayist, died 1916.
I have had a quiet but very happy Christmas.

NICCOLO MACHIAVELLI
Political theorist, died 1530.
I desire to go to hell and not to heaven. In the former place I shall enjoy the company of Popes, Kings and Princes, while in the latter are only beggars, monks and apostles.

SIR JAMES MACKINTOSH
Historian and essayist, died 1832.
Happy, happy!

A. T. MAHAN
Writer on sea power, died 1914.
Looking out of his window at the garden . . .
If a few more quiet years were granted me, I might see and enjoy these things, but God is just and I am content.

LOUIS MANDRIN
Brigand, executed 1755.
Ah, what a moment, great God! And one I ought to have foreseen.

ANDREW MARVELL, SR
Killed 1641. Marvell, father of the poet, stepped on board a ferry with this comment. The boat promptly sank . . .
Ho for heaven!

COTTON MATHER
Divine, died 1728.
Is this dying, is this all? Is this what I feared when I prayed against a hard death? Oh, I can bear this, I can bear it!

RICHARD MATHER
Puritan clergyman, died 1669. Asked how he felt? . . .
Far from well, yet better than my iniquities deserve.

PHILIP MELANCHTHON
German humanist, died 1568. Asked what he needed . . .
Nothing else but heaven.

ALICE MEYNELL
Poet and essayist, died 1922.

This is not tragic. I am happy.

JOHN STUART MILL
Political thinker, died 1873.

My work is done.

LADY MARY WORTLEY MONTAGU
Essayist, died 1762.

It has all been very interesting.

HANNAH MORE
American poet, died 1833.

Joy!

JEAN VICTOR MOREAU
French general, died 1813. Dying in exile,
Moreau sent his last words to Napoleon . . .

Say to the Emperor that I go to the tomb with the same feelings
of veneration, respect and devotion that he inspired in me the
first time I saw him. I have nothing to reproach myself with.

SAMUEL MORSE
Pioneer of telegraphy, died 1872. Being told 'This is
the way we doctors telegraph' to allay his fears
of the instruments . . .

Very good.

ARTHUR MURPHY
British dramatist, died 1805.

Taught half by reason, half by mere dismay. To welcome death
and calmly pass away.

GIAMBATTISTA NANI
Died 1678.

How beautiful!

RICHARD NEWTON
Divine, died 1753.

I am going, going to glory. Farewell sin, farewell death. Praise the Lord.

TORLOGH O'CAROLAN
Irish bard, died 1838.
Calling for a last tot of whiskey . . .

It would be hard if such friends should part at least without kissing.

CHARLOTTE ELIZABETH, DUCHESSE D'ORLEANS
Her last letter . . .

Thank God, I am prepared to die, and I only pray for strength to die bravely. It is not bad weather although today a fine rain is setting in. But I do not think any weather will help me. Many complain of coughs and colds, but my malady lies deeper. Should I recover you will find me the same friend as ever. Should this be the end, I die with full faith in my Redeemer.

WILLIAM OUGHTRED
Mathematician, died 1660.
Hearing that King Charles II had been restored . . .

And are you sure he is restored? Then give a glass of sack to drink his Sacred Majesty's health.

ROBERT OWEN
Socialist and philanthropist, died 1858.

Relief has come!

SILVIO PELLICO
Italian poet, died 1854.

Oh Paradise, Paradise! At last comes to me the grand consolation. My prisons disappear, the great of earth pass away, all before is rest.

PABLO PICASSO
Artist, died 1973.

Drink to me.

ALBERT PIKE
American poet, died 1891. Written in Hebrew ...

Peace, peace, peace.

SIR ISAAC PITMAN
The inventor of shorthand, died 1897.

To those who ask how Isaac Pitman passed away, say peacefully and with no more concern than passing from one room into another to take up some further employment.

SANZIO RAPHAEL
Italian artist, died 1520.

Happy.

MADAME RECAMIER
Literary hostess and beauty, died 1849.

We shall meet again.

ERNEST RENAN
French writer, philologist and historian, died 1892.

I have done my work. It is the most natural thing in the world to die. Let us accept the laws of the Universe – the heavens and the earth remain.

SIR JOSHUA REYNOLDS
British artist, died 1792.

I have been fortunate in long good health and constant success and I ought not to complain. I know that all things on earth must have an end and now I am come to mine.

CHRISTINA ROSSETTI
Poet, died 1894.

I love everybody. If ever I had an enemy I should hope to meet and welcome that enemy in heaven.

DANTE GABRIEL ROSSETTI
Poet and painter, died 1882.

Then you really think I'm dying? At last you think so. But I was right from the first.

☠

BISHOP SANDERSON
Divine, died 1663.

My heart is fixed, oh God. My heart is fixed where true joy is to be found.

MARSHAL SAXE
French soldier, died 1750.

I have had a beautiful dream.

PAUL SCARRON
French dramatist, died 1660.

I would never have thought it was so easy to laugh at the approach of death.

CARL SCHURZ
American politician, died 1906.

It is so simple to die.

JUNIPERO SERRA
Spanish missionary, died 1784.

Now I shall rest.

WILLIAM HENRY SEWARD
*American statesman, died 1872. His daughters asked
if he had any last messages for them? . . .*

Nothing. Only 'Love one another'.

ALGERNON SIDNEY
*Executed 1683. Condemned for his role in the
'Rye House Plot' against Charles II.
The executioner asked 'Will you rise again?' . . .*

Not until the general Resurrection.

REV. EDWARD SMEDLEY
Poet, died 1836.

Be always thankful.

ARTHUR STANLEY
Dean of Westminster, died 1881.
I am perfectly happy, perfectly satisfied. I have no misgivings.

SIR JOHN STEWART
Last words established his son as his legal heir . . .
. . . Lady Jane Douglas, my lawful spouse, did, in the year
1748, bring to the world my two sons, Archibald and Sholto and
I firmly believe the children were mine, as I am sure they were
hers. Of the two sons, Archibald is the only one in life now. I
make this declaration as stepping into eternity before the witnesses afore-mentioned . . .Jo. Stewart.

EMMANUEL SWEDENBORG
Swedish philosopher, scientist and mystic, died 1772.
It is well. I thank you. God bless you.

☠

JOHN TAYLOR
'The Water Poet', died 1653.
How sweet it is to rest.

ELLEN TERRY
British actress, died 1928.
Scribbled in the dust of her bedside table . . .
Happy.

WILLIAM S. THAYER
Doctor, died 1932.
This is the end and I am not sorry.

'BIG BILL' THOMPSON
Mayor of Chicago, died 1944.
Reassuring his aides that his affairs were all in order . . .
Everything is all set, Jim . . . that's right, that's right.

JOHN TOLAND
Deist, died 1722. Asked if he wanted anything ? . . .
I want nothing but Death.

☠

SIR HARRY VANE
Puritan leader, executed 1662.

Why should we shrink from death. I find it rather shrinks from me than I from it.

JOSEPH DE VEUSTER
'Father Damien', died 1889.

Well, God's will be done and He knows best. My work, with all its faults and failures, is in His hands. Before Easter I shall see my Saviour.

EUGENE VIDOCQ
Theif turned detective, died 1857.

How great is the forgiveness for such a life.

GENERAL LEW WALLACE
American religious author, died 1905.
The author of 'Ben Hur' told his wife . . .

We shall meet in heaven.

GEORGE WASHINGTON
American President, died 1799.

Doctor, I die hard, but I am not afraid to go.

ETHEL WATERS
Blues singer, died 1977.
Interviewed shortly before her death . . .

I'm not afraid to die, honey. In fact I'm kind of looking forward to it. I know that the Lord has his arms wrapped around this big, fat sparrow.

THOMAS E. WATSON
US Senator, died 1922.

I am not afraid, I am not afraid to die.

ISAAC WATTS
Nonconformist schoolmaster and composer of hymns, died 1748.

It is a great mercy to me that I have no manner of fear or dread of death. I could, if God please, lay my head back and die without terror this afternoon.

WILLIAM WEBSTER
Died 1758.

Peace.

CHARLES WESLEY
Methodist leader and hymn composer, died 1788.

I shall be satisfied with thy likeness – satisfied.

JOHN WESLEY
Methodist leader and preacher, died 1791.

The best of all is that God is with us.

WILLIAM WHITAKER
Divine, died 1595.

Life or death is welcome to me and I desire not to live but so far as I may be serviceable to God and His church.

PHILIP WICKSTEED
Dante scholar.

Hurrah, hurrah!

WILLIAM WILBERFORCE
Anti-slavery campaigner, died 1833.

Heaven!

JOHN SHARP WILLIAMS
US Senator, died 1932.

I've done things that seemed at the time worth doing. I think that if a man can get to my age and, looking back, believe a majority of things he did were worth the effort, he has nothing to regret.

THOMAS WOOLSTON
British theologian, died 1733.

This is a struggle which all men go through and which I bear not only with patience but with willingness.

Sir Henry Wooton
Died 1639.

I now draw near to the harbour of death – that harbour that will rescue me from all the future storms and waves of this restless world. I praise God and am willing to leave it. I expect a better, that world where dwelleth righteousness, and I long for it.

Eugene Ysaye
Belgian violinist, died 1929. He had his Fourth Sonata played for his enjoyment . . .

Splendid, the finale just a little too fast.

THE SHOW MUST GO ON

JANE ADDAMS
Temperance campaigner, died 1935.
Offered spirits as a restorative . . .
Always, always water for me!

ANONYMOUS FRENCH ARISTOCRAT
Guillotined 1794. Refusing a glass of rum . . .
I lose all sense of direction when I am drunk.

HONORÉ DE BALZAC
French novelist, died 1850.
Summoning one of his own fictional creations . . .
Send for Bianchon!

HENRI BARBUSSE
French novelist, died 1935. Barbusse wrote on military themes
and died still urging the escalation of world-wide conflicts . . .
Telephone and say they must still enlarge it. Always larger,
broader, more universal. It is the only way of saving the world.

PHINEAS T. BARNUM
America's supreme showman, died 1901.
How were the circus receipts tonight at Madison Square
Garden?

CLARENCE BARRON
Publisher of the Wall Street Journal, *died 1928.*
What's the news?

JOHANN BASEDOW
Educational reformer, died 1790.
I want an autopsy made for the benefit of my fellow men.

WARNER BAXTER
Film star, died 1951. Invited to make up
his own epitaph for a fanzine . . .
Did you hear about my operation?

GEORGE M. BEARD
Surgeon, died 1883.
Tell the doctors it is impossible for me to record the thoughts of a dying man. It would be interesting to do so, but I cannot. My time has come. I hope others will carry on my work.

ROBERT BENCHLEY
American humorist, died 1945. Benchley had been
reading a book called 'Am I Thinking' during his
final illness. His comment adorned the title page . . .
No. And supposing you were?

CONSTANCE BENNETT
Film star, died 1965. Invited to contribute her own
epitaph to a fanzine . . .
Do not disturb.

JOSH BILLINGS
(H. W. Shaw) American humorist, died 1885.
His final public lecture . . .
My doctors East ordered a rest of brain, but you see I do not have to work my brain for a simple lecture – it comes spontaneously.

FRANZ BOAS
Anthropologist, died 1942.
It isn't necessary to wear oneself out repeating that racism is either a monstrous error or a shameless lie. The Nazis themselves have recently had to appreciate the accuracy of the facts that I have brought together on the European immigrants of America.

BARON CHRISTIAN BUNSEN
Prussian diplomat and scholar, died 1860.
Died as he greeted guests . . .

Very kind, very glad . . .

THOMAS CAMPBELL
Poet, died 1844. Campbells' friends were not sure
whether the poet was dead or merely silent. In the hope
of a response they asked who was the real author of
one of his poems. The poet proved himself still alive
when he heard another name mentioned . . .

No. It was one Tom Campbell.

ALONZO CANO
'The Spanish Michelangelo', died 1677. The sculptor refused
the ornate crucifix his confessor was offering . . .

Vex me not with this thing, but give me a simple cross that I may
adore it both as it is in itself and as I can figure it in my mind.

ISAAC CASAUBON
Huguenot scholar and theologian, died 1614. Asked on his
deathbed which religion – Protestant or Catholic –
he finally believed . . .

Then you think, my Lord, that I have all along been a dissem-
bler in a matter of the greatest moment?

CATO THE CENSOR
Suicide 149 BC.

Shut the door.

RENE DE CHATEAUBRIAND
Pioneer of the French romantic movement, died 1848.
Hearing of the outbreak of fighting in Paris . . .

I want to go there.

ANTON PAVLOVICH CHEKHOV
Russian dramatist, died 1904. Calling for a last drink . . .

I am dying. I haven't drunk champagne for a long time.

HANNAH CHICKERING
American prison reformer.

Say only that I was at peace. More than this, if repeated, might indicate a deeper spiritual experience than I ever had.

DAVID CHYTRAUS
Historian, died 1600.
Chytraus had finished his final manuscript . . .

I have concluded the history of this century and put the finishing touches to it and not another word will I write.

GEORGE COGHILL
Naturalist, died 1941.
Taking a glass of peppermint water from the nurse . . .

Why, that's what we used to give to babies.

HARRY COHN
Hollywood movie magnate, died 1958. Cohn's last words were not recorded, but comic Red Skelton provided what many would have found an apt epitaph as he surveyed the crowds at Cohn's funeral . . .

It proves what they say: give the public what they want to see and they'll come out for it.

SPENCER COLE
Divine.

I should like to finish my exposition of the Twenty-Second of Revelation.

JEAN-BAPTISTE COROT
French artist, died 1875.

In spite of myself, I go on hoping. I hope with all my heart that there will be painting in heaven.

ALEISTER CROWLEY
'The Great Beast', mystic and black magician, died 1947.
The final paragraph of his autobiographical 'Confessions' . . .

What may befall, I know not, and I have almost ceased to care. It is enough that I should press towards the mark of my high calling, secure in the magical virtue of my oath: 'I shall endure unto the End'.

LADY EMERALD CUNARD
Socialite, died 1948. Turning down the teaspoon
of champagne her maid was offering . . .
No. Open a bottle for the nurse and yourself.

DANIEL DEFOE
British novelist, died 1731.
I do not know which is more difficult in a Christian life – to live well or to die well.

JOHN DUBOS
Died 1742.
Death is a law and not a punishment. Three things ought to console us for giving up life – the friends we lost, the few persons worthy of being loved whom we leave behind us, finally the memory of our stupidities and the assurance that they are now going to stop.

HENRI DUNANT
Pioneer of the Red Cross, died 1910. A follower of the faith
of the earliest Christians, he rejected the rites of the later
faith . . .
I wish to be carried to my grave like a dog without a single one of your ceremonies which I do not recognize. I trust to your goodness faithfully to respect my last earthly request. I count upon your friendship that it shall be so. Amen. I am a disciple of Christ as in the First Century and nothing more.

ISADORA DUNCAN
Interpretative dancer, killed 1927.
Adieu my friends, I go on to glory!

JOSEPH DUVEEN
Art dealer, died 1939. Referring to his living beyond
all medical prognoses, rather than his ability to sell art to
the rich . . .
Well, I fooled them for five years.

AMELIA EARHARDT
Pilot, killed 1937. Her last letter to her husband . . .

Please know that I am quite aware of the hazards. I want to do it because I want to do it. Women must try to do things as men have tried. When they fail, their failure must be but a challenge to others.

CHARLES D'EVERERUARD
Gourmet, died 1703. His confessor asked him
if he would be reconciled with Christ ? . . .

With all my heart I would be fain reconciled with my stomach which no longer performs its usual functions.

HORACE FABOR
'The Silver King', died 1899. To his wife, who believed him
and still died in abject poverty thirty-six years later . . .

Hang on to the Matchless [mine]. It will make millions again.

FRANCOIS FENELON
French divine and religious theorist, died 1715.

Lord, if I am still necessary to Thy people, I refuse not to labour for the rest of my days. Thy will be done!

KATHLEEN FERRIER
Opera singer, died 1953.

Now I'll have eine kleine pause.

W. C. FIELDS
American film comic, died 1946. Referring to his lifelong
bête noire among cities, the great performer chose this epitaph . . .

On the whole, I'd rather be in Philadelphia.

MME DE FONTAINE-MARTEL
Literary hostess. Asking what time it was ?
Then reminded herself . . .

God be blessed! Whatever the hour there is always a rendezvous going on.

BENJAMIN FRANKLIN
American diplomat and writer, died 1790. Aged 25,
Franklin composed this possible epitaph for himself . . .
The body of Ben Franklin, Printer, (like the cover of an old book, its contents torn out and stripped of its lettering and gilding) lies here, food for worms. But the work shall not be lost, for it will (as he believed) appear in a new and more elegant edition, revised and corrected by the Author.

CLARK GABLE
Film star, died 1960. Gable died while shooting
'The Misfits' with Marilyn Monroe. The last words
he spoke on camera were suitably symbolic . . .
Marilyn Monroe: How do you find the way back in the dark? Clark Gable: Just head for the big star straight on. The highways under it take us right home.

GALILEO GALILEI
Astronomer, died 1642. Galileo was forced to recant his new
and accurate theories – that the earth moves around the sun
and not vice versa – but he remained privately defiant . . .
Yet it still moves.

JOHN GARFIELD
Film star, died 1952. Garfield died in bed, but not alone.
A Hollywood wit suggested this epitaph . . .
Died in the saddle.

GEORGE GIPP
American football star, died 1920. Gipp died of pneumonia
after the 1920 college season. He left this last request with
Notre Dame's legendary coach Knute Rockne . . .
One day, when the going is tough and a big game is hanging in the balance, ask the team to win one for the Gipper. I don't know where I'll be, Rock, but I'll know about it and I'll be happy.

WILLIAM GODWIN
Political philosopher, died 1836. Last entry in his diary . . .
Cough, snow.

GEN. GEORGE WASHINGTON GOETHALS
Builder of the Panama Canal, died 1928.
Dying in New York City . . .

Let me stay here. If I stay here, I'll be much nearer to West Point.

CARY GRANT
Movie star. Invited to write his own epitaph
for a fanzine . . .

He was lucky, and he knew it.

JOSEPH GREEN
Surgeon, died 1863. Green checked his own pulse . . .

Congestion . . . stopped.

RUFUS W. GRISWOLD
Edgar Allen Poe's literary executor, died 1857.

Sir, I may not have been always a Christian, but I am very sure that I have been a gentleman.

☠

WILLIAM HAINES
Star of the silent movies.
Invited to write his own epitaph for a fanzine . . .

Here's something I want to get off my chest.

MARK HANNA
American politician, died 1904.
Asked if he wanted a handkerchief, joked back . . .

Yes, I would like one, but I suppose I cannot have it. My wife takes them all.

CALVIN S. HARRINGTON
Classical scholar.

As it was in the beginning, is now, and ever shall be, world without end, Amen.

JOEL CHANDLER HARRIS
American humorous author, died 1908.

I am about the extent of a tenth of a gnat's eyebrow better.

WILLIAM HARRISON
American President, died 1841.

I wish you to understand the true principles of government, I wish them carried out. I ask nothing more.

JOHANN HERDER
German poet and critic, died 1803.

Refresh me with a great thought.

THEODOR HERZL
Zionist leader, died 1904. To his son . . .

Your brethren are dispersed throughout the whole world. If you want to, you will find them. I have found them too, because I have been looking for them. Think of it and don't forget that your people need young, healthy strength and that you are heir to the name Herzl.

HERMANN HESSE
German novelist, died 1961. Last line of his final poem . . .

One more summer and another winter.

JACOB HILTZHEIMER
Philadelphia diarist. His last entry referred to the epidemic that killed him . . .

Deaths today – sixty-six.

ADOLF HITLER
Nazi dictator, suicide 1945. Hitler's final political testament, dictated in his bunker before he killed himself and his wife . . .

Above all I enjoin the governments of the nation and the people to uphold the racial laws and to resist mercilessly the poisoner of all nations, international Jewry. Berlin, 29 April 1945 0400 hours. My wife and I choose to die in order to escape the shame of overthrow or capitulation. It is our wish for our bodies to be cremated immediately on the place where I have performed the greater part of my daily work, during twelve years of service to my people.

HENRY FOX, 1ST BARON HOLLAND
Died 1774. Sociable to the last . . .

If Mr Selwyn calls again, show him up. If I am alive I shall be delighted to see him, and if I am dead he would like to see me.

BURTON HOLMES
Lantern lecturer. Thinking of the ultimate show – heaven . . .
How I could pack them in with that one!

WINIFRED HOLTBY
British novelist, died 1935.
Announcing her intention to get married . . .
Not an engagement – just an understanding.

THOMAS HOOD
Editor and humorist, died 1845.
Watching the application of a mustard plaster to his foot . . .
There's very little meat for the mustard.

HOWARD HUGHES
Recluse, millionaire, film and plane maker, died 1977.
Hughes' last public statements came in a special
telephone interview in 1972, held to disprove any claims that a
fraudulent 'biography' by Clifford Irving was his true story . . .
I am certainly not happy about my condition. I mean I'm not in
any seriously disparaging . . .or, that's not the word. What the
hell is the word I'm looking for? I am not in any seriously
derogatory . . .er, that's not the word either. I'm not in any
seriously deficient, now there's the word! I'm not in a deficient
condition . . . I'm not going to continue being quite as reclusive
as I have been, because it has apparently attracted so much
attention that I have just got to live a somewhat modified life
in order not to be an oddity . . . for one thing I would like to see
an accurate story of my life printed.

WILLIAM HUNTER
Professor of anatomy, died 1783.
If I had the strength to hold a pen, I would write how easy and
pleasant it is to die.

☠

JOHANN GEORGE JACOBI
Lyric poet, died 1919. After finishing on New Year's Eve
a poem about New Year's Day . . .
I shall not in fact see the New Year which I have just com-
memorated. I hope, at least, it is not apparent in the poem how
elderly I am.

JOHN JAY
American politician, died 1829.

I would have my funeral decent, but not ostentatious. No scarfs, no rings. Instead, thereof, I give two hundred dollars to any one poor deserving widow or orphan of this town whom my children shall select.

SIR WILLIAM JOHNSON
British agent to the Iroquois Indians, died 1774.
To his halfbreed son, Joseph, a Mohawk chief ...

Joseph, control your people. I am going away.

WILLIAM KEYSERLING
Jewish philanthropist.

We must save Jewish lives.

RONALD KNOX
British religious writer, died 1957. Asked if he would
like to hear someone read a portion of his version of the Bible? ...

Awfully jolly of you to suggest it though.

BERNARD DE LA VILLE COMTE DE LACEPEDE
Naturalist and writer, died 1825.
Called for an unfinished manuscript and told his son ...

Charles, write in large letters the word End at the foot of the page.

THOMAS DE LAGNY
French mathematician, died 1734.
Asked on his deathbed for the square of 12 ...

144.

JIMMY LEE LAINE
Blues pianist. Died still playing the piano ...

Let it roll! Let it roll!

HEDY LAMARR
Film star. Invited to compose her own epitaph
for a fanzine ...

This is too deep for me.

GERTRUDE LAWRENCE
British actress, died 1952.
Starring in 'The King and I' she remained generous to the end . . .
See that Yul (Brynner) gets star billing. He has earned it.

ANTON VAN LEEUWENHOEK
Pioneer microscopist, died 1723.
Hoogvliet, my friend, be so good as to have those two letters on
the table translated into Latin . . . Send them to the Royal Society
in London.

DR LUDWIG LEICHHARDT
Australian explorer, died 1848.
Leichhardt was lost – this was his last letter . . .
The only serious accident that has happened was the loss of a
spade, but we are fortunate to make it up on this station. Though
the days are still very hot, the beautiful nights are cool and be-
numb the mosquitoes which have ceased to trouble us. Myriads
of flies are the only annoyance we have. Seeing how much I
have been favoured in my present progress, I am full of hopes
that our Almighty Protector will allow me to bring my darling
scheme to a successful termination. Your most sincere friend,
Ludwig Leichhardt.

DAVID LIVINGSTONE
Explorer of Africa, died 1873. Last entry in his journal . . .
Knocked up quite, and remain = recover sent to buy milch
goats. We are on the banks of the River Molilamo.

MARTIN LUTHER
Founder of Protestantism, died 1546.
Asked whether he still held his revolutionary beliefs ? . . .
Yes!

STEPHEN MACKENNA
British novelist, died 1956. Letter from hospital . . .
Dear Peggy, I cannot resist, tho' I mean to see no one, never no
more. But you mustn't bring me anything whatever. I abhor
grapes, am worried by flowers, can't read magazines. I'm greatly
touched by your goodness, Peggy. Probably you could come any
hour, arranging things over the telephone with Sister, you know

the ropes. But Regular Visiting Fixtures: Sunday 2-3½. Tuesd. and Frid. 5-6. I wept when I got you. S.M.K. What a howling swell of an address you have acquired. God save us.

ANDRE MAGINOT
French military planner, died 1932. To President Laval . . .

For me, this is the end, but you – continue!

INCREASE MATHER
American divine, died 1723.

Be fruitful.

W. SOMERSET MAUGHAM
British novelist and short story writer, died 1965.

Dying is a very dull, dreary affair. And my advice to you is to have nothing whatever to do with it.

VLADIMIR MAYAKOWSKI
Russian poet, suicide 1930.
His last note warned against imitating him . . .

I don't recommend it for others.

H. L. MENCKEN
American editor, critic and social commentator, died 1956.
'The Sage of Baltimore', stricken by paralysis,
composed his own epitaph . . .

If, after I depart this vale, you remember me and have some thought to please my ghost, forgive some sinner and wink your eye at some homely girl.

ELIE METCHNIKOFF
Russian basteriologist, died 1916.

You remember your promise? You will do my post-mortem? And look at the intestines carefully, for I think there is something there now.

EDNA ST VINCENT MILLAY
American poet, died 1950.
Left a note for her maid as she went to bed . . .

Dear Lena, The iron is set too high. Don't put it on where it says 'Linen' or it will scorch the linen. Try it on 'Rayon' and then perhaps on 'Woollen'. And Lena, be careful not to burn your fingers when you shift it from one heat to another. It is 5.30 and I have been working all night. I am going to bed. Good morning.

WILSON MIZNER
Hollywood wit, died 1933. To his doctor . . .
Well, doc, I guess this is the main event.
Rejecting an attending priest . . .
Why should I talk to you? I've just been talking to your boss.

DUC DE MONTMORENCY
Constable of France, killed 1567.
Facing death on the scaffold . . .
Do you think a man who has known how to live honourably for eighty years does not know how to die for a quarter of an hour.

WILLIAM DE MORGAN
Potter and novelist, died 1917. De Morgan was at work on this manuscript at his death . . .
Pinning her faith on this, she passed into the passage, where he ought to have been, the import of her demeanour being that her shrewder insight would at once discern the whereabouts of . . .

WOLFGANG AMADEUS MOZART
Composer, died 1791. Playing his 'Requiem' . . .
Did I not tell you I was writing this for myself.

MARGARET NOBLE
'Nivedita', campaigner for Indian independence, died 1911.
The ship is sinking, but I shall see the sun rise.

GEORGE ORWELL
Journalist and writer, died 1949.
Final entry in his working notebook . . .
At fifty, everyone has the face that he deserves.

THOMAS PAINE
Radical political theorist and pamphleteer, died 1809.
His doctor observed 'Your belly diminishes' ...
And yours augments.

COURTLANDT PALMER
Founder of the Nineteenth Century Club.
I want you to say that you have seen a free-thinker die without
fear of the future, and without changing his opinion.

DOROTHY PARKER
Writer and wit, died 1967.
To Beatrice Ames, a few days before her lonely death ...
I want you to tell me the truth. |Did Ernest (Hemingway)
really like me?

THOMAS LOVE PEACOCK
*Novelist and poet, killed 1866. Peacock was burnt to death,
refusing to give up his efforts to save his library from the flames* ...
By the immortal God, I will *not* move!

GEORGE WASHINGTON PLUNKITT
Tammany Hall boss.
Now, in conclusion, I want to say I don't own a dishonest dollar.
If my worst enemy was given the job of writing my epitaph
when I'm gone, he could do no more than write 'George W.
Plunkitt: He Seen His Opportunities and He Took 'Em'.

☻

FRANCOIS RABELAIS
French satirist and doctor, died 1553.
Ring down the curtain, the farce is over.
His will concluded ...
I have nothing. I owe much. The rest I leave to the poor.

WILLIAM CHAPMAN RALSTON
Comstock Lode speculator, died 1875.
Keep these for me. There are valuable papers in my pocket.

GRANTLAND RICE
American sports columnist, died 1954.
The end of his last column, on baseball star Willie Mays . . .
Willie, at least, has a golden start.

HENRY CRABBE ROBINSON
Foreign correspondent and diarist, died 1867. His last diary
entry approved of fellow writer Matthew Arnold . . .
He thinks of Germany as he ought, and of Goethe with high admiration. On this point I can possibly give him assistance, which he will gladly – but I feel incapable to go on.

AUGUSTE RODIN
French sculptor, died 1917.
And people say that Puvis de Chavannes is not a fine artist.

HAROLD ROSS
Founder and editor of the New Yorker, *died 1951. His last phone*
conversation from his hospital bed to George S. Kaufman . . .
I'm up here to end this thing and it may end me too. But it's better than going on this way. God bless you, I'm half under the anaesthetic now.

MEYER AMSCHEL ROTHSCHILD
Banker, died 1874. Rothschild called his five sons
together and gave them instructions to be faithful to the
law of Moses, to remain united until the end and
to consult their mother on all actions . . .
Observe these three points, and you will soon be among the richest, and the world will belong to you.

DAMON RUNYON
American humorist, died 1946.
You can keep the things of bronze and stone and give me one man to remember me just once a year.

CHARLES, ABBÉ SAINT-PIERRE
Writer on social questions, died 1814.
Told his priest that he had only gone through the
Last Rites for the sake of his family . . .
I am only to be reproached for this action. I do not believe a word
of all this. It was a vile concession for the family, but I wanted
to be the confessor of truth all my life.

SAMSON
Killed c. 1155 BC.
Let me die with the Philistines.

FRA PAOLO SARPI
Venetian scholar, died 1623. His last thoughts were of Venice . . .
Be thou everlasting.

E. W. SCRIPPS
Journalist, died 1926.
Too many cigars this evening, I guess.

HENRY SEGRAVE
British sportsman, killed 1930.
Segrave was attempting to break the world speedboat
record when his boat crashed . . .
Did we do it?

WILLIAM SHAKESPEARE
Dramatist, died 1616.
Shakespeare left no recorded last words, but the inscription on
his gravestone has provided his final message to the world . . .
Good friend, for Jesus sake forbear
To dig the dust enclosed here.
Blest be the man yt pares these stones,
And curst be he yt moves my bones.

GEORGE BERNARD SHAW
Dramatist, journalist and Fabian, died 1950. To his nurse . . .
Sister, you're trying to keep me alive as an old curiosity. But
I'm done, I'm finished. I'm going to die.

SISERA
Biblical soldier, killed.
To Jael, who killed him in his sleep with a hammer and nail . . .
Stand in the door of the tent, and it shall be, when any man
doth come and enquire of thee and say, 'Is there any man here?'
that thou shalt say 'No'.

SIDNEY SMITH
Editor and wit, died 1845.
His wife told him that he had mistakenly drunken some ink . . .
Bring me all the blotting paper there is in the house!

C. P. STANTON
Killed 1847.
Stanton was resting by his camp fire after making three
arduous rescue trips through the Donner Pass
for avalanche victims . . .
Yes, I'm coming soon.

ELIZABETH CADY STANTON
American feminist, died 1902.
Still campaigning for women's rights, she sent this plea to
President Theodore Roosevelt . . .
Abraham Lincoln immortalized himself by the emancipation of
four million Southern slaves. Speaking for my suffrage coadju-
tors, we now desire that you, Mr President, who are already
celebrated for so many honourable deeds and worthy utterances,
immortalize yourself by bringing about the complete emancipation of thirty-six million women.

ALEXANDER H. STEPHENS
American statesman, died 1883.
But I carried it individually by six hundred majority.

LEWIS STONE
Film star, died 1953.
Invited to compose his own epitaph for a fanzine . . .
A gentleman farmer goes back to the soil.

LUCY STONE
Suffragist, died 1893.
Make the world better!

LYTTON STRACHEY
Biographer and critic, died 1932.
If this is dying, I don't think much of it.

CHARLES SUMNER
American politician, died 1874.
Do not let the Civil Rights bill fail!

☠

ARCHIBALD CAMPBELL TAIT
Archbishop of Canterbury, died 1882.
His last note was to Queen Victoria . . .
A last memorial of twenty-six years of devoted service, with earnest love and affectionate blessing on the Queen and her family. A. C. Cantuar.

BAYARD TAYLOR
American traveller and author, died 1878.
I want . . . oh, you know what I mean . . . the stuff of life!

THEOPHRASTUS
Greek philosopher, died 287 BC. Leaving his pupils . . .
Farewell, and may you be happy. Either drop my doctrine, which involves a world of labour, or stand forth its worthy champion, for you will win great glory. Life holds more disappointment than advantage. But as I can no longer discuss what we ought to do, do you go on with the inquiry into right conduct.

DYLAN THOMAS
Poet, died 1953.
I've had eighteen straight whiskies, I think that's the record . . . After 39 years, this is all I've done.

JAMES THURBER
Cartoonist and humorist, died 1961.
God bless . . . God damn . . .

HERBEOT BEERBOHM TREE
British actor, died 1917.
Thinking of his forthcoming role . . .
I shall not need to study the part at all. I know it already.

HARRY S. TRUMAN
American President, died 1972. A view of his life ...
There is an epitaph in Boot Hill cemetery in Arizona which reads 'Here lies Jack Williams – he done his damnedest. What more can a person do?' Well, that's all I could do. I did my damnedest and that's all there is to it.

VOLTAIRE
(Francois Marie Arouet) Writer, satirist and philosopher, died 1778.
To the priest who was hoping for a deathbed conversion ...
In the name of God, let me die in peace!
Looking at the lamp which flared up at his side ...
The flames already?

KARL WALLENDA
Highwire virtuoso, killed 1978.
Wallenda, like so many of his wire-walking family, was killed on the job, promoting a circus in Puerto Rico ...

The only place I feel alive is the high wires.

WALTER WHITE
Black leader, died 1954.
Asked by his daughter whether he liked her dress, White mocked the current McCarthyite witch hunts ...
I plead the Fifth Amendment.

OSCAR WILDE
Dramatist and wit, died 1900.
Noting the turn of the century ...
It would really be more than the English could stand if another century began and I were still alive. I am dying as I have lived – beyond my means.
Alternatively ...
Either this wallpaper goes, or I do.

WENDELL WILKIE
American diplomat.
Still talking politics in a last note . . .
I enjoyed our talk this morning very much. Frankly I cannot answer your ultimate question [as to whom he would support] because I have not yet fully decided.

MARY WOLLSTONECRAFT
Pioneer feminist, died 1797.
I know what you are thinking of, but I have nothing to communicate on the subject of religion.

ALEXANDER WOOLCOTT
Journalist, broadcaster, wit, died 1941.
To a hospital visitor when he was ill just before his death . . .
I have no need of your God damned sympathy. I only wish to be entertained by some of your grosser reminiscences.
To helpers who tried to save him when
he collapsed during his radio show . . .
Get back in there. Never mind me. Go back in there!

SOMEBODY HELP ME

HENRY ADAMS
American author, died 1918. To his secretary ...
Dear child, keep me alive.

DUCHESS OF ANGOULEME
Died 1619.
My God, I am going to beg pardon for my sins. Help thy humble servant in this moment which is to be decisive for me for all eternity.

QUINTUS AURELIUS
Roman patrician, suicide.
The Emperor suspected Aurelius of treason ...
Woe is me, My Alban farm has informed against me.

DON CARLOS OF AUSTRIA
Pretender to the Spanish throne, died 1909.
God be propitious to me, a sinner.

MAX BAER
Heavyweight boxer, died 1959.
Oh God, here I go!

LOUIS BARTHOU
French politician, killed 1934.
The French Foreign Minister was unfortunately accompanying
King Alexander I of Yugoslavia when fascist assassins killed
them both ...
I can't see what's happening now. My eyeglasses, where are my eyeglasses?

SAM BASS
Outlaw, killed 1878.
Bass refused to talk to the lawman who shot him down . . .
Let me go, the world is bobbing around.

AUBREY BEARDSLEY
Artist and illustrator, died 1898.
Fortunately, this deathbed demand went unheeded.
I am imploring you – burn all the indecent poems and drawings.

HENRY BEAUFORT
Divine, died 1447. After so saintly a life,
did Beaufort see the devil on his deathbed? . . .
I pray you all pray for me . . . Away! Away! Why thus do you look at me?

GENERAL LUDWIG BECK
German officer, executed 1944. After the Stauffenberg
plot against Hitler failed, ageing General Beck tried to shoot
himself. Two attempts failed – a soldier had to finish him off . . .
If it doesn't work this time, then please help me.

WILLIAM BECKFORD
Patron of the Arts and writer, died 1844.
Writing to his daughter . . .
Come quick, quick!

JUDAH BENJAMIN
American lawyer, died 1884.
What I require is warmth. Will it never come?

JOSEPH BODWELL
Governor of Maine. Asking to be helped back into a chair . . .
Get me there quickly!

JUNIUS BRUTUS BOOTH
American actor-manager, died 1852.
Pray, pray, pray.

LUCREZIA BORGIA
Italian intriguer, died 1519.
To Pope Alexander VI, her father . . .
Most Holy Father and Honoured Master. With all respect I kiss

your Holiness' feet and commend myself in all humility to your holy mercy. Having suffered for more than two months, early in the morning of the 14th present, as it pleased God, I gave birth to a daughter and hoped then to find relief from my sufferings. But I did not and shall be compelled to pay my debt to nature. So great is the favour that our merciful Creator has shown me, that I approach the end of my life with pleasure, knowing that in a few hours, after receiving for the last time all the sacraments of the church, I shall be released.

DAVID G. BRODERICK
US Senator, died 1859.

I die. Protect my honour.

GUILLAUME DODE DE LA BRUNERIE
French general, died 1851.

The doctors still assert that the enemy is retreating. I believe, on the contrary, that we are, as it were on the eve of a battle. God knows what tomorrow will bring.

GEORGE VILLIERS, 2ND DUKE OF BUCKINGHAM
Favourite of Charles II, died 1687.

My distemper is powerful. Come and pray for the departing soul of poor, unhappy Buckingham.

SIR GEORGE BURNS
Shipowner, died 1890.

Lord Jesus, come, come . . . I am waiting, I am ready. Home, home. Give me patience to wait thy time, but Thou knowest what I suffer.

ROBERT BURNS
Scottish poet, died 1796.

Don't let the awkward squad fire over me.

SIR RICHARD BURTON
Explorer and writer, died 1890. His wife refused to give him any medicines without the presence of a doctor, by which time it was too late . . .

Quick Puss! Chloroform, ether . . . or I am a dead man!

☠

BARON ARTHUR CAPEL
Supporter of King Charles I, beheaded 1649.
God Almighty staunch this blood. God Almighty staunch this issue of blood. This will not do the business. God Almighty, find another way to do it.

ENRICO CARUSO
Opera singer, died 1921.
Doro, I can't get my breath!

PHOEBE CARY
American poet, died 1871.
Oh God have mercy on my soul.

RUFUS CHOATE
American Congressman, died 1859.
I don't feel well. I feel faint.

MARY CLEMMER
Writer, died 1884. Taking a glass of water ...
Thanks.

CHARLES COFFIN
American war correspondent, died 1916.
If it were not for this pain I should get up and write.

LADY JANET COLQUHOUN
Author of religious tracts, died 1846.
Looking for her grandson ...
Where is he? I cannot see him!

PRINCE HENRI DE CONDE
French aristocrat, died 1588.
Hand me my chair, I feel extremely weak.

URIEL DA COSTA
Writer and convert, died 1860.
There you have the true story of my life. I have shown you what role I played in this vain world-theatre and in my unimportant and restless life. Now fellow men, make your just and dispassionate judgement, speaking freely according to the truth as becomes men who are really men. If you find something which

arouses your sympathy, then realize and mourn the sad lot of Man which you share. And let there be no confusion about this: the name that I bore as a Christian in Portugal was Gabriel da Costa. Among the Jews – would that I had never got involved with them – I was known, by a small change, as Uriel.

REV. BENJAMIN CUTLER
Lift me up, life me right up.

💀

JEFFERSON DAVIS
President of the Confederacy, died 1889.
Refusing a dose of medicine . . .
Please excuse me, I cannot take it.

SIR JAMES RADCLIFFE, EARL OF DERWENTWATER
Jacobite rebel, beheaded 1716. To his executioner . . .
I am but a poor man. There's ten guineas for you. If I had more I would give it to you. I desire you to do your office so as to put me to the least misery you can.

CHARLES DICKENS
Novelist, died 1870.
To his friends who were trying to lay him on a sofa . . .
On the ground!

HENRY H. DIXON
American sportswriter, died 1870.
Oh God, I thank thee, I could not bear much more.

HENRY DORNEY
Died 1863.
I am almost dead. Lift me up a little higher.

BISHOP DUPANLOUP
Clergyman, died 1878.
When people offered to pray for him . . .
Yes, yes . . .

MADAME DUPIN
Mother of Georges Sand, died 1865.
Comb my hair.

💀

JOHN ELIOT
Missionary to the Indians, died 1690. To a friend . . .
You are welcome to my very soul. Please retire into my study
for me and give me leave to be gone.

HENRY FAWCETT
British statesman, died 1884.
The best things to warm my hands with would be my fur gloves.
They are in the pocket of my coat in the dressing-room.

'BIG JIM' FISK
*Speculator, assassinated 1872. Fisk was killed by his
ex-partner Med Stokes, no one came to his rescue . . .*
For God's sake, will nobody help me!

ANDREW FLETCHER OF SALTOUN
Scottish patriot, died 1716.
Asked by Lord Sunderland for any last wishes . . .
I have a nephew who has been studying the law. Make him a
judge when he is fit for it.

DANIEL C. FRENCH
American sculptor, died 1931. To his nurse . . .
You're very good to me.

HENRY FUSELI
British artist, died 1825.
Is Lawrence come, is Lawrence come?

DAVID GARRICK
British actor, died 1779.

Oh dear . . .

PAUL GAUGUIN
French artist, died 1903.
*Alone on his tropical paradise, Gauguin sent off a note
to a nearby missionary, but he was
dead before help could arrive . . .*
Dear M. Vernier, Would it be troubling you too much to ask you

to come and see me. My eyesight seems to be going and I cannot walk. I am very ill.

BARON LOUIS DE GEER
Swedish statesman, died 1896.
My God, have pity on me. Do not visit on me suffering beyond my strength . . .Oh Christ! Thou hast suffered still more for me.

JOHANN WOLFGANG VON GOETHE
German dramatist, died 1832.
More light!

JOSEPH GOLDBERGER
Medical researcher, died 1929. To his wife . . .
Mary, don't leave me. You have always been my rock, my strength. Mary, we must have patience.

ULYSSES S. GRANT
American President, died 1885.
Water!

AUGUSTUS GRANVILLE
Italian patriot.
Light, all light.

💀

FITZ-GREENE HALLECK
Poet, died 1867. To his wife . . .
Maria, hand me my pantaloons if you please.

THOMAS HALYBURTON
Divine, died 1712.
Pray! Pray!

CYRUS HAMLIN
American missionary, died 1900. Hamlin wanted to sit one last time in the chair he had sat in as a boy . . .
Put me there.

WARREN G. HARDING
American President, died 1923.
That's good. Go on. Read some more.

BENJAMIN HARRISON
American President, died 1901. To his wife . . .
Are the doctors here?

FERDINAND RUDOLPH HASSLER
Engineer, died 1843.
My children! My papers!

LAFCADIO HEARN
American writer, died 1904.
Ah, because of the sickness.

W. E. HENLEY
British poet, died 1903. A letter to Charles Whibley . . .
Dear Boy, I'd give much to see you just now. When can you
come? I can't get to town, being kind of broken-hearted or I'd
tryst you there. But I want your advice and, if I can get it, your
help. And I want the first of these things soon. The sooner the
better. W.E.H.

HENRY THE LION
Duke of Saxony and Bavaria, died 1195.
God be merciful to me a sinner.

WILHELM HEY
German poet, died 1854.
A last poem for the two men who had assisted him . . .
So you my nurses dear
In these last difficult days,
In bitter parting here
Show me your loving ways.
The love so tenderly given
And yet such strength behind,
A brief foretaste of heaven,
Is what it brings to mind.

BENJAMIN HILL
US Senator, died 1882.
Almost home.

HARRY HOUDINI
(Erich Weiss) Escapologist, died 1926.
I am tired of fighting. I guess this thing is going to get me.

ROBERT HOUSMAN
Divine. Receiving a gift of violets . . .

I shall never again see the spot where those flowers grew. Give him my best thanks for the present.

BARON FRIEDRICH VON HUGEL
Catholic theologian, died 1925. To his nurse . . .

Pray for me.

THOMAS HUTCHINSON
Royal governor of Massachusetts, died 1780.

Help me!

BRIAN JONES
Rock musician, killed 1969. A final telegram
before he died in his swimming pool . . .

Don't judge me too harshly.

'JOSELITO'
(Jose Gomez) Bull fighter, killed 1920.

Mother, I'm smothering!

ADONIRAM JUDSON
Missionary, died 1850. Judson was worried about
the hot Burmese climate affecting his body . . .

Brother Ranney will you bury me? Bury me? Quick, quick!

JOSEPH KARGE
Linguist. Karge had been reading about death on his travels . . .

I have but one desire concerning it – that it come suddenly and without warning.

JOHN KITTO
British theologian, died 1854.

Pray God to take me soon.

THEOPHILE LAENNEC
Inventor of the Stethoscope, died 1826.
The doctor took off his rings before lying down to die ...
It would be necessary soon that another do me this service. I do
not want anyone to have the bother of it.

SIDNEY LANIER
American poet, died 1881.
Refusing a soothing drink ...
I can't.

D. H. LAWRENCE
British author, died 1930.
I think it is time for morphine.

GIACOMO LEOPARDI
Italian poet and scholar, died 1837.
I can't see you any more.

AMY LOWELL
American poet, died 1925.
Pete – a stroke! Get Eastman!

☠

WILLIAM H. McGUFFEY
Author of primary readers, died 1873.
Oh that I might once more speak to my dear boys. But Thy will
be done.

HORACE MANN
British diplomat, died 1786. To his wife ...
Sing to me, if you have the heart.

HENRY, CARDINAL MANNING
Died 1892. To Sir Andrew Clark ...
Is there any use in your coming tomorrow? Then mind you,
Sir Andrew, come at nine tomorrow.

JEAN PAUL MARAT
French Revolutionary leader, assassinated 1793.
As Charlotte Corday struck her blows, Marat called to his lover ...
Help, my dear, help!

JOHN CHURCHILL, 1ST DUKE OF MARLBOROUGH
Soldier and statesman, died 1722.
When it was suggested he should go to bed . . .
Yes.

LORENZO DE MEDICI
Ruler of Florence, died 1492.
Asked whether he still liked his food? . . .
As a dying man always does.

'OWEN MEREDITH'
(Lord Lytton) British poet, died 1891.
I feel thirsty and I should be glad to drink something.

JOAQUIN MILLER
American poet, died 1913.
Take me away, take me away.

JOHN A. MOREHEAD
Lutheran leader, died 1866.
On the day of his wife's burial . . .
Will you do me a favour? Will you kindly ask my physician how
long before I shall join my Nellie?

JOHN PIERPOINT MORGAN
American millionaire, died 1913.
Don't baby me so!

☠

DANIEL O'CONNELL
Irish leader, died 1847.
My dear friend, I am dying. Jesus, Jesus, Jesus . . .

'OUIDA'
(Louise de la Ramee) British novelist, died 1908.
I have been very ill these days and my maid is of the opinion that
I shall never get well. The weather is intensely cold and at St
Remo it is so warm and brilliant. It is odd that there should be
so great a difference. Excuse this rough word – I am ill and
cannot write.

☠

JAN PADEREWSKI
Musician and statesman, died 1941.
Aked if he would like some champagne? . . .

Please.

THOMAS NELSON PAGE
Novelist and diplomat, died 1877.

Here Alfred, take this spade.

LOUIS PASTEUR
Scientist, died 1895. Offered a glass of milk . . .

I cannot.

JOHN PAYNE
British poet and translator, died 1800.

Have you got the sheets? Did you get the pillow-cases?

BOIES PENROSE
American politician, died 1921. To his black valet . . .

See here, William, see here. I don't want any of your damned lies. How do I look? Am I getting any better? The truth now . . . All right, William. When you go to church tomorrow, pray for me too.

PEPONILA
Wife of the Gallic rebel Sabinus. Pleading with
Emperor Vespasian to spare her family . . .

These little ones, Caesar, I bore and reared in the monument (where Sabinus had hidden) that we might be a greater number to supplicate you.

CLARETTA PETACCI
Mistress to Mussolini, killed 1945.

Mussolini must not die!

MARSHAL PETAIN
French soldier, died 1951

Do not weep, do not grieve.

MADAME DE POMPADOUR
Patron of the arts, died 1764.
As the priest was leaving her room . . .
One moment, M. le Curé, and we will depart together.

JOSEPH PULITZER
American newspaper owner, died 1911.
To the friend who was reading to him . . .
Softly, quite softly.

☻

ANNE RADCLIFFE
British novelist, died 1823. Taking a little food . . .
There is some substance in that.

RICHARD III
'Richard III' by William Shakespeare.
A horse, a horse, my kingdom for a horse!

W. GRAHAM ROBERTSON
British author, died 1948. Final instructions . . .
I should like the ashes to be buried or otherwise disposed of at
the crematorium, with no tombstone nor inscription to mark the
place of burial. No funeral, no mourning, no flowers. By request.
If these arrangements are carried out one may perhaps manage
to die without making a public nuisance of oneself. W. Graham
Robertson.

COMMODORE JOHN RODGERS
American naval officer, died 1882.
Butler, do you know the Lord's Prayer? Then repeat it for me.

FRANKLIN DELANO ROOSEVELT
American President, died 1945.
I have a terrific headache.

THEODORE ROOSEVELT
American President, died 1919.
Please put out the light.

NICHOLAS RUBINSTEIN
Brother of the pianist, Anton, died 1881.

Oysters! Nothing will do me as much good as a dozen cold oysters and an ice afterwards.

☻

JOSE DE SAN MARTIN
South American soldier and statesman, died 1850.
To his brother . . .

Mariano – back to my room!

FRIEDRICH SCHLEIERMACHER
German theologian, died 1834.

Now I can hold out here no longer. Lay me in a different posture.

OLIVE SCHREINER
South African author, died 1920. A final letter . . .

I long to see the stars and the veldt. One day I will go up to Matjesfontein just for one day, if I can find anyone to take me. It doesn't seem to me that this is Africa. A Happy New Year, my dear one.

GENERAL WINFIELD SCOTT
American soldier, died 1866.

Peter, take good care of my horse.

ANTHONY ASHLEY COOPER, 7TH EARL OF SHAFTESBURY
Philanthropist, died 1885.
Handed something by his valet . . .

Thank you.

JOHN SHERMAN
American politician, died 1900.

I think you had better send for the doctor. I feel so faint.

SIR STANLEY SPENCER
British artist, died 1959.
To the nurse who had just given him an injection . . .

Beautifully done.

Count Friedrich Stolberg

German poet, died 1821. To his doctor . . .

Tell me, will it truly be all over tomorrow or the next day. Praise God! Thanks, thanks! I thank you with all my heart! Jesus be praised!

Talleyrand

French statesman, died 1838.

Do not keep me in suspense.

Jeremy Taylor

Bishop of Dromore, died 1667.

Bury me at Dromore.

Samuel Tilden

American politician, died 1886.

Water!

Henry Timrod

American divine, died 1867.

Failing to swallow a drink on his deathbed . . .

Never mind. I shall soon drink of the river of eternal life.

Gitanillo de Triano

Matador, killed 1931. Killed in the ring . . .

Tell them to moisten my mouth. Moisten my mouth a little.

Paul Verlaine

French poet, died 1896.

Don't sole the dead man's shoes yet.

Alfred de Vigny

French poet, died 1863.

Pray for me. Pray to God for me.

JAMES J. WALKER
American politician, died 1946.
A staunch democrat, he resisted his nurse's advice
to lie back until she admitted to sharing his party beliefs . . .
In that case I shall abide by the wishes of a fair constituent.

ROBERT WALKER
Died 1951. Following this request Walker received a shot
of sodium amytal which induced a coma and in due course, death.
I feel terrible, doc. Do something quick!

BOOKER T. WASHINGTON
Campaigner for Black rights, died 1915.
Take me home. I was born in the South, I have lived and
laboured in the South, and I wish to die and be buried in the
South.

GEORGE WASHINGTON
American President, died 1799.
Let me go quietly. I cannot last long.

WILLIAM C. WHITNEY
American politician, died 1904.
Don't get angry nurse. I love my son and daughter. It does me
good to chat with them.

CHARLES WOLFE
Irish poet and clergyman, died 1823.
Close this eye. The other is closed already. Now farewell.

REV. JOHN WOOD
Naturalist, died 1889.
Give me a large cup of tea.

ELINOR WYLIE
American poet, died 1928. Offered a glass of water . . .
Is that all it is?

☠

WILLIAM L. 'CAP'N BOB' YANCEY
American lawyer, died 1863.

I will just lie here for a few minutes. I will stay here a little while just to please you. Don't leave me, little lady. I love to watch your bright young face. Two things in this world I have always loved – a bright, young face and walking in the sunshine.

ABD ALLAH BEN ZOHAR
Killed in battle.

No one need ask where Abd Allah is. Whoever wants him will meet him in the first ranks. Oh my Lord, the troops of Syria are assailing me in great numbers and have already torn aside part of the veils that cover thy sanctuary. Oh Lord, I am weak and oppressed on all sides. Send thy phalanxes to my aid.

FEAR AND LOATHING

PIERRE ABELARD
Founder of Scholastic Theology, died 1142.
I don't know! I don't know!

COUNTESS JEANNE DU BARRY
Mistress of LouisXV, guillotined 1793.
You are going to hurt me! Oh, please, do not hurt me!

FREDERIC BASTIAT
French economist, died 1850.
I am not able to explain myself.

WILLIAM BATTIE
Died 1776.
Young man, you have heard, no doubt, how great are the terrors of death; this night will probably offer you some experience. But you may learn, and may you profit by the example, that a conscientious endeavour to perform his duties will ever close a Christian's eyes with comfort and tranquility.

LUDWIG VAN BEETHOVEN
Composer, died 1827.
Refusing a glass of wine for which he had asked . . .
Too bad, too bad! It's too late!

ARNOLD BENNETT
British novelist, died 1931.
Everything has gone *wrong*, my girl!

PIERRE BERANGER
French poet, died 1857.

Today, on the day of his Epiphany, my Lord Jesus Christ will appear to me: either for glory, as I in my repentance should like, or for condemnation, as others would hope and as I fear.

GEORGES BIZET
Composer, died 1875.

I am in a cold sweat. It is the sweat of death. How are you going to tell my father?

MARY BLANDY
Murderer, hanged 1752. Mary had poisoned her father ...

Gentlemen, don't hang me high for the sake of decency – I am afraid I shall fall.

ANNE BOLEYN
Second wife of Henry VIII, beheaded 1536.

The executioner is, I believe, an expert ... and my neck is very slender. Oh God, have pity on my soul!

CESARE BORGIA
Soldier and tyrant, killed in battle 1507.

I die unprepared.

JACQUES BOSSUET
French preacher, died 1704.

I suffer the violence of pain and death, but I know whom I have believed.

PRINCE LOUIS DE BOURBON
Killed 1560. The Prince's request was ignored by his captor ...

Mercy, mercy, mercy My Lord of Chemberg. I am your prisoner.

GEORGE BRIGGS
Governor of Massachusetts, died 1861. To his son ...

You won't leave me again, will you?

CHARLOTTE BRONTË
British novelist, died 1855.
She had only been married one year ...

Oh, I am not going to die, am I? He will not separate us, we have been so happy.

237

Rev. Abel Brown
Abolitionist, killed by the mob.
Must I be sacrificed? Let me alone, every one of you!

Georg Buchner
German dramatist, died 1837.
We do not suffer too much. We suffer too little. For it is through suffering that we attain God. We are death, dust and ashes. How should we dare to complain.

Saul Budgett
American merchant, died 1851.
Oh dear . . .

Hans von Bulow
Musician, died 1894. Asked how he felt . . .
Bad.

☠

Georges Cadoudal
A plotter against Napoleon, executed 1804.
Rejecting advice to repeat the 'Hail Mary' so as to protect
himself 'now and at the hour of our death' . . .
For what? Isn't this the hour of my death?

John Calvin
Protestant reformer, died 1564.
Thou bruisest me, O Lord, but it is enough for me to feel that it is Thy hand.

George Campbell
Outlaw, killed 1881. To Marshall Dallas Stoudenmire,
who shot him in the Battle of Keating's Saloon in El Paso . . .
You big sonofabitch, you murdered me!

Roger Casement
Irish patriot, shot as a spy 1916.
From his last letter to his sister . . .
It is a cruel thing to die with all men misunderstanding.

FREDERIC CHOPIN
Composer, died 1849. His last written request . . .
The earth is suffocating. Swear to make them cut me open, so I won't be buried alive.

AUGUSTIN COUCHY
Mathematician, died 1857.
No, I do not suffer much . . . Jesus, Mary and Joseph!

☠

ROBERT DAMIENS
'Robert the Devil', assassin of Louis XV
tortured to death 1757. Damiens was chained to a red hot steel 'bed' and his entrails were slowly torn out . . .
Oh death, why art thou so long in coming. May God have pity on me and Jesus deliver me!

HART P. DANKS
Unfinished note . . .
It's hard to die alone and . . .

ENGELBERT DOLLFUSS
Chancellor of Austria, assassinated 1934.
Children, you are so good to me. Why aren't the others? I have only desired peace. We have never attacked anybody. We have always fought to defend ourselves. May God forgive them.

GASTON DOUMERGUE
President of the French Republic, assassinated, 1937.
Doumergue refused to see a doctor, fearing that . . .
He put me in the discard.

☠

'GEORGE ELIOT'
(Mary Ann Evans). British novelist, died 1880.
Tell them I have a great pain in the left side.

EBENEZER ELLIOTT
'The Corn Law Rhymer', died 1849.
A strange sight, sir – an old man unwilling to die.

HENRY VENN ELLIOTT
Divine, died 1865.

Suffer me not from any pains of death to fall from Thee.

☠

ELIZA FENNING
Murderer, hanged 1815.
Fenning died on the gallows, though popular
opinion had found her innocent . . .

I am innocent!

MARSHALL FIELD II
Merchant, died accidentally 1906.

I do not know how this happened. I can account for it in no way. It was an accident. What are the chances of my recovery, Doctor?

BENJAMIN FRANKLIN
American diplomat, died 1790.

A dying man can do nothing easy.

MELVIN FULLER
American jurist, died 1910.

I am very ill.

☠

CAPTAIN ALLEN GARDINER
Missionary, died 1851.
Starving to death, wrote his last letter . . .

My dear Mr Williams, The Lord has seen fit to call home another of our little company. Our dear departed brother left the boat on Tuesday at noon, and has not since returned. Doubtless he is in the presence of his Redeemer, whom he served so faithfully. Yet a little while, and through grace we may join that blessed throng to sing the praises of Christ throughout eternity. I neither hunger nor thirst, though five days without food. Marvellous loving kindness to me a sinner! Your affectionate brother in Christ . . .

PIERS GAVESTON
*Favourite of Edward II, killed 1312. Gaveston was
killed by a group of nobles who resented his influence . . .*
Oh noble Earl, spare me!

VINCENT VAN GOGH
Artist, suicide 1890.
Now I want to go home. Don't weep. What I have done was
best for all of us. No use. I shall never get rid of this depression.

☠

RICHARD HALLIBURTON
Lost at sea, 1939. Last message . . .
Southerly gales, squalls, lee rail under water, wet bunks, hard
tack, bully beef. Wish you were here, instead of me.

HENRY HAMMOND
Divine, died 1660.
Lord make haste!

ROBERT HARE
Wesleyan minister, died 1611.
There is a long dreary lane in every life, called 'Suffering',
which I now seem to have entered.

WARREN HASTINGS
Governor-General of India, died 1818.
Surely at my age it is time to go. God only can do me good.
My dear, why wish me to live to suffer thus ? None of you know
what I suffer.

BENJAMIN HAYDON
British artist, suicide 1846.
God forgive me. Amen.

PHILIP HENRY
Dissenter, died 1696.
Oh death where is thy . . .

SAINT HILARY
Bishop of Poitiers, died 468.
Soul, thou has served Christ these seventy years and art thou
afraid to die ? Go out soul, go out!

REVEREND ROWLAND HILL
Clergyman, died 1833.

Christ also hath suffered for sins, the just for the unjust, that he might bring us unto God.

SIDNEY HILLMAN
Labour leader, died 1946.

I feel like hell. I'm going to lie down again.

HOKUSAI
Japanese painter, died 1849.

If heaven had only granted me five years more, I could have become a real painter.

THOMAS HOLCROFT
Novelist and playwright, died 1809.
Talking about his pain . . .

How tedious. My affections are strong.

VICOMTESSE D'HOUDETOT

I am sorry for myself.

☠

HENRIK IBSEN
Playwright, died 1906.
Rejecting those who said he might get better . . .

On the contrary!

WASHINGTON IRVING
American essayist, died 1859.

Well, I must arrange my pillows for another night. When will this end?

☠

FRIEDRICH JACOBS
German classical philologist, died 1819.
Recited Latin verses . . .

Who would wish, indeed, to prolong pain, the breath failing all too gradually? Better to die in death, than to drag out a dead life, the senses buried in the limbs.

WILLIAM JAY
Dissenting minister, died 1853.
Oh, none of you know what it is to die.

RICHARD JEFFERIES
Writer on nature, died 1887.
Yes, yes, that is so. Help, Lord, for Jesus' sake. Darling, good-bye. God bless you and the children, and save you all from such great pain.

LORD FRANCIS JEFFREY
Jurist and critic, died 1850.
Writing about a dream he had had about political journals . . .
I read the ideal copies with a good deal of pain and difficulty, owing to the smallness of the type, but with great interest and, I believe, often for more than an hour at a time, forming a judgement of their merits with great freedom and acuteness, and often saying to myself 'This is very cleverly thought out, but there is a fallacy in it, for so and so . . .'

STONE JOHNSON
American professional footballer, killed in a game.
Oh my God, oh my God! Where's my head? Where's my head?

☠

JOSEPH LAKANAL
Educator, died 1845. To his doctor . . .
Your attentions will not save me. I feel that there is no more oil in the lamp.

CHARLES LAMB
British poet, died 1834.
My bedfellows are cramp and cough – we three all in one bed.

JULIE DE LESPINASSE
French beauty and courtesan, died 1776.
Am I still alive?

MRS LINN LINTON
Novelist, died 1898.
I am very forlorn at the present moment and wish I was at Malvern. Oh, don't I just!

HENRY LONGFELLOW
American poet, died 1881. To his sister . . .

Now I know that I must be very ill, since you have been sent for.

JEAN-BAPTISTE LULLY
Composer and director of the Paris Opera, died 1687.

Sinner, thou must die.

☻

MADAME DE MAINTENON
Second wife of Louis XIV, died 1719.
Asked to bless his daughters of whom she had been governess . . .

I am not worthy.

MANOLETE
Bull fighter, killed in the bullring, 1947.

I can't feel anything in my right leg. I can't feel anything in my left leg. Doctor, are my eyes open? I can't see!

CARDINAL MAZARIN
Prime Minister of France, died 1661.

Oh my poor soul, what is to become of thee? Whither wilt thou go?

HORTENSE MAZARIN
Sister of the Cardinal, died 1699.
After she died her creditors seized her corpse . . .

Debt!

GEORGE MEREDITH
Novelist and poet, died 1909.
Mentioning his doctor's opinion . . .

I'm afraid Sir Thomas thinks very badly of my case.

COUNT MIRABEAU
Leader of the French Revolution, died 1791.

Are you not my doctor and my friend? Did you not promise to save me from the pain of such a death? Do you wish me to carry away regret for having given you my confidence?

MARIA MONTESSORI
Educator, died 1952.

Am I no longer of any use, then?

JOHN MOTLEY
Diplomat and historian, died 1877.

I am ill, very ill. I shall not recover.

FREDERIC MOYSE
Murderer, executed by the guillotine.
Moyse had killed his own son . . .

What! Would you execute the father of a family?

MODEST MUSSORGSKY
Composer, died 1881.

It is the end. Woe is me!

☠

HARRIET NEWELL
Missionary, died 1812.

The pain, the groans, the dying strife. How long oh Lord, how long?

FRANCIS NEWPORT
Militant atheist, died 1692.

Oh, the insufferable pangs of hell and damnation!

CHARLES NODIER
French man of letters, died 1844.

It is very hard, my children, I no longer see you. Remember me, love me always.

☠

PHIL OCHS
Folk singer, suicide 1975.
A message from the stage at his last concert . . .

One day you'll read about it: Phil Ochs, A Suicide at 35.

FRANCIS OLIVER
Chancellor of France, died 1560.
Oliver condemned many innocents on the orders of
the corrupt Cardinal, Lorrain . . .
Cardinal, thou wilt make us all be damned.

AMELIA OPIE
Novelist and poet, died 1853.
Sending a message to anyone who asked after her . . .
Tell them I have suffered great pain, but I think on Him who
suffered for me. Say that I am trusting in my Saviour and ask
them to pray for me.

☠

DOROTHY PARKER
Poet, writer and wit, died 1967.
Asked to compose her own epitaph . . .
Excuse my dust.

WILLIAM PATTISON
Poet, died 1727. Starving to death, he sent this last note . . .
Sir, if you was ever touched with a sense of humanity, consider
my condition. What I am, my proposals will inform you. What
I have been, Sidney College in Cambridge can witness, but what
I shall be some few hours hence, I tremble to think. Spare my
blushes – I have not enjoyed the common necessaries of life for
these two days and can hardly hold to subscribe myself, Yours
etc.

BRIAN PICCOLO
American professional footballer, died of cancer, 1968.
To his girlfriend . . .
Can you believe it Joy? Can you believe this shit?

EDGAR ALLEN POE
American writer, died 1849.
Lord help my poor soul.

WILLIAM POPE
*Atheist, died 1797. Pope led an atheistic cult who delighted
in desecrating religious places and objects and at whose
meetings a bible was ritually kicked around the floor . . .*

I have done the damnable deed. The horrible damnable deed. I
cannot pray God will have nothing to do with me. I will not have
salvation at his hands. I long to be in the bottomless pit, the lake
which burneth with fire and brimstone. I tell you I am damned.
I will not have salvation. Nothing for me but hell. Come eternal
torments! Oh God do not hear my prayers for I will not be
saved. I hate everything that God has made!

JOHN RANDOLPH OF ROANOKE
*American politician, died 1833.
Traditionally he ordered a secretary . . .*

Write that word 'remorse' and show it to me.
But in reality said . . .

Dying. Home . . . Randolph and Betty, my children, adieu!
Get me to bed at Chatham or elsewhere, say Hugh Mercer's or
Minor's. To bed I conjure you all!

LOUIS, DUC DE RICHELIEU
*French aristocrat, died 1789.
Dying on the eve of the French Revolution . . .*

What would Louis XIV have said?

RAINER MARIA RILKE
German poet, died 1926.

I still think of the world, poor shard of a vessel that remembers
being of the earth. But how it abuses our senses and their
dictionary – the pain that turns their pages.

JOSE RIZAL
National hero of the Philippines, died 1896.

Oh Father how terrible it is to die. How one suffers! Father, I
forgive everyone from the bottom of my heart. I have no resentment against any one, believe me, your reverence.

FREDERICK ROBERTSON
Divine, died 1853.

I cannot bear it. Let me rest. I must die. Let God do his work.

LOUIS FRANCOIS, DUC DE ROHAN-CHABOT
Archbishop of Besançon, died 1648.
I am nothing, nothing, less than nothing!

ANTON RUBINSTEIN
Pianist and composer, died 1894.
I am suffocating! A doctor! Quick! A doctor!

JOHN RYLAND
Baptist minister, died 1825.
No more pain.

RAPHAEL SABATIER
French surgeon, died 1811. To his son . . .
Contemplate the state to which I am fallen and learn to die.

DONATIEN ALPHONSE FRANCOIS, MARQUIS DE SADE
French philosopher, died 1814.
The conclusion of his will . . .
The ground over my grave shall be sprinkled with acorns so that all traces of my grave shall disappear so that, as I hope, this reminder of my existence may be wiped from the memory of mankind.

RICHARD SAVAGE
British poet, died 1743. To his gaoler . . .
I have something to say to you, sir . . . 'Tis gone!

THOMAS SCOTT
US Congressman/Lawyer, died 1887. To the priest . . .
Begone, you and your trumpery! Until this moment I believed that there was neither a God nor a hell. Now I know and feel that there are both and that I am doomed to perdition by the just judgment of the Almighty.

RICHARD SHERIDAN
British dramatist, died 1816.
I am absolutely undone.

SIWARD
Earl of Northumberland, died 1055.

Shame on me that I did not die in one of the many battles that I have fought, but am reserved to die with the disgrace of the death of a sick cow! At least put on my armour of proof, gird the sword by my side, place the helmet on my head, let me have my shield in my left hand and my gold-inlaid battle-axe in my right hand, that the bravest of soldiers may die in a soldier's garb.

PETER SPENGLER
Martyr.

It is all one, for shortly I must have forsaken this skin, which already hangeth to my bones. I know well that I am a mortal and a corruptible worm, and have nothing in me but corruption. I have long time desired my latter day, and have made my request that I might be delivered out of this mortal body, to be joined with my Saviour Christ. I have deserved through my manifold sins committed against my Saviour Christ, my cross, and my Saviour Christ hath borne the cross, and hath died upon the cross, and for my part I will not glory in any other thing, but only in the cross of Jesus Christ.

BARUCH SPINOZA
Philosopher, died 1677.

God have mercy upon me and be gracious to me – a miserable sinner.

EDMUND CLARENCE STEDMAN
Poet and editor, died 1908.

Twenty-seven letters! What is the use!

ROBERT LOUIS STEVENSON
Novelist and travel writer, died 1894.

My head, my head!

SIR ARTHUR SULLIVAN
Composer, died 1900.

My heart, my heart!

☠

FRANCIS TALMA
French actor, died 1826.

The worst is, I cannot see.

MATTHEW TINDALL
Militant atheist, died 1733.

Oh God, if there be a God, I desire thee to have mercy on me!

REV. AUGUSTUS TOPLADY
Composer of hymns, died 1778. Asked if he were in pain? . . .

It is delightful.

BERENGER DE TOURS
Theologian, died 1088.
His writing had been banned by the Vatican . . .

I shall not long hesitate between conscience and the Pope, for I shall soon appear in the presence of God to be acquitted, I hope, to be condemned, I fear.

GASTON TRUPHENE
Murdered 1928. Truphene was trying to collect a debt when his killer, the Parisian jeweller Mestorino, smashed his skull with a jeweller's mandrel, used for holding steady pieces for engraving or cutting . . .

There are 300,000 francs, you can take them all!
And to Mestorino's sister-in-law, who stood by and watched . . .
Suzanne, I have a sister like you. Take pity on me!

IVAN TURGENEV
Russian writer, died 1883. Letter to Tolstoy . . .

I can neither walk, eat, nor sleep. It tires me even to mention all this. My friend, great writer of the Russian land, heed my request. Let me know whether you receive this sheet and permit me once more closely, closely to embrace you, your wife and all yours. I can no more. I am tired.

☠

WILLIAM H. VANDERBILT
American millionaire, died 1899.

I have had no real gratification or enjoyment of any sort more than my neighbour down the block who is worth only half a million.

LEONARDO DA VINCI
Draughtsman, anatomist, scientist, artist, died 1519.

I have offended God and mankind because my work did not reach the quality it should have.

☠

JOHN GREENLEAF WHITTIER
American poet, died 1892.

No, no!

SONNY BOY WILLIAMSON
Blues musician, killed 1948.

Lord have mercy.

DR JOHN WOLCOT
'Peter Pindar', satirist, died 1819.
Asked what could be done to help him? . . .

Give me back my youth.

☠

GIACOMO ZANE
Italian poet, died 1560.

I should like to live.

DAVID ZEISBERGER
Missionary, died 1808.

I have reviewed my whole life and found that there is much to be forgiven.

LOOK BACK
IN ANGER

AGRIPPINA
Mother of the Emperor Nero, killed 59AD.
Smite my womb!

GABRIELE D'ANNUNZIO
Italian poet and novelist, died 1938.
I'm bored, I'm bored!

ARATUS
Poisoned 213 BC. Staring at the blood he was coughing up . . .
These, Oh Cephalon, are the wages of a King's love.

☠

ANTOINE BARNAVE
French politician, guillotined 1793.
This, then, was my reward.

ALEXANDER GRAHAM BELL
Inventor of the telephone, died 1922.
So little done, so much to do.

ALBAN BERG
Composer, died 1936. Advised to relax . . .
But I have so little time!

BESTOUJEFF
*Russian revolutionary, hanged 1926. He was hanged
alongside Count Pestel (see p 153) and his rope also broke . . .*
Nothing succeeds with me. Even here I meet with disappointment.

ELISA BONAPARTE
Sister of Napoleon, died 1820.
Someone told her that nothing was as certain as death . . .
Except taxes.

PAULINE BONAPARTE
Napoleon's favourite sister, died 1825.
I always was beautiful.

TYCHO BRAHE
Danish astronomer, died 1601.
Let me not seem to have lived in vain.

RICHARD BROCKLESBY
Physician, died 1797.
To the servants who were helping him undress . . .
What an idle piece of ceremony this buttoning and unbottoning
is to me now.

STOPFORD BROOKE
Died 1816. Hearing the news read to him . . .
It will be a pity to leave all that.

ROBERT BURNS
Scottish poet, died 1796.
Receiving a bill sent to his deathbed . . .
That damned rascal Matthew Penn!

CAIUS CASSIUS
Leader of the plot to kill Julius Caesar, suicide 42 BC.
Through too much fondness for life I have lived to endure the
sight of my friend taken by the enemy before my face.

PAUL CEZANNE
French artist, died 1906.
Recalling the name of the Director of the Museum at Aix
who had once refused to exhibit his works . . .
Pontier! Pontier!

ROCH CHAMFORT
French writer, died 1794.
Ah my friend, I am about to leave this world where the heart
must either be broken or be brass.

253

CHARLES CHURCHILL
Satirist, died 1764.

What a fool I have been.

GROVER CLEVELAND
American President, died 1908.

I have tried so hard to do right.

REV. DR JOHN COLBATCH
Lawyer, died 1748.
He remembered a far off legal wrangle over a Latin tag . . .

Arrogat, my lord!

AUGUSTE COMTE
French philosopher, died 1857.

What an incomparable loss.

ANN COPPOLA
Wife of gangster 'Trigger Mike' Coppola, suicide 1962.
Her suicide note . . .

Mike Coppola – Someday, somehow, a person, or God, or the law shall catch up with you, you yellow-bellied bastard. You are the lowest and biggest coward I have ever had the misfortune to meet.

CRATO OF THEBES
Greek Philosopher, died 300 BC.
Referring to his crooked back . . .

Ah, poor humpback. Thy many long years are at last conveying thee to the tomb. Thou shalt soon visit the palace of Pluto.

LORD HENRY DARNLEY
Killed probably on the orders of Mary, Queen of Scots, 1567.
He quoted the Sixtieth Psalm against the Queen . . .

It is not an open enemy that has done me this dishonour, for then I could have borne it. It was even thou, my companion, my guide and my own familiar friend.

JAMES DEAN
Film star, killed 1955.
Dean was talking shortly before his fatal car crash . . .
My fun days are over.

JOHN DENNIS
Poet, died 1734. Told on his deathbed that someone
published a book of poems under his name . . .
By God! That could be no-one but that fool S—!

JOHN DENTON
Died 1709.
I wish I could once more recall
That bright and blissful joy.
And summon to my weary heart
The feelings of a boy.
But now on scenes of past delight
I look and feel no pleasure.
As misers on their bed of death
Gaze coldly at their treasure.

CAMILLE DESMOULINS
Leader of the French Revolution, guillotined 1794.
Oh my poor wife. Poor people . . . how they have deceived you.

DENIS DIDEROT
French philosopher, died 1784.
Taking an apricot that his wife had offered . . .
But what the devil do you think that will do to me?

ALEXANDER DUMAS
French dramatist and novelist, 'Dumas Père', died
complaining to his son that he would never find out
how 'The Count of Monte Cristo' ended . . .
I shall never know how it all comes out.

MARQUIS JOSEPH DUPLEIX
Colonialist, died 1763. In a letter to the French Government . . .
I have sacrificed my youth, my fortune, my life to enrich my
nation in Asia. Unfortunate friends, too weak relations, devoted
all their property to the success of my projects. They are now in
misery and want. I have complied with all the judiciary forms. I

have demanded as the last of the creditors, that which is due to me. My services are treated as fables, my demand is denounced as ridiculous, I am treated as the vilest of mankind. I am in the most deplorable indigence. The little property that remains to me has been seized. I am compelled to ask for decrees for delay in order not to be dragged to prison.

JAMES B. EADS
Engineer, died 1887.
I cannot die. I have not finished my work.

POPE EUGENIUS IV
Gabriele Condolmere, died 1447.
Oh Gabriele, how much better it would have been for thee and how much more it would have promoted thy soul's welfare if thou had never been raised to the Pontificate, but had been content to lead a quiet and religious life in a monastery.

JOHN GALSWORTHY
British novelist, died 1933.
Beyond speech, Galsworthy scribbled a dying note . . .
I have enjoyed too pleasant circumstances.

STEPHEN GARDINER
Bishop, burnt 1555. Expressing his sorrow at
ever denying the supremacy of the Catholic church . . .
I have denied with Peter, I have gone out with Peter, but not yet have I wept with Peter.

GERONIMO
Chief of the Apache Indians, died 1909.
Interviewed before his death . . .
I want to go back to my old home before I die. Tired of fight and want to rest. I asked the Great White Father to allow me to go back, but he said no.

NICHOLAS GOGOL
Russian novelist and dramatist, died 1852.
Quoting the Old Testament . . .
And I shall laugh a bitter laugh.

OLIVER GOLDSMITH
Dramatist, novelist and biographer, died 1774.
Asked whether his mind was at rest? . . .

No, it is not.

POPE GREGORY VII
Died 1085.

I have loved righteousness and hated iniquity, therefore I die in exile.

REINIER DE GROENVELD
Dutch leader.

Oh God, what a man I was once and what am I now? . . . Patience.

HUGO GROTIUS
(Hugo de Groot) Dutch jurist, statesman and scholar, died 1645.

By understanding many things I have accomplished nothing.

JAROSLAV HASEK
Czech author, died 1923. Rebuking the doctor
who refused him one last drink of brandy . . .

But you're cheating me!

HILDEBRAND
Died 1035.

I have loved justice and hated iniquity and therefore I die in exile.

JAMES HOGG
Poet, died 1835. Died of hiccups . . .

It is a reproach to the faculty that they cannot cure the hiccup.

OLIVER WENDELL HOLMES
Jurist and son of the poet, died 1935.
Before his final incarceration in an oxygen tent . . .

Lot of damn foolery.

DAVID HUME
British philosopher, died 1776.
I am dying as fast as my enemies, if I have any, could wish, and as cheerfully as my best friends could desire.

ANDREW JACKSON
American President, died 1845.
I have only two regrets – that I have not shot Henry Clay or hanged John C. Calhoun.

JEZEBEL
Died 9th Century BC.
Has Zimri peace who slew his master.

FATHER JOSEPH
'The Grey Eminence', influence on Richelieu, died 1638.
Render an account! Render an account!

JAMES JOYCE
Irish novelist, died 1941.
Does nobody understand?

FRANZ KAFKA
Writer, died 1924.
Demanding that all his papers should be burnt . . .
There will be no proof that I ever was a writer.

JOHN KEATS
British poet, died 1821. Inscribed on his gravestone . . .
Here lies one whose name was writ in water.

CAPTAIN WILLIAM KIDD
Pirate, hanged 1701. Kidd had only surrendered
on the sure promise of a free pardon . . .
This is a very false and faithless generation.

KUANG-HSU
Chinese Emperor, died 912.
This wish was never carried out . . .
We were the second son of the Prince Ch'un when the Empress
Dowager selected Us for the Throne. She has always hated Us,
but for Our misery of the past ten years, Yuan Shi Kai is respon-
sible and none other. When the time comes I desire that Yuan
be summarily beheaded.

FRANCOIS DE MALHERBE
Poet, died 1628.
To the priest who was eulogising heaven . . .
Hold your tongue! Your wretched style disgusts me.

GEORGE BROWNE MACDONALD
Rudyard Kipling's grandfather, died 1868.
Lord, what things I lie here and remember.

KARL MARX
German political theorist, died 1883. Asked by his
housekeeper if he had a last message to the world . . .
Go on, get out! Last words are for fools who haven't said enough.

TOMMASO MASANIELLO
Italian soldier, killed 1646.
His own troops assassinated him . . .
Ungrateful traitors.

LOUIS B. MAYER
Hollywood movie magnate, died 1957.
Mayer left no last words, but an anonymous wit claimed . . .
The only reason so many people attended his funeral was that
they wanted to make sure he was dead.

H. L. MENCKEN
Editor, critic, essayist and wit, died 1956.
To James T. Farrell . . .
Remember me to my friends, tell them I'm a hell of a mess.

JEAN MESSELIER
Anarchist, died 1733. Voltaire published his will . . .
I should like to see, and this will be the last and most ardent of my desires. I should like to see the last king strangled with the guts of the last priest!

HENRI MURGER
Author, died 1861.
Referring to his 'Scènes de la vie de Bohéme' . . .
No more music, no more commotion, no more Bohemia.

☠

ADAM NARUSEWICZ
Polish historian, died 1796.
Regretting dying with his work incomplete . . .
Must I leave it unfinished?

☠

POPE PIUS X
Died 1914.
The Pope refused to bless the armies of the Holy Roman Empire, then had a fatal heart attack after dismissing the Emperor Franz Joseph . . .
Get out of my sight! Get out of my sight! Away! Away! We grant blessing to no one who provokes the world to war.

☠

CECIL RHODES
Colonizer, died 1902.
Turn me over, Jack.
Traditionally Rhodes is also supposed to have said
So little done, so much to do.

LEGH RICHMOND
Author of moral tracts, died 1827.
It will be all confusion. The church! There will be such confusion in my church!

☠

Sandro Sandri
Italian Fascist war correspondent, killed reporting
the Chinese-Japanese War 1937.

They've killed me this time. What an end. In another nation's ship, in this country.

Sir Edward Shackleton
Explorer, died 1922. Complaining to his doctor . . .

You are always wanting me to give up something. What do you want me to give up now?

'Suspinianus'
(Johann Spiessheimer) Viennese humanist.
Writing to a fellow humanist, Johann Brassican . . .

That you have not visited me in my grievous and deadly sickness – what even strangers do – will be noted at the appointed time. Through my man-servant I informed myself of your situation and sent you wine and other good things. By your behaviour you have marked yourself out as a sneak and an intriguer, and I shall see that posterity knows about it. What is another man to you? In order that you may be aware of my intention, even when my hand is a corpse's, I am putting it in writing. Let it be goodbye, then. It goes badly with me, but I am what I always was.

Hannen Swaffer
British journalist, died 1962. It is not known
whether he referred to his nurse, his life or whatever . . .

What a cow!

Jonathan Swift
Satirist, died 1745.

I am dying like a poisoned rat in a hole. I am what I am! I am what I am!

Toussaint l'Ouverture
Led the revolt of slaves in Haiti, died 1803.
To his gaolers . . .

Nothing can compare with the humiliation to which you subjected me. You have taken away my watch and the money I had in my pocket. I hereby serve notice on you that these objects are my personal property and that I will call you to account for them on the day I am executed, when I shall expect you to remit them to my wife and children.

WILLIAM TWEED
'Boss' of Tammany Hall, New York, died 1870.
Tweed was referring to his old partners and rivals . . .
Tilden and Fairchild, they will be satisfied now.

@

GENERAL CHARLES DE VILLARS
French soldier, died 1734.
Talking about the Duke of Berwick who died in battle,
while de Villars died in bed . . .
I always deemed him more fortunate than myself.

@

HENRY WAINWRIGHT
Murderer, hanged 1875. Public executions were
no longer performed, but Wainwright's death was
watched by some hundred officials, pressmen and
friends of the warden . . .
You curs! So you have come to see a man die!

ALL MY OWN WORK

JULIUS AGRESTIS
Suicide, 69 AD.
Charged with treason, he proved his loyalty in death . . .
Since you (Emperor Vitellius) require some decisive proof and
I can no longer serve you in any other way, either by my life or
death, I will give you a proof which you can believe.

ANONYMOUS
San Francisco dishwasher, suicide by hanging.
That's all folks!

ANONYMOUS
Banker, suicide. Suicide note . . .
Sorry to be a nuisance this way. Call — [name of undertakers].

ANONYMOUS
17 year old girl cited by Dostoevsky, suicide.
I am undertaking a long journey. If I should not succeed, let
people gather to celebrate my resurrection with a bottle of
Cliquot. If I should succeed, I ask that I be interred only after
I am altogether dead, since it is particularly disagreeable to
awake in a coffin in the earth. It is not chic!

ANONYMOUS
Doctor, suicide. Suicide note.
Waiting. Feeling very happy. First time I ever felt without worry,
as if I were free. My heart must be strong. It won't give up.
Pulse running well. I feel fine. When will it be over?

ANONYMOUS
American worker, suicide. Suicide note . . .

My small estate I bequeath to my mother; my body to the nearest accredited medical school; my soul and heart to all the girls; and my brain to Harry Truman.

ANONYMOUS
Hollywood failure, suicide. Suicide note . . .

I tried so hard to make a comeback. Exit, Act III.

ANONYMOUS
Found on a wall in an empty house in Hampstead, London.

Why suicide? Why not?

�احی

BARNETT BARNATO
Adventurer, suicide by jumping off ship 1897.

What is the time?

PAUL BERN
Husband of Jean Harlow, suicide by slashing his wrists 1932.
He killed himself two months after their marriage
ceremony because of his impotence . . .

Dearest Dear, Unfortunately this is the only way to make good the frightful wrong I have done you. And to wipe out my abject humiliation.

☠

CLIVE OF INDIA
Suicide by stabbing, 1774.
When asked to sharpen a pencil, he picked up the
penknife and stabbed himself . . .

To be sure.

GNAIUS DOMITIUS CORBULO
Suicide, 67 AD. Ordered to kill himself by Nero,
who suspected him of treason . . .

Well deserved.

HART CRANE
American writer, suicide by jumping off ship 1932.
Goodbye, everybody!

RENE CREVEL
Surrealist painter, suicide by gas 1920s.
Is it true . . . that one commits suicide for love, for fear, for
syphilis? It is not true. Suicide is a means of selection. Those
men commit suicide who reject the quasi universal cowardice of
struggling against a certain spiritual sensation so intense that it
must be taken until further notice as a sensation of truth. Only
this sensation permits the acceptance of the most obviously just
and definitive of solutions – suicide.

DEMOSTHENES
*Athenian orator, suicide 322 BC. Killed himself
rather than be captured by the Macedonians . . .*
Now, as soon as you please, you may commence the part of
Creon in the tragedy, and cast out this body of mine unburied.
But, O gracious Poseidon, I for my part while I am still alive
will arise and depart out of this sacred place, though Antipater
and the Macedonians have not left so much as Thy temple
unpolluted.

GEORGE EASTMAN
American Scientist, suicide 1932.
To my friends: my work is done. Why wait?

JAMES V. FORRESTAL
Admiral's son, suicide 1949.
Quoting Sophocles as his suicide note . . .
Woe to the mother in her close of day
Woe to her desolate heart and temples grey
When she shall hear
Her loved one's story whispered in her ear
'Woe, woe!' will be the cry
No quiet murmur like the tremulous wail.

FANNY GODWIN
Illegitimate daughter of Mary Wollstonecraft and
William Godwin, suicide. Suicide note . . .

I have long determined that the best thing I could do was to put an end to the existence of a being whose birth was unfortunate, and whose life has only been a series of pains to those persons who have hurt their health in endeavouring to promote her welfare. Perhaps to hear of my death may give you pain, but you will soon have the blessing of forgetting that such a creature ever existed.

JOSEPH GOEBBELS
Hitler's propaganda chief, suicide 1945.

This is the worst treachery of all. The generals have betrayed the Fuhrer. Everything is lost. I shall die together with my wife and family. You will burn our bodies. Can you do that?

MAGDA GOEBBELS
Wife of Joseph Goebbels, suicide 1945.

You see, we die an honourable death. If you should ever see Harald again [son from her first marriage, a war prisoner,] give him our best and tell him we died an honourable death.

FITZHUGH C. GOLDSBOROUGH
Suicide 1911. Obsessed with his sister, he killed a man
he thought had insulted her in a book . . .

Here I go!

TONY HANCOCK
British comedian, overdosed 1968. His last TV monologue
in 1964 proved an ironic farewell . . .

What have you achieved? What have you achieved? You lost your chance, me old son. You contributed absolutely nothing to this life. A waste of time you being here at all. No place for you in Westminster Abbey. The best you can expect is a few daffodils in a jam jar, a rough hewn stone bearing the legend 'He came and he went' and in between – nothing! Nobody will even notice you're not here. After about a year afterwards somebody might say down the pub 'Where's old Hancock? I haven't seen him around lately.' 'Oh, he's dead y'know.' 'Oh, is he?'. A right raison d'être that is. Nobody will ever know I existed. Nothing to leave behind me. Nothing to passon. Nobody to mourn me. That's the bitterest blow of all.

HANNIBAL
Carthaginian general, suicide 183 BC.

Let us ease the Romans of their continual dread and care, who think it long and tedious to await the death of a hated old man. Yet Titus will not bear away a glorious victory, nor one worthy of those ancestors sent to caution Pyrrhus, an enemy and conqueror too, against the poison prepared for him by traitors.

BARON JAMES A. HARDEN-HICKEY
Soldier of fortune, suicide. Suicide note to his wife . . .

My Dearest, No news from you although you have had plenty of time to write; Harvey has written me that he has no one in view at present to buy my land. Well, I shall have tasted the cup of bitterness to the very dregs, but I do not complain. Goodbye. I forgive you your conduct towards me and trust you will be able to forgive yourself. I prefer to be a dead gentleman to a living blackguard like your father.

HEINRICH HIMMLER
Commander of the S.S., suicide by poison 1945.

I am Heinrich Himmler!

HUGO VON HOFMANNSTHAL
Austrian poet and playwright, died 1929.
His letter on his son's suicide . . .

Good friend, I sincerely hope it goes well with you. Yesterday afternoon a great misfortune visited our Rodauner House. During a bad, oppressive thunderstorm our poor Franz took his life with a shot in the temple. The motive for this dreadful deed lies darkly deep: in the depths of character and of fate. There was no external motive. We had eaten together as usual, en famille. There is something infinitely sad and infinitely noble in the way the poor child went. He was never able to share his thoughts. So his departure was silent too – Raymond is with us. In all friendship, Hugo von Hofmannsthal.

CHRIS HUBBOCK
American newsreader, suicide by shooting 1970.
She made the news when she shot herself in
the head on a prime time news programme . . .

And now, in keeping with Channel 40's policy of always bringing you the latest in blood and guts, in living colour, you're about to see another first – an attempted suicide.

JUDAS ISCARIOT
Suicide 1st Century

I have sinned in that I have betrayed the innocent blood.

HEINRICH VON KLEIST
German dramatist and poet, suicide 1811.
Suicide letter to his sister . . .

I cannot die without, contented and serene as I am, reconciling myself with all the world and, before all others, with you, my dearest Ulrike. Give up the strong expressions which you resorted to in your letter to me: let me revoke them; truly, to save me, you have done all within the strength, not only of a sister, but of a man – all that could be done. The truth is, nothing on earth can help me. And now good-bye: may Heaven send you a death even half equal to mine in joy and unutterable bliss: that is the most heart-felt and profoundest wish that I can think of for you. Your Henry. Stimmung, at Potsdam, on the morning of my death.

GUNTHER VON KLUGE
German Field-Marshal, suicide 1944.
Suicide note addressed to Hitler . . .

I depart from you my Fuhrer, as one who stood nearer to you than perhaps you realized in the consciousness that I did my duty to the utmost. Heil, my Fuhrer, von Kluge, Field-Marshal. 18 August 1944.

CAROLE LANDIS
American film star, suicide 1948.

Dearest Mommie. I'm sorry, really sorry to put you through this. But there is no way to avoid it. I love you darling. You have been

the most wonderful Mom ever. And that applies to all our family.
I love each and every one of them dearly. Everything goes to
you. Look in the files and there is a will which decrees everything. Goodbye my angel. Pray for me.

DR ROBERT LEY
*Nazi war criminal, suicide by hanging 1945. His suicide
note written before hanging himself in his cell . . .*
The fact that I should be a criminal, that I can't stand.

VACHELL LINDSAY
American poet, suicide by drinking a bottle of Lysol 1931.
They tried to get me – I got them first!

LUCAN
*Suicide 65 AD.
His own verse 'Pharsalia' provided a farewell message . . .*
Asunder flies the man
no single wound the gaping rupture seems
where trickling crimson flows the tender streams
but from an opening horrible and wide
a thousand vessels pour the bursting tide
at once the winding channel's course was broken
where wandering life her mazy journey took.

CHARLOTTE MEW
English poetess, suicide 1928.
Don't keep me, let me go.

RICHARD MIDDLETON
English poet and story writer, suicide 1641. Suicide note . . .
Good-bye! Harry. I'm going adventuring again, and thanks to
you I shall have some pleasant memories in my knapsack. As for
the many bitter ones, perhaps they will not weigh so heavy now
as they did before. 'A broken and contrite heart, oh Lord, Thou
shalt not despise.' Richard.

HUGH MILLER
*Scottish geologist and man of letters, suicide 1856.
Suicide letter to his wife . . .*
Dearest Lydia, My brain burns, I must have walked; and a fear-

ful dream rises upon me. I cannot bear the horrible thought. God and Father of the Lord Jesus Christ, have mercy upon me. Dearest Lydia, dear children, farewell. My brain burns as the recollection grows. My dear wife, farewell, Hugh Miller.

JULIANA MOHAUPT
Niece of German author Stifter, suicide by drowning,
age 17. Suicide note . . .
I am going to my mother in the great Service.

EUGENE O'NEILL JR
Greek scholar, suicide. Suicide note . . .
Never let it be said of O'Neill that he failed to empty a bottle. Ave atque vale.

MAJOR JOHN ONEBY
Murderer, suicide 1727. Oneby killed his victim in a tavern
brawl, he committed suicide in his cell in Newgate,
but first left a note for his gaolers . . .
Give Mr Akerman, the turnkey below stairs half a guinea, and Jack who waits in my room five shillings. The poor devils have had a great deal of trouble with me since I have been here.

JULES PASCIN
Artist, suicide by hanging 1930. Wrote this in blood
on the wall before hanging . . .
Adieu Lucy.

CESARE PAVESE
Italian writer, suicide by overdose 1950. His final
diary entry . . .
The thing most feared in secret always happens; all it needs is a little courage. The more the pain grows clearer and definite, the more the instinct for life reasserts itself and the thought of suicide recedes. It seemed easy when I thought of it. Weak women have done it. It needs humility, not pride. I am sickened by all this. No words. Action. I shall write no more.

JACQUES RIGAUT
Surrealist painter, suicide.

Suicide is a vocation.

ERWIN ROMMEL
German general, suicide 1944. Explaining his suicide,
which was ordered by Hitler, to his son . . .

To die by the hand of one's own people is hard.

ROLAND DE LA PLATIERE
Suicide 1793. His wife, Madame Roland, was
guillotined in 1793 . . .

After my wife's murder, I would not remain any longer in a
world so stained with crime.

BOURG SAINT- EDME
French man of letters, suicide. Suicide note to his children . . .

At four o'clock or at 4.15 I will carry out my design, if everything
goes right. I am not afraid of death, since I am seeking it, since
I desire it! But prolonged suffering would be frightful. I walk;
all ideas vanish. I think only of my children. The fire is dying
out. What a silence all around! Four o'clock. I hear the chimes.
Soon comes the moment of sacrifice. I put my snuff box in my
desk drawer. Good-bye my dearest daughters! God will pardon
my sorrows. I put my spectacles in the drawer. Good-bye, once
more, good-bye, my darling children! My last thought is yours,
for you are the last flutterings of my heart.

LUCIUS ANNAEUS SENECA
Roman philosopher, suicide, 65 AD. While bleeding, he
entered a pool of heated water, with which he sprinkled
the nearest of his slaves . . .

I offer this liquid as a libation to Jupiter the Deliverer.

SIMON
A monk, suicide by poison 1216. He drank poisoned
wine in order to get King John of England to drink it . . .

If it shall like your princely majesty, here is such a cup of wine
as ye never drank a better before in all your lifetime; I trust this
wassail shall make all England glad.

SOCRATES
Greek philosopher, suicide by drinking hemlock 399 BC.
Crito, I owe a cock to Asclepius. Will you remember to pay the debt.

SOPHONISBA
Wife of Masinissa, suicide by poison. Her husband was ordered
to surrender her to the Romans, but rather than this
fate he sent her a dose of poison which she voluntarily
drank . . .
If my husband has for his new wife no better gift than a cup of death, I know his will and accept what he bestows. I might have died more honourably if I had not wedded so near to my funeral.

FILIPPO STROZZI II
Florentine intriguer against the Medicis, suicide 1538.
He backed a defiant note with a line from Virgil
carved with his sword on the prison wall . . .
If I have not known how to live, I shall know how to die. May some avenger rise from my bones !

THERAMENES
Athenian statesman and general, suicide by drinking
hemlock 5th Century BC. He toasted his accuser . . .
This to the health of the lovely Critias !

PAETUS THRASEA
Roman senator and Stoic, suicide 66 AD. Ordered
by Nero to kill himself . . .
We pour out a libation to Jupiter the Deliverer. Behold, young man, and may the gods avert the omen, but you have been born into times in which it is well to fortify the spirit with examples of courage.

HENNING VON TRESCKOW
General and one of the Stauffenberg plotters against
Hitler, suicide 1945. He chose suicide rather than execution . . .
The worth of a man is certain only if he is prepared to sacrifice his life for his convictions.

JACQUES VACHE

*Surrealist painter, suicide. He fulfilled his wish in all
points: killing himself with two university friends . . .*

I shall die when I want to die. And then I shall die with someone
else. To die alone is boring. I should prefer to die with one of
my best friends.

LUPE VELEZ

Hollywood filmstar, suicide 1944. Suicide note . . .

To Harald, May God forgive you and forgive me too but I prefer
to take my life away and our baby's before I bring him with
shame or killing him, Lupe.

And on the back of this note . . .

How could you, Harald, fake such a great love for me and our
baby when all the time you didn't want us. I see no other way
out for me so goodbye and good luck to you. Love, Lupe.

VIRGINIA WOOLF

English novelist, suicide by drowning 1941.

I have a feeling I shall go mad. I cannot go on any longer in these
terrible times. I hear voices and cannot concentrate on my work.
I have fought against it but cannot fight any longer. I owe all my
happiness to you, but cannot go on and spoil your life.

TAKI ZENZABURO

Japanese officer of the Prince of Bizen, suicide by hara-kiri.

I, and I alone, unwarrantably gave the order to fire on the
foreigners at Kobe, and again as they tried to escape. For this
crime I disembowel myself, and I beg you who are present to do
me the honour of witnessing the act.

STEFAN ZWEIG

*Austrian philosopher, suicide 1942. Sickened by the state
of Europe under fascism . . .*

I believe it is time to end a life which was dedicated only to
spiritual work, considering human liberty and my own as the
greatest wealth in the world. I leave an affectionate goodbye to
all my friends.

A FOND FAREWELL

FIFTH EARL OF ABERDEEN
British aristocrat, died 1864. Asked how he felt ...
Perfectly comfortable.

ABIGAIL ADAMS
Wife of US President John Adams, died 1818.
Do not grieve my friend, my dearest friend. I am ready to go.
And John, it will not be long.

ALICE ADAMS
Lover, but never wife, of Nathan Hale.
Where is Nathan?

JOHN QUINCY ADAMS
American President, died 1848.
This is the last of earth. I am content.

JOSEPH ADDISON
British essayist, died 1719.
See in what peace a Christian can die.

ALFRED ADLER
Pioneer psychologist, died 1937. To his son ...
Kurt.

THOMAS B. ALDRICH
American author and journalist, died 1907.
In spite of it all, I am going to sleep.

VITTORIO ALFIERI
Italian dramatist, died 1803.

Clasp my hand, dear friend, I am dying.

JOHN PETER ALTGELD
Governor of Illinois, died 1902. To his last visitor . . .

How d'you do, Cushing. I am glad to see you.

ANAXAGORAS
*Greek philosopher, died 428 BC. Asked what he felt
would be his best memorial . . .*

Give the boys a holiday.

AGRIPPA D'AUBIGNE
Huguenot leader and poet, died 1630. A final verse . . .

It comes at last the happy day
Let there be given
To God in heaven
While we learn pleasure in His way.

JOHN BACHMAN
Lutheran minister, died 1874.

I love her. I love you all.

RICHARD BARHAM
*Author of 'The Ingoldsby Legends', died 1845.
Final line of his final poem . . .*

Here is rest.

MAURICE BARING
Novelist, died 1945. Asked what he wanted for lunch . . .

Anything you would like me to have.

ISAAC BARROW
Scholar and preacher, died 1677.

I have seen the glories of the world.

JOHN BARRYMORE
American actor, died 1942. To his brother, Lionel . . .
You heard me, Mike.
To his old friend Gene Fowler . . .
Tell me Gene, is it true that you're the illegitimate son of
Buffalo Bill?

SIR CHARLES BELL
Anatomist, died 1842. To his wife . . .
Hold me in your arms.

GENERAL LUDWIG VON BENEDEK
Died 1881. Telegraph to his wife . . .
Relieved to hear you feel better. I had a very bad night. Am now
strong. Your poor Louis.

ANTHONY BENEZET
Philanthropist, died 1784. To his wife . . .
We have lived long in love and peace.

PARK BENJAMIN
*American journalist, died 1864. His wife asked him
'Do you know me?' . . .*
Why should I not know you, Mary?

MONSIGNOR ROBERT BENSON
Clergyman, died 1914.
Arthur! Don't look at me. Nurse, stand between my brother
and me! Jesus, Mary and Joseph, I give you my heart and soul.

JEREMY BENTHAM
Political theorist, died 1832.
I now feel that I am dying. Our care must be to minimize pain.
Do not let the servants come into the room and keep away the
youths. It will be distressing to them and they can be of no
service.

HECTOR BERLIOZ
Composer, died 1869.
One thousand greetings to Balakirev.

THEODORE BEZA
Protestant theologian, died 1605. Still worrying for
Geneva, the home of his faith . . .
Is the city in full safety and quiet?

WILLIAM BLAKE
Poet, died 1827. To his wife, who asked whose songs he was
singing . . .
My beloved, they are not mine, no, they are not mine.

MARSHAL BLUCHER
Prussian general, died 1819. To an aide . . .
Nostitz, you have learned many a thing from me. Now you are to
learn how peacefully a man can die.

EDWIN BOOTH
Actor, died 1893. Asked how he felt by a grandson . . .
How are yourself, old fellow?

WILLIAM BOOTH
Founder of the Salvation Army, died 1912. To his son . . .
I am leaving you a bonnie handful. Railton will be with you.

ALEXANDER BORODIN
Russian composer, died 1887. Writing to his wife about
a ball to which he was going and at which he would die . . .
I shall say no more about it and leave the description of the
festivity to the more expert pen of other correspondents.

HENRY BOWDITCH
Divine, died 1911. Asked whether he suffered . . .
No dear. Wish that the end would come.

SAUL BOWLES
American journalist, died 1915. To his nurse . . .
You may be sure that in another world there is always one soul
praying for you.

JOHANNES BRAHMS
Composer, died 1897. Enjoying his last glass of wine . . .
Ah, that tastes nice. Thank you.

ANNE BRONTË
Author, died 1849.

Take courage Charlotte, take courage!

SIR JAMES BROOKE
Colonial official, died 1868. Starting a letter that he could not finish . . .

My dear Arthur . . .

RUPERT BROOKE
Poet, died 1915. Greeting a final visitor . . .

Hullo.

ROBERT BROOKINGS
American philanthropist, died 1932.

I have done everything I wanted to do. This is the end.

ELIZABETH BARRETT BROWNING
Poet, died 1861. Asked how she was feeling . . .

Beautiful.

ROBERT BROWNING
Poet, died 1889. Hearing that his last volume of poems 'Asolando' was proving popular . . .

How gratifying.

JOHANN BUCHER
Jurist, died 1892.

Now farewell. Permit me to close my tired eyes and sleep.

WILLIAM CECIL, LORD BURLEIGH
Elizabethan statesman, died 1598. Leaving his affairs in the hands of his Steward . . .

I have ever found thee true to me and now I trust thee with all.

AARON BURR
American politician, died 1836.

Madame.

FERUCCIO BUSONI
Pianist, died 1924. To his wife . . .

Dear Gerda, I thank you for every day we have been together.

☠

WILLIAM CADOGAN
2nd Earl, died 1797. To his servants . . .

I thank you all for your faithful services. God bless you.

EDMUND CAMPION
Jesuit martyr, executed 1581. Asked on the scaffold
for which Queen – Elizabeth or Mary – he prayed . . .

Yes, for Elizabeth, your Queen and my queen, whom I wish a
long quiet reign with all prosperity.

CHARLES CARROLL
American Revolutionary soldier, died 1832.

Thank you, doctor.

ALICE CARY
American poet, died 1871.

I want to go away.

MIGUEL DE CERVANTES
Spanish author, died 1616. To his patron . . .

Already my foot is in the stirrup. Already, great Lord and master, the agonies are upon me as I send these lines. Yesterday
they administered to me the Last Rites. Today I am writing this.
Time is short. Agony grows. Hope lessens. Only the will to live
keeps me alive. Would that life might last until I might kiss the
feet of your excellency. Seeing your excellency back in Spain,
hale and hearty, might restore me to life. But if it be decreed
that I must die, heaven's will be done. May your excellency
know at least what my wish was and know also that he had in
me a servant so faithful as to have wished to have served your
excellency even after death.

THOMAS CHALMERS
Scottish divine, died 1847.

A general goodnight.

PHILIP STANHOPE, 4TH EARL OF CHESTERFIELD
Statesman and writer, died 1773. Attentive to the
needs of others even on his deathbed . . .

Give Dayrolles a chair.

HENRY CLAY
American politician, died 1852.

I believe, my son, that I am going. Now I lay me down to sleep.

FRANCIS COBBE
Philanthropist and religious writer, died 1904.
His last letter . . .

I am touched by your affectionate words, dear Blanche, but nobody must be sorry when that time comes, least of all those who love me.

GEORGE M. COHAN
American showman, died 1942. Of his wife . . .

Look after Agnes.

SAMUEL TAYLOR COLERIDGE
Poet, died 1834. Making provision for his favourite
servant . . .

I beg, expect and would fain hope of them [his family] according to their means such a contribution as may suffice collectively a handsome Legacy for that most faithful, affectionate and disinterested servant Harriet Macklin. Henry can explain. I have never asked for myself. Samuel Taylor Coleridge.

CALVIN COOLIDGE
American President, died 1933.

Good morning, Robert.

SIR ARTHUR CONAN DOYLE
British author, died 1930. To his wife . . .

You are wonderful.

SIR ASTLEY COOPER
British surgeon, died 1841.

Goodbye, God bless you.

JOHN J. CRITTENDEN
Kentucky politician, died 1863. To a servant . . .

Tom, come and raise me up and arrange my pillow. That's right Tom.

JOHN CROKER
Politician and critic, died 1857. To a servant . . .
Oh, Wade . . .

JOHN CROME
British landscape artist, died 1821.
Oh Hobbima, Hobbima, how I do love thee.

HARVEY CUSHING
*American surgeon, died 1939. To his nephew who was
adjusting his bedclothes . . .*
Pat, you have the touch. You're a good doctor.

JOHN A. DAHLGREN
Armament inventor, died 1870. To his wife . . .
Madeline, I will take nothing more until you go to your breakfast, which you must require.

MARQUISE DU DEFFAND
*French literary hostess, died 1780. Refusing to accept
a priest as confessor . . .*
I shall confess to my friend, the Duc de Choiseul.

RUDOLF DIESEL
Engineer, died 1913. His last letter . . .
Greetings and a kiss. In fondest love, Your father.

GRACE DODGE
*American philanthropist, died 1914. Asking after some
guests whom she was too ill to meet herself . . .*
And were they happy?

STEPHEN A. DOUGLAS
American politician, died 1861. His final advice to his sons . . .
Tell them to obey the laws and respect the Constitution of the United States.

ERNEST DOWSON
*Poet, died 1900. To Mrs Robert Sherard,
who had nursed him . . .*
You are like an angel from heaven. God bless you!

MICHAEL DRAYTON
Poet, died 1631. To his patron's daughter,
Anne Rainsford . . .

So all my thoughts are pieces but of you
Which put together make a glass so true
As I therein no other's face but yours can view.

💀

EDWARD EDWARDS
Pioneer of Public Libraries, died 1886. To his landlady,
who had just bathed his feet . . .

I am much obliged to you – very . . .

SIR CHARLES ELIOT
Diplomat and scholar, died 1931.

I see Mother.

JOHN LOVEJOY ELLIOTT
Founder of the Ethical Culture Movement, died 1925.

The only things I have found worth living for, and working for,
and dying for, are love and friendship.

RALPH WALDO EMERSON
American philosopher and poet, died 1882.

Goodbye, my friend.

EPICURUS
Greek philosopher, died 270 BC.

Now farewell, remember all my words.

CHRISTMAS EVANS
Welsh preacher, died 1838.

Goodbye. Drive on.

💀

PAOLO FARINATO
Italian painter, died 1606.

Now I am going.
His sick wife joined him in death, saying . . .
I will bear you company, my dear husband.

WILBUR FISK
American scholar, died 1839. Asked by his wife if he
recognized her . . .

Yes, love, yes.

MARJORY FLEMING
Youthful prodigy, died 1811. Dying at eight years old . . .
Oh mother, mother . . .

EDWIN FORREST
Actor, died 1872.
God bless you, my dear and much valued friend.

GEORG FORSTER
Traveller and writer, died 1794. His last letter home . . .
It's true, isn't it, my children, that two words are better than
none? I haven't strength to write more. Goodbye. Keep away
from illness. A kiss for my little darlings.

STEPHEN FOSTER
American composer, died 1864. The creator of 'ragtime'
music died in poverty. This note was found in his pocket . . .
Dear friends and gentle hearts.

MARGARET FOX
Wife of George Fox, the Quaker leader, died 1702.
To her daughter . . .
Take me in thy arms, I am in peace.

ANATOLE FRANCE
French scholar and satirist, died 1924.
So this is what it is like to die. It takes a long time. Maman!

☠

LEON GAMBETTA
French politician, died 1882. When a visitor fainted at
seeing him so near the end . . .
Good heavens, has he hurt himself?

COUNT AGENOR DE GASPARIN
Died 1871. To his wife, who wished to walk up the
steps behind him . . .
No, you know I like to have you go before me.

MRS ANNE GILBERT
Author of children's books, died 1904. Kissing her
daughter twice after she had arranged her mother's hair . . .
That's for thank you . . . That's for goodnight.

THOMAS GRAY
Poet, died 1771.

Molly, I shall die.

ANTHONY N. GROVES
Missionary, died 1853. To his son . . .
Now my precious boy, I am dying; be a comfort to your beloved
mother, as your dear brothers Henry and Frank have been to me.
And may the Lord Himself bless you and make you His own.
May the Lord give you the peace and joy in Himself that He has
given me, for these are true riches. What would thousands of
gold and silver be to me now. Now I give you a father's blessing.

JOHN GUNTHER, JR
Son of the journalist.
Mother . . . Father . . .

JOSEPH J. GURNEY
Quaker philanthropist, died 1847. To his wife . . .
I think I feel a little joyful, dearest.

☠

FRANK HARRIS
Editor and bon viveur, died 1931. To his wife . . .
Nellie, my Nellie – I'm going!

MRS NATHANIEL HAWTHORNE
To her husband . . .
I am tired – too tired – I am – glad to go – I only – wanted to live
– for you – and Rose . . . Flowers, flowers.

HELOISE
Lover of Pierre Abelard, died 1164.
In death at last let me rest with Abelard.

EDWIN P. HOOD
Congregational divine and author, died 1885.
Oh God! Oh God! My wife! My wife!

☠

Sir Elijah Impey
*Judge, died 1809. Apologizing for leaning too heavily
on a nurse who was helping him into bed . . .*

Did I hurt you, my dear?

☠

Andrew Jackson
American President, died 1845.

Oh do not cry. Be good children and we shall all meet in heaven.

Marshal Joseph Joffre
French soldier, died 1931. To his confessor . . .

I have not done much evil in my life and I have sincerely loved
my wife.

Samuel Johnson
*Biographer, essayist, lexicographer and wit, died 1784.
To his wife . . .*

God bless you, my dear.

☠

Francis Adrian van der Kemp
Last letter . . .

Now I must close. I can scarcely distinguish one letter from
another. Whatever may happen I know you remain unalterably
my friend, as, so long as I draw breath, I shall be yours. Once
again, farewell.

James Kent
American jurist, died 1847.

Go, my children. My object in telling you this is that, if anything happens to me, you might know, and perhaps it would
console you to remember, that on this point my mind is clear;
I rest my hopes of salvation on the Lord Jesus Christ.

Thomas King
Unitarian minister, died 1864. Taking a last look at his son . . .

Dear little fellow, he is a beautiful boy.

RICHARD KNILL
Dissenting minister, died 1857. To his daughter . . .
How are you, Mary?

💀

MME DE LAFAYETTE
French writer, died 1693. To her husband . . .
Is it then true? You have loved me? How happy I am! Kiss me!
What a blessing. How happy I am to be yours!

EDWARD LEAR
Author of 'Nonsense' verses, died 1888. To his servant . . .
I cannot find words sufficient to thank my good friends for the
good they have always done me. I did not answer their letters
because I could not write, as no sooner did I take a pen in my
hand than I felt as if I were dying.

PRINCESS DOROTHEA DE LIEVEN
*Russian diplomat, died 1857. A note to her friend
Francois Guizot . . .*
I thank you for twenty years of affection and happiness. Don't
forget me. Goodbye. Goodbye.

GEORGE, 1ST BARON LYTTLETON
*Patron of the Arts, died 1773. Final advice to his
son-in-law . . .*
Be good, be virtuous, my Lord. You must come to this.

💀

O. O. McINTYRE
American newspaper columnist, died 1938. To his wife . . .
Snooks, will you please turn this way. I like to look at your face.

SIR MORELL MACKENZIE
Laryngologist, died 1892. Referring to his brother, a doctor . . .
Yes, send for Stephen.

DOLLY MADISON
Wife of American President James Madison, died 1849.
My poor boy.

MAURICE MAETERLINCK
Belgian poet and dramatist, died 1949.
For me this is quite natural. It is for you that I am concerned.

OTTMAR MERGENTHALER
Inventor of Linotype printing, died 1899. To his family . . .
Emma, my children, my friends, be kind to one another.

HENRY MILLER
Theatre Manager, died 1874. To his son . . .
Gilbert, poor Dodd.

WILLIAM MORRIS
Poet, decorator, printer and socialist, died 1896.
In a letter to Lady Burne-Jones . . .
Come soon, I want a sight of your dear face.

REV. WILLIAM MUHLENBERG
Clergyman, died 1877. To his last visitor . . .
Good morning.

ED MURROW
American broadcaster, died 1965. To his wife . . .
Well Jan, we were lucky at that.

REV. EDWARD NARES
Clergyman, died 1841.
Goodbye.

WACLAV NIJINSKY
Ballet dancer, died 1950.
Mamasha!

LORD NORTHCLIFFE
British press magnate, died 1922. Final orders for his
funeral and obituary . . .
I wish to be laid as near Mother as possible at North Finchley.
I do not wish anything erect from the ground or any words
except my name, the year I was born and this year on the stone.
In *The Times* I should like a page reviewing my life work by

someone who really knows, and a leading article by the best man available on the night.

JOHN BOYLE O'REILLY

Poet and editor, died 1890.

Yes, Mamsie dear, I have taken some of your sleeping medicine. I feel tired now, and if you will let me lie down on that couch, I will go to sleep right away . . . Yes my love! Yes, my love!

SIR WILLIAM OSLER

Professor of Medicine, died 1919. Talking to his doctor as if he were still a child . . .

Nighty-night, a-darling.

BASS OUTLAW

Gunfighter. Died 1894.

Gather my friends around me, for I know that I must die.

CHARLES S. PARNELL

Irish patriot, died 1891. The mythical speech ran . . .

Let my love be given to my colleagues and to the Irish people.

But Parnell actually said . . .

Kiss me, sweet wifie, and I will try to sleep a little.

SPRINGETT PENN

Son of William Penn of Pennsylvania.

Let my father speak to the doctor and I'll go to sleep.

GEORGE LAWRENCE PILKINGTON

Ugandan pioneer.

Thank you my friends, you have done well to take me off the battlefield. Now give me rest.

JAMES K. POLK

American President, died 1849. To his wife . . .

I love you Sarah. For all eternity, I love you.

NOAH PORTER

Lexicographer, died 1892. To a child . . .

Go call your mother, wake her up. I want to consult with her.

WILLIAM H. PRESCOTT
American historian, died 1859. Amused that his wife
could remember the name of a diplomat that
he had forgotten . . .

How came *you* to remember ?

MARCEL PROUST
French novelist, died 1922. To his brother, who asked
if he were hurting Proust . . .

Yes, Robert dear, you are.

GIACOMO PUCCINI
Composer of operas, died 1924.

My poor Elvira, my poor wife.

ALEXANDER PUSHKIN
Russian novelist, died 1837.

Farewell, my friends.

☠

JOHN RADCLIFFE
Physician to Queen Anne, died 1714. Letter to his sister . . .

I have nothing further than to beseech the Divine Being who is
the God of the living to prosper you and all my relations with
good and unblameable lives, that when you shall change the
world you are now in for a better, we may all meet together in
glory and enjoy these ineffable delights which are promised to
all that love Christ's coming. Till then, my dear, dear Milly, take
this as a last farewell from your Affectionate and Dying Brother,
J. Radcliffe. N.B. The Jewels and Rings in my gilt cabinet, not
mentioned in my will, I hereby bequeath to you.

JOHN RAY
Naturalist, died 1705.

When you happen to write to my singular friend Dr Hotton, I
pray tell him that I received his most obliging and affectionate
letter for which I return thanks and acquaint that I am not able
to answer it.

THOMAS READ
American poet, died 1872.

Sweet are the kisses of one's friends.

THOMAS WILLIAM ROBERTSON
British dramatist, died 1871. To his son . . .

Goodbye, my son, and God bless you. Come and see me tomorrow. If I don't speak, don't be frightened, and don't forget to kiss your father.

EDWIN ARLINGTON ROBINSON
American poet, died 1935.

We'll have our cigarettes together . . . Goodnight.

JOHN, EARL OF ROCHESTER
Poet, died 1680.

Has my friend left me? Then I shall die shortly.

MRS ROSE RODIN
Wife of the sculptor Auguste Rodin, died 1917.

I don't mind dying, but it's leaving my man. Who will look after him. What will happen to the poor thing?

GIOACCHINO ROSSINI
Italian composer of operas, died 1868. His wife's name . . .

Olympe.

BENJAMIN RUSH
American Revolutionary leader, died 1813. To his son . . .

Be indulgent to the poor.

LORD JOHN RUSSELL
Father of Bertrand Russell, died 1931.

It is all done. Goodbye my little dears for ever.

☻

GEORGES SAND
(Amandine Dudevant)
French novelist, died 1876. To her family . . .

Farewell, I am going to die. Goodbye Lina, goodbye Maurice, goodbye Lolo, good . . .

SAPPHO
Greek poet, died c. 7th Century BC. A farewell poem
to her daughter . . .
For it is not right that in the house of song there be mourning.
Such things befit not us.

CLARA SCHUMANN
German pianist, died 1896.
You two must go to a beautiful place this summer.

JOHANN GOTTFRIED SEUME
German poet, died 1810. When asked if he wanted anything . . .
Nothing, dear Weigel. I only wanted to tell you that you
shouldn't be annoyed if I say some things I wouldn't say in a
different situation. I take a guilt with me. You I cannot repay.
My eyes grow dim.

SEVERUS
Died 390. To his wife and daughter, who had already
been buried in the family mausoleum . . .
My dear ones, with whom I have lived in love for so long, make
room for me, for this is my grave and in death we shall not be
divided.

KONSTANTIN STANISLAVSKY
Dramatic theorist, died 1938. Talking about his sister . . .
I've lots to say to her, not just something. But not now. I'm sure
to get it all mixed up.

HARRIET BEECHER STOWE
American author, died 1896. To her nurse . . .
I love you.

ROBERT A. TAFT
US Senator, died 1953. To his wife . . .
Well, Martha! Glad to see you looking so well.

WILLIAM DESMOND TAYLOR
Hollywood star, died 1922. Taylor died in mysterious circumstances. Fellow star Mary Miles Minter alleged that she heard his corpse speak to her from the coffin . . .
I shall love you always, Mary!

GENERAL REGIS DE TROBRIAND
Led the Army of the Potomac. Letter to an aide . . .
You will understand, dear Bonnaffon, that in such condition it is out of the question for me to receive any visit, or even to designate any possible time of meeting, as by that time it is as likely that I may be underground as on it. Farewell then, or 'au revoir', as the case may turn. Anyhow, I remain, Yours faithfully, R. de Trobriand.

MARTIN TROMP
Dutch admiral, died 1653. To his family . . .
Take courage children. Act so that my end will be glorious, as my life has been.

MADAME TUSSAUD
Founder of the Waxworks, died 1850. To her two sons . . .
I divide my property equally between you, and implore you, above all things, never to quarrel.

MARK TWAIN
American humorist, died 1910. To his daughter, Clara . . .
Goodbye. If we meet . . .

JULES VERNE
French adventure novelist, died 1905. To his children . . .
Honorine, Mechel, Valentine, Suzanne – are you here ?

JAKOB WASSERMANN
German novelist, died 1934. His companion's name . . .
Marta.

LOUISA, MARCHIONESS OF WATERFORD
Oh darling Adelaide, goodness and beauty, beauty and goodness
– those are ever the great things!

WALT WHITMAN
American poet and socialist, died 1892.
Oh dear, he's a good fellow.

SIR WILLIAM WILDE
*Surgeon, father of Oscar Wilde, died 1876. Listening
to the noise from his son's party ...*
Oh those boys, those boys!

ALFRED WILLIAMS
British poet, died 1905. To his wife ...
My dear, this is going to be a tragedy for us both.

WOODROW WILSON
American President, died 1924. His wife's name ...
Edith.

THOMAS WOLFE
American novelist, died 1938. Greeting his late wife ...
All right Mabel, I am coming.

CARDINAL WOLSEY
Henry VIII's main opponent over Protestantism, died 1530.
Master Kingston, farewell. My time draweth on fast. Forget not
what I have sent and charged you withal. For when I am dead
you shall, peradventure, understand my words better.

GRANT WOOD
American painter, died 1942. His sister's name ...
Nan.

WILLIAM WORDSWORTH
British poet, died 1850. Asking for his sister ...
God bless you. Is that you, Dora?

WILLIAM WYCHERLY

Dramatist, died 1716. Asked by his young wife
what were his last wishes . . .

My dear, it is only this: you will never marry an old man again.

WILLIAM YANCEY

American politician, died 1863. To his wife . . .

Sarah!

INDEX

Ariosto, Ludovico 32
Armistead, General Lewis 102
Armstrong, Major Herbert 138
Arnaud, Angelique 48
Arnold, Benedict 138
Arnold, Dr Thomas 32
Arria 123
Artagerses 83
Arundel, Earl of 48
Arvers, Felix 9
Ascham, Roger 48
d'Aste, Cardinal 48
d'Astros, Cardinal 48
Atcheson, George C. 32
Atticus, Titus Pomponius 83
Aubigne, Agrippa d' 275
Audubon, John J. 179
Augustus, Emperor of Rome 83
Aurelius, Marcus 83
Aurelius, Quintus 219
Aurungzebe, Emperor of
   Hindustan 83
Austen, Jane 32
Austria, Don Carlos of 219
Averill, Jim 160

Barbar, 1st Mogul Emperor 84
Babington, Anthony 139
Bachman, John 275
Bacon, Francis 179
Baedecker, Dr Frederick 48
Baer, Max 219
Baesell, Major Norman 179
Bagehot, Walter 179
de Bailli, 'La Rivière' 10
Bailly, Jean Sylvain 139
Bainham, James 139
Balboa, Vasco Nunez de 139
Baldwin, Elias 179
Balzac, Honoré de 198
Bancroft, George 10
Bannister, John 48
Barbusse, Henri 198
Barham, Richard 275
Baring, Maurice 275
Barker, Arizona 'Ma' 123
Barnato, Barnett 264
Barnave, Antoine 252

Barneveldt, Johann 10
Barnum, Phineas T. 198
Barre, Chevalier de la 139
Barrie, Sir James M. 10
Barron, Clarence 198
Barrow, Isaac 275
Barry, Countess Jeanne du 236
Barrymore, John 180, 276
Barrymore, Lionel 180
Barton, Clara 10
Barthou, Louis 219
Basedow, Johann 199
Bashkirtseff, Marie 32
Bass, Sam 220
Bastiat, Frederick 236
Battie, William 236
Baxter, Richard 48
Baxter, Warner 199
Bayard, General George 102
Bayard, Seigneur de 110
Beard, George M. 199
Beardsley, Aubrey 220
Beaton, Cardinal 48
Beatrix, Grand Duchess of
   Bavaria 84
Beauchamp, Jereboam 139
Beaufort, Henry 220
Beaumont, Rev. Joseph 49
Beaverbrook, Lord 32
Beck, General Ludwig 220
Becket, Thomas à 131
Beckford, William 220
Bede, The Venerable 49
Bedell, Bishop 49
Beddoes, Thomas L. 10
Bedoyere, Count Charles de 123
Beecher, Catherine 160
Beecher, Henry Ward 32, 180
Beecher, Lyman 180
Beerbohm, Max 10
Beethoven, Ludwig van 160, 236
Behaine, Bishop 10
Bell, Alexander Graham 252
Bell, Sir Charles 276
Bellingham, John 139
Benchley, Robert 199
Benedek, General Ludwig
   von 276

Benedict, Brevet-Brigadier-General Lewis 102
Benezet, Anthony 276
Benjamin, Judah 220
Benjamin, Park 276
Bennett, Arnold 236
Bennett, Constance 199
Benson, Colonel G. E. 103
Benson, Monsignor Robert 276
Bentham, Jeremy 276
Beranger, Pierre 237
Berg, Alban 252
Bergerus 49
Berlioz, Hector 276
Bern, Paul 264
Bernard, Claude 32
Bernadette of Lourdes 70
Bernard, Saint 70
Bernadotte, Count 131
Berry, Charles Duc de 49
Berulle, Cardinale de 49
Bessarion, Johann 49
Bestoujeff 252
Bevan, Aneurin 160
Bewgill, Rev. John 132
Beza, Theodore 277
Bickersteth, Edward 49
Billings, Josh 199
Billy the Kid (William Bonney) 123
Biron, Duc de Lanzon de 139
Bismarck, Count Otto von 110
Bizet, Georges 237
Blackie, John 50
Blake, William 277
Blandy, Mary 237
Blaurer, Ambrosius 50
Blomfield, Bishop 50
Blood, Thomas 160
Blucher, Marshal 277
Blum, Robert 111
Bluntschli, Johann 50
Boas, Franz 199
Bodwell, Joseph 220
Boehm, Jacob 33
Boerhaave, Herman 50
Bogue, David 160
Boileau, Nicholas 161

Boleyn, Anne 237
Bolingbroke, Henry, Viscount 50
Bolivar, Simon 33
Bonaparte, Elisa 253
Bonaparte, Emperor Napoleon 111
Bonaparte, Pauline 253
Boniface, Saint 71
Bonnet, Charles 33
Booth, Edwin 277
Booth, John Wilkes 111
Booth, Junius Brutus 220
Booth, General William 277
Borgia, Cesare 237
Borgia, Lucrezia 220
Borne, Ludwig 11
Borodin, Alexander 277
Borromeo, Saint Carlo 71
Bosco, Saint John 71
Bossuet, Jacques 237
Bottomley, Horatio 161
Boufflers, Chevalier de 161
Bouhours, Dominique 180
Bourbon, Prince Louis de 237
Bourg, Anne du 11
Bouvier, Auguste 30
Bow, Clara 161
Bowditch, Henry 277
Bowditch, Nathaniel 11
Bowles, Saul 277
Boyle, Robert 50
Bozzari, Marcos 111
Brace, Charles 11
Bradford, Alder 50
Bradford, Andrew 33
Bradford, John 139
Brahe, Tycho 253
Brahms, Johannes 277
Brainerd, David 51
Brandt, General Karl 111
Brasidas 161
Brecht, Bertold 161
Breitinger, Johann 51
Bremer, Frederika 51
Brereton, William 140
Briggs, George 237
Brindley, James 11

Harris, Joel Chandler 205
Harrison, Benjamin 226
Harrison, General Thomas 146
Harrison, William 206
Harvey, William H. 185
Hasek, Jaroslat 257
Hassler, Ferdinand 226
Hastings, Warren 241
Hauff, Wilhelm 58
Hauser, Kaspar 38
Havelock, Sir Henry 106
Havergal, Francis 58
Hawker, R. S. 58
Hawthorne, Mrs Nathaniel 284
Hay, Will 17
Haydn, Franz Joseph 168
Haydon, Benjamin 241
Hayes, Rutherford B. 168
Haynes, Rev. Lemuel 58
Hazlitt, William 185
Hearn, Lafcadio 226
Heath, Neville 146
Heber, Reginald 17
Hecker, Father Isaac 59
Heckewelder, John 17
Heine, Heinrich 168
Heloise 284
Hemans, Felicia 59
Henderson, Alexander 185
Henderson, Ebenezer 59
Hendricks, Thomas 185
Henley, Rev. John 38
Henley, W. E. 226
Henri IV, King of France 90
Henrietta, Duchess of Orléans 90
Henry II, King of England 91
Henry IV, King of England 91
Henry V, King of England 91
Henry VIII, King of England 91
Henry, Prince of Wales 91
Henry IV, Holy Roman Emperor 91
Henry, the Lion of Saxony and Bavaria 226
Henry, Matthew 185
Henry, O. 38
Henry Patrick 185
Henry, Philip 241

Herbert, Edward 18
Herbert, George 185
Herbert, Sidney 185
Herder, Johann 206
Herrick, Myron T. 168
Hervey, James 59
Herzi, Theodor 206
Hesse, Hermann 206
Hessus, Helius 59
Hewitt, Abram S. 18
Hey, Wilhelm 226
Heylin, Peter 59
Hickok, Richard Eugene 146
Hickok, 'Wild Bill' 126
Hilary, Saint 241
Hildebrand, Pope 257
Hill, Benjamin 226
Hill, Rev. Rowland 242
Hill, Ureli 186
Hillary, Richard 169
Hillman, Sidney 242
Hilton, John 18
Hiltzheimer, Jacob 206
Himmler, Heinrich 267
Hindenberg, Airship 59
Hindenberg, Paul von 169
Hingoro, Rahim 146
Hirobumi Ito, Prince 134
Hitler, Adolf 206
Hobbes, Thomas 39
Hoche, Lazare 116
Hodge, Charles 39
Hodgson, Francis 59
Hoeffle, General Herman 116
Hofer, Andreas 127
Hoffman, Eugene A. 186
Hofmannsthal, Hugo von 267
Hogg, James 257
Hokusal 242
Holcroft, Thomas 242
Holliday, 'Doc' 127
Holloway, John 147
Holmes, Burton 207
Holmes, Oliver Wendell 257
Holst, Gustav 169
Holtby, Winifred 207
Holty, Ludwig 18
Hood, Edwin P. 284

Meynell, Alice 190
Michelangelo Buonarroti 172
Michelet, Jules 41
Middleton, Richard 269
Mihajlovic, Draza 118
Mill, John Stuart 190
Millay, Edna St Vincent 210
Miller, Henry 287
Miller, Hugh 269
Miller, Joaquin 229
Mirabeau, Count 244
Mitchell, Silas Weir 41
Mitford, Mary Russell 173
Mizner, Wilson 211
Mohammed 76
Mohaupt, Juliana 270
Moleneux, Thomas 135
Molière (Jean Baptiste Poquelin) 173
Moltke, Helmut von 22
Moncey, Marshal 107
Monica, Saint 77
Monmouth, James, Duke of 150
Montagu, Lady Mary Wortley 190
Montcalm, Marquis de 107
Montefiore, Sir Moses 63
Montesquieu, Comte 63
Montessori, Maria 245
Montez, Lola 22
Montezuma II, Emperor of the Aztecs 97
Montfort, Simon de 107
Montmorency, Duc Henry II de 150
Montmorency, Duc de 211
Montrose, James, Earl of 151
Moody, Blair 173
Moody, Dwight 41
Moran, Thomas B. 129
More, Hannah 190
More, Thomas 151
Moreau, Jean Victor 190
Morehead, John A. 229
Morgan, J. P. 229
Morgan, William De 211
Moriale, Fra 151
Morris, Gouverneur 22

Morris, William 287
Morse, Samuel 190
Morton, Oliver 22
Motley, John 245
Moyse, Frederic 245
Mozart, Wolfgang Amadeus 211
Mudgett, Herman 151
Muhlenberg, Rev. William 287
Munro, H. H. (Saki) 173
Munsterberg, Hugo 173
Murat, Joachim, 'King of Naples' 97
Murger, Henri 260
Murphy, Arthur 190
Murrieta, Joaquin 129
Murrow, Ed 287
Musset, Alfred de 22
Mussorgsky, Modest 245
Mussolini, Benito 151

Nadir Shah 135
Nani, Giambattista 190
Napoleon II, Duke of Reichstadt 97
Napoleon III 97
Nares, Rev. Edward 287
Narusewicz, Adam 260
Narvaez, Ramon 173
Neander, Johann 23
Nelson, Earle 151
Nelson, Horatio, Lord 119
Newell, Harriet 245
Newport, Francis 245
Newton, John 63
Newton, Sir Isaac 23
Newton, Sir Richard 191
Ney, Marshal 151
Nicholl, Sir William Robertson 173
Niebuhr, Barthold Georg 23
Nuinsky, Waclav 287
Noble, Margaret 211
Nodier, Charles 245
Nolan, Captain Lewis 107
Northcliffe, Lord 287
Nothnagel, Hermann 23
Noyes, John 152

Segrave, Henry 214
Selwyn, Bishop George 43
Senancour, Etienne 65
Seneca, Lucius Annaeus 271
Serment, Mlle Louise 44
Serra, Junipero 193
Seton, Elizabeth 65
Seume, Johanne G. 291
Servetus, Michael 156
Severus 221
Severus, Emperor of Rome 99
Seward, William Henry 193
Sforza, Galeazzo 136
Shackleton, Sir Edward 261
Shaftesbury, 7th Earl of 232
Shakespeare, William 214
Sharp, William 44
Shaw, George Bernard 214
Sheppard, Jack 156
Sheridan, Richard Brinsley 248
Sherman, John 232
Sherwood, Mrs Mary Martha 66
Sickingen, Franz von 66
Sidney, Algernon 193
Sidney, Sir Philip 108
Simon 271
Simonides 108
Sisera 215
Siward, Earl of Northumberland 249
Sixtus, Bishop 79
Smalridge, Bishop 175
Smedley, Rev. Edward 193
Smith, Captain E. J. 130
Smith, Adam 26
Smith, Al 26
Smith, Joseph 137
Smith, Perry Edward 156
Smith, Sidney 215
Snyder, Ruth 156
Socrates 272
Somerset, Henry Beaufort, Duke of 156
Sophonisba 272
Southcott, Joanna 44
Spencer, Henry 156
Spencer, Sir Stanley 232
Spengler, Peter 249

Spies, August 157
Spinoza, Baruch 249
Stafford, Earl of 157
Stambouloff, Stefan 120
Stanford, Mrs L. 66
Stanislaus I, King of Poland 99
Stanislavsky, Konstantin 291
Stanley, Arthur 194
Stanley, Sir Henry 44
Stanton, C. P. 215
Stanton, Elizabeth Cady 215
Starkweather, Charlie 157
Starr, Belle 44
Stauffenberg, Count Klaus von 120
Stedman, Edmund Clarence 249
Stein, Gertrude 44
Steinmetz, Charles P. 26
Stephen, Saint 79
Stephens, Alexander H. 215
Sterne, Laurence 26
Stevenson, R. L. 249
Stewart, Sir John 194
Stolberg, Count Friedrich 233
Stone, Lewis 215
Stone, Lucy 215
Stonehouse, Sir James 66
Stowe, Harriet Beecher 291
Strachey, Lytton 216
Strafford, Earl of 157
Strathcona and Mount Royal, Baron Donald 66
Strauss, Mrs Isadore 130
Strauss, Johann 26
Straw, Jack 157
Streicher, Julius 157
Strindberg, August 27
Strozzi, Filippo 272
Stuart, General J. E. B.
Suckel, Fritz 157
Sudbury, Simon of 66
Sullivan, Sir Arthur 249
Sumner, Charles 216
Sun-Yat-Sen 120
Surratt, Mary 157
Sutter, John 176
Suspinianus 261
Svetchine, Sofia Soymanoff 176

Fiction

☐	**Options**	Freda Bright	£1.50p
☐	**The Thirty-nine Steps**	John Buchan	£1.50p
☐	**Secret of Blackoaks**	Ashley Carter	£1.50p
☐	**The Sittaford Mystery**	Agatha Christie	£1.00p
☐	**Dupe**	Liza Cody	£1.25p
☐	**Lovers and Gamblers**	Jackie Collins	£2.50p
☐	**Sphinx**	Robin Cook	£1.25p
☐	**Ragtime**	E. L. Doctorow	£1.50p
☐	**The Rendezvous**	Daphne du Maurier	£1.50p
☐	**Flashman**	George Macdonald Fraser	£1.50p
☐	**The Moneychangers**	Arthur Hailey	£2.25p
☐	**Secrets**	Unity Hall	£1.50p
☐	**Simon the Coldheart**	Georgette Heyer	95p
☐	**The Eagle Has Landed**	Jack Higgins	£1.95p
☐	**Sins of the Fathers**	Susan Howatch	£2.50p
☐	**The Master Sniper**	Stephen Hunter	£1.50p
☐	**Smiley's People**	John le Carré	£1.95p
☐	**To Kill a Mockingbird**	Harper Lee	£1.75p
☐	**Ghosts**	Ed McBain	£1.25p
☐	**Gone with the Wind**	Margaret Mitchell	£2.95p
☐	**The Totem**	David Morrell	£1.25p
☐	**Platinum Logic**	Tony Parsons	£1.75p
☐	**Wilt**	Tom Sharpe	£1.50p
☐	**Rage of Angels**	Sidney Sheldon	£1.75p
☐	**The Unborn**	David Shobin	£1.50p
☐	**A Town Like Alice**	Nevile Shute	£1.75p
☐	**A Falcon Flies**	Wilbur Smith	£1.95p
☐	**The Deep Well at Noon**	Jessica Stirling	£1.95p
☐	**The Ironmaster**	Jean Stubbs	£1.75p
☐	**The Music Makers**	E. V. Thompson	£1.75p

Non-fiction

☐	**Extraterrestrial Civilizations**	Isaac Asimov	£1.50p
☐	**Pregnancy**	Gordon Bourne	£2.95p
☐	**Jogging from Memory**	Rob Buckman	£1.25p
☐	**The 35mm Photographer's Handbook**	Julian Calder and John Garrett	£5.95p
☐	**Travellers' Britain**	} Arthur Eperon	£2.95p
☐	**Travellers' Italy**		£2.50p
☐	**The Complete Calorie Counter**	Eileen Fowler	75p

☐	**The Diary of Anne Frank**	Anne Frank	£1.50p
☐	**Linda Goodman's Sun Signs**	Linda Goodman	£2.50p
☐	**Mountbatten**	Richard Hough	£2.50p
☐	**How to be a Gifted Parent**	David Lewis	£1.95p
☐	**Symptoms**	Sigmund Stephen Miller	£2.50p
☐	**Book of Worries**	Robert Morley	£1.50p
☐	**The Hangover Handbook**	David Outerbridge	£1.25p
☐	**The Alternative Holiday Catalogue**	edited by Harriet Peacock	£1.95p
☐	**The Pan Book of Card Games**	Hubert Phillips	£1.75p
☐	**Food for All the Family**	Magnus Pyke	£1.50p
☐	**Everything Your Doctor Would Tell You If He Had the Time**	Claire Rayner	£4.95p
☐	**Just Off for the Weekend**	John Slater	£2.50p
☐	**An Unfinished History of the World**	Hugh Thomas	£3.95p
☐	**The Third Wave**	Alvin Toffler	£1.95p
☐	**The Flier's Handbook**		£5.95p

All these books are available at your local bookshop or newsagent, or can be ordered direct from the publisher. Indicate the number of copies required and fill in the form below   7

....

Name...
(Block letters please)

Address..

_____

Send to Pan Books (CS Department), Cavaye Place, London SW10 9PG
Please enclose remittance to the value of the cover price plus:
35p for the first book plus 15p per copy for each additional book ordered
to a maximum charge of £1.25 to cover postage and packing
Applicable only in the UK

While every effort is made to keep prices low, it is sometimes
necessary to increase prices at short notice. Pan Books reserve
the right to show on covers and charge new retail prices which
may differ from those advertised in the text or elsewhere